DUNCAN McLAREN is the author of *Personal Delivery*, a blend of autobiography, fiction and contemporary art, as well as being a regular contributor to the *Independent on Sunday* and art magazines. He is presently researching the life and work of Evelyn Waugh.

From the reviews of *Looking for Enid*

'A strikingly inventive and unusual portrait.' **Sunday Times**

'An impressionistic, fan's-eye view of the Blyton phenomenon... an original idea and McLaren does it well.' **Sunday Telegraph**

'A charming exploration of the links between autobiography and fiction.' **TLS**

'This is one of those rare biographies where you learn as much about the biographer as about his subject. In this anarchic, inventive tome Duncan McLaren tries to find out more about this fascinating woman who wrote over 600 books. An imaginative take on what made Blyton tick.' **Good Book Guide**

'The inventive tale of how fine art critic Duncan McLaren set off on a mysterious adventure to find out who children's writer Enid Blyton really was... A spiffing idea, and amusing view and an entertaining book.' **Oxford Times**

'McLaren's colloquially written biography leads the reader on an intricate, deeply personal trail to places where the author spent her fascinating life... An informative, nostalgic biography and an eccentric Blyton mystery pastiche.' **London Lite**

'There is something moving about this enterprise. McLaren, a genuine enthusiast, readily refers to "the trainspotting sector of my brain" and maintains an ironic awareness of what he is doing: "'You great Theophilus Goon' I shout, as we walk through the rose trellis" just about sums up the tone of this demented but heartfelt exploration.' **Guardian**

'Remember the Famous Five? Secret Seven? The Golliwogs and Noddy? We all loved Enid Blyton's books until the politically correct brigade swung into action and we had to pretend we never did. Now McLaren offers lapsed devotees a chance to catch up with our Enid and to discover how the torrent of stories came to her.' **www.pensioneronline.com**

LOOKING FOR
ENID

THE MYSTERIOUS AND INVENTIVE LIFE OF ENID BLYTON

DUNCAN MCLAREN

Portobello
BOOKS

First published by Portobello Books Ltd 2007
This paperback edition published 2008

Portobello Books Ltd
Twelve Addison Avenue
Holland Park
London
W11 4QR, UK

A CIP catalogue record is available from the British Library

9 8 7 6 5 4 3 2 1

ISBN 978 1 84627 116 8

www.portobellobooks.com

Designed in ITC Charter and Monotype Baskerville by
Geoff Green Book Design

Typeset by Avon DataSet Ltd, Bidford on Avon, Warwickshire

Printed in Great Britain by
Clays Ltd, St Ives plc

FOREWORD

Dear Readers,

Here is the latest Enid adventure. The same characters appear in it, of course. Enid herself, her favourite Fatty, young Bets, Hugh (called Goon for fun), Thomas the father and Kenneth the dog. Like all the other Enid books this one is complete in itself. I hope you will find it the most exciting yet.

The earlier titles are:

Enid on a Treasure Island
Enid Goes Adventuring Again
Enid Runs Away On Her Own
Enid Goes to Smuggler's Top
Enid Goes Off in a Caravan
Enid on Kirrin Island Again
Enid Goes Off to Camp
Enid Gets Into Trouble
Enid Falls Into Adventure
Enid on a Hike On Her Own
Enid Has a Wonderful Time

Enid Goes Down to the Sea
Enid Goes to Mystery Moor
Enid Has Plenty of Fun
Enid on a Secret Trail
Enid Goes to Billycock Hill
Enid Gets Into a Fix
Enid on Finniston Farm
Enid Goes to Demon's Rocks
Enid Has a Mystery to Solve
Enid is Together Again

Good luck to you all,
from

Duncan McLaren

CONTENTS

Beginnings   1

Chapter One: In Beaconsfield   11

Chapter Two: In Beckenham   46

Chapter Three: In Bourne End   93

Chapter Four: In and around Blairgowrie   152

Chapter Five: In and around Swanage   201

Chapter Six: In George MacDonald   272

Endings   306

Acknowledgements   318

LIST OF ILLUSTRATIONS

Facing page

THIS IS HER FATTY (from *Five on Kirrin Island Again*)   30

THIS IS HER BETS (from *Five Go Off To Camp*)   50

THIS IS HER HUGH (from *Five on Kirrin Island Again*)   100

THIS IS HER FATHER (from *Five on Kirrin Island Again*)   167

THIS IS HER KENNETH (from *Five Fall Into Adventure*)   232

THIS IS HER GEORGE (from *Five Go to Mystery Moor*)   290

SHE IS ASLEEP (from *The Little Girl at Capernaum*)   316

BEGINNINGS

1

The boy is in the library. It is not the first time he has been in the book-filled building in the middle of the bleak council estate, but it may be the second.

This time it is easier. Previously he was directed to the card index and had to finger his way through the tightly packed, neatly typed items until he got to the name 'Blyton, Enid'. Once he had established that the library did own several Famous Five books, the next task was to find out where exactly the Blytons were shelved, and which Fives were in stock.

No flicking to and fro within the card index this time around. The boy goes straight to the shelf of books that had so mesmerised him before. He instantly registers that there are two Fives, both new to him. After a short period revelling in his excitement, he reluctantly considers the books one at a time. *Five Go To Mystery Moor* shows tomboy George and another of the Five on a horse, running away from something that can only be half-glimpsed in the mist. The other is *Five Have a Wonderful Time*. On the cover of this book, George – surrounded by the rest of the Five sitting on grassy ground – is looking through binoculars at an old castle tower in the distance. The boy wonders if the boy-girl is being dazzled by the sun, which is big in the sky and is directly under the author's name.

The boy has to decide which book to borrow. He thinks it is great that he is getting to borrow either of these beautiful objects. But both have the distinctive signature of the author on the front, both are about the fantastic Five, and he does not know which of the books he can bear to put back on the shelf. The truth is, he can't bear to put either of them back.

His mother appears and asks why he hasn't chosen a book yet. The boy tells her the difficulty. She suggests that they take *both* books and put one on her own ticket. What an absolutely brilliant idea! But will the librarian be taken in by the scheme? The boy's mother does not want to discuss it. She is in a hurry to get home. She walks him to the desk and the boy watches in trepidation as the card for one of the books *(Wonderful Time)* is taken from the flap on the inside of its front cover and inserted into his own blue linen-covered ticket. The card from *Mystery Moor* is then removed and placed inside the slot of his mother's red ticket. And both the red and blue tickets are filed away behind the desk.

'Here. You can carry them as it's you who's going to be reading them,' says the mother, as much to the librarian as to the boy. The boy blushes as he takes hold of the books. But it seems that the official is not going to cross-question them as to exactly who is going to be reading which book when. The boy is ready to promise that he won't read *Five Go To Mystery Moor* until his mother has quite finished with it, in the hope that this will satisfy the rules of the organisation. No need for any such declaration, apparently. The boy thinks, not for the first time, that it is blooming marvellous having such a genius for a mother.

NOVEMBER, 1968

Unbeknown to the boy in the local library, the author of the books that have so transfixed him during his tenth year dies in a nursing home in London, aged 71.

2

SUMMER, 2002

The man has been walking the streets of London for about an hour, thinking about the text he is writing for a contemporary artist. He needs to switch off from that now, and has walked far enough for one afternoon, so he goes into a charity shop as a way of clearing his mind and turning himself around.

Standing in front of a rickety bookcase, a particular blue spine catches his eye. Perhaps it is the unusual combination of dark shade and glossiness that attracts his interest. He plucks it from its default position, but finds that it is a Noddy book. He is about to put it back unopened when he changes his mind. Something about the author's signature on the cover makes him open the book after all.

The man is looking at a full-page image of Noddy driving a little yellow car with red mudguards. Noddy is sitting behind the steering wheel, wearing his blue, pointed hat, cheerfully singing for his two female passengers. The man turns the page and the lyrics to Noddy's song become apparent:

> 'Oh little Miss Rabbit, and little Miss Bear,
> I really do think
> They're a nice little pair.
> I do love their noses,
> I do love their ears,
> It *is* fun to see them,
> They really are DEARS.'

The man is not sure if he has the *time* or *energy* for whatever it is that is happening in his mind. But he flicks on in any case. The next full-page image shows Noddy's guardian, Big-Ears, as he pegs out washing on a line while standing on a stool. The white-bearded pixie's mouth is crammed full of pegs but he manages to give Noddy some sage advice: 'Hold some pegs in your mouth while you hang up the curtains.' Wide-eyed Noddy drinks in these words. By the next page he has fallen off the stool and swallowed at least one peg.

Two minutes of looking through the playfully subversive book – voraciously sampling paragraphs and images – is enough for the man to realise he has rediscovered something from his past. Yes, however dimly remembered, he knows this Toyland laid out in front of him as a panoramic image on the end-papers. He has occupied that space in his imagination. How does he account for this? He must have read – or been read – the book, or series of books, as an infant. The books must then have been disposed of before they'd been re-read as a slightly older child. Certainly, the man had not known that Noddy had been part of his inheritance. He is aware that he read Enid Blyton's Famous Five books and some of her other adventure stories as an older child. The present discovery means that Blyton must have been an influence on him for a significant proportion of his formative years, far more than any other writer or artist.

The man can't move from the spot now. Half-way through the sixty-page book, Noddy appears in his House-For-One, a bed-sit not unlike the one the man currently occupies. Solid-seeming single bed... uncarpeted floorboards... bowl of sugar-cubes resting on tableclothed table... teapot in tea-cosy. Actually, the room might be more accurately described to himself as a cross between his Aunt Meg's parlour set out for a high tea in Blairgowrie, circa 1965, and van Gogh's bedroom in the Yellow House in Arles. Perhaps, just perhaps, the early experience of reading about and seeing images of House-For-One accounts for why he had been so keen on the picture *The Artist's Bedroom* when he'd come across it a few years later.

The man is out of the shop now, having exchanged 40p for the precious jewel in the plastic bag. Soon his walking has found its usual rhythm. But his mind has gone into hiding where it will remain until he has had a rest and a mug of tea back at base. For the moment, all it can come up with is the question: 'Who the hell was Enid Blyton?'

It would have surprised the man to be told that another three years would pass before his curiosity had matured sufficiently for him to set about answering that question.

3

I'm sitting in my study with a library copy of *Enid Blyton: the Biography* by Barbara Stoney. It's the standard biography of the world-famous children's writer, indeed it's the only comprehensive one. There is also a book written by Enid's younger daughter, one by her literary agent, and a treatise written by a lecturer in librarianship. But these are partial accounts, limited in scope. This is the book that surveys her whole life, and on its cover a smartly dressed middle-aged woman, holding a pencil, looks up from the sheaf of pages resting on her lap. Enid smiles into the eyes of the reader. 'Trust me,' she seems to say. Well, I do trust her, but not because of this carefully contrived pose. Besides, trust isn't the word. Awe is the word. Having read this book, I am in awe of Enid Blyton's creativity and want to know a lot more about it.

Whatever the merits of the text itself, the highlight of the Barbara Stoney biography has to be Appendix 10, which consists purely of a list of the books that Enid Blyton published. She went from producing a few titles per year in the early twenties, to a peak of thirty-odd books annually around 1950. There are 600 books on the list altogether! And every one of those that I have read so far gives the impression that the writing of each one was a constant joy.

Almost as interesting is the foreword written by Gillian Baverstock, the older of Enid's daughters. Gillian inherited her mother's papers, and has retained the copyright of the Stoney book. After Enid's death in 1968 there were many requests for permission to write a biography. Stoney had been working on the life of a master thatcher, which meant a visit to Old Thatch, Bourne End, one of the houses in which Enid lived. It was here Gillian met Barbara Stoney and was won over by the biographer's instinctive knowledge of what life must have been like for Enid and family while living in that house.

The biography, which takes a chronological approach, using numbered but untitled chapters, was published in 1974. Eighteen years later, in the light of Enid's continued popularity with readers, Stoney added a four-page update. This dealt with both the discovery of one of Enid's diaries (most of them had been destroyed by her second husband) and the publication of the sad and critical memoir by Enid's younger daughter, Imogen. Fine, but why are there no other major biographies of one of the twentieth century's most prolific and unobtrusively influential writers from between 1968 and now? Presumably because the personal papers and copyright remain with a party or parties unwilling to give the permissions necessary for further 'official' biographies, while unsanctioned books have tended to explore the dead-end – as far as I'm concerned – of political-correctness issues. No doubt the day will come when a new comprehensive biography will be attempted, and hopefully this will incorporate the views of both daughters in a more integrated way. Unfortunately, I can't wait for that. Or, rather, I feel motivated to embark on an investigation of my own, focusing on Enid's rampant creativity and her books.

There are several reasons for this, which I had better acknowledge from the start. Although I've written several books myself, only *Personal Delivery* has been accepted by a literary publisher, and sales of it were nothing special. I don't feel bitter about this, but some sense of disappointment must lie close to the surface of what I might call my mid-life contentment. Perversely, when I consider Enid Blyton's astonishing success with both publishers and public, it makes me want to clap my hands. I think this must be because my relationship with her as a reader goes back so far, and has bitten so deep, that I feel it's somehow all in the family. In any case, from whatever combination of admiration, affection, jealousy and the wish to emulate, the phrase 'Enid Blyton' gets my creative juices spurting. I trust I can take advantage of this.

It would be wrong to make too much of the contrast between my publishing history and that of Enid Blyton, because in recent years a lot of my texts have appeared in the art world. For example, Grizedale Arts asked me to go to their base in the Lake District and to write about whatever I wanted. At dinner on the first night of my residency, I was sitting beside the curator of Brantwood, the house overlooking Coniston Water in which the Victorian art critic and social reformer John Ruskin lived for the second half of his phenomenally creative life. Soon I found myself fascinated by Ruskin's unhappy sexuality and his prodigious output as a writer. The resulting novella, *The Strangled Cry of the Writer-in-Residence*, was the first time I had written about a fellow writer, but I thoroughly enjoyed the experience and feel Grizedale Arts made a good job of producing the book. There are 2,000 copies currently stored at the art centre. After a year or two the director of the organisation will deem them shed-soiled and the books will be pitched into Coniston Water. And that'll be fine by me. Though, of course, it's not ideal.

For a writer, there is so much more to be gained from the art world than publishing opportunities. A couple of months ago I was a passenger on a trip to France. The party was organised by artists Nina Pepys and Karen G. They raised the money for fifty individuals to do the journey in a buttercup yellow coach that had 'IN REMEMBRANCE OF THINGS PAST' emblazoned down one side of it, and 'WE ARE NOT AFRAID OF MARCEL PROUST' down the other. It turned heads did that luxury coach, whether it was swishing down the motorway towards the Dover end of the Channel Tunnel or parked in the middle of the French *campagne*.

The artists' programme involved taking the party to Illiers, the real-life equivalent of Combray, where Proust's book's narrator spends his summers as a child. Then the coach went on to 'Balbec' on the Normandy coast where adolescent Marcel falls in love with the teasing Albertine. The trip culminated in Paris, with the coach illegally parked on the Boulevard Haussman, where, in a cork-lined room, Proust spent most of his last years writing and rewriting his monster novel sequence.

Part of the idea was to see whether visiting these sites added to an appreciation of the books or simply distracted from them. For most of us, the visits added truckloads. If you believe, from inclination and experience, that biography adds to your appreciation of an author's fiction, then the case for studying the actual places – the buildings and localities – where an author lived his-or-her one-and-only life, is already made.

There was also a dissenting faction on the bus, the Alain de Botton School of Thought, as it was affectionately known. According to this, we shouldn't be looking at Proust's world through our own eyes, but our own world through his eyes. Well, many of the coach party were all for seeing our own world through Proust's eyes. But first we had to see his world through our own eyes before we could more properly adjust to his way of seeing. Swann's Way or the Guermantes Way? We tried them both, as a group and as individual hikers. We walked the walks and we talked the talk. And many of us went back to our thick books with renewed appetite for Proust's prose and his personality.

The artists had given places on the trip to three sets of people. The first group consisted of individuals who were into Proust in a literary way. The second lot knew something of Nina and Karen's previous work – in other words they were along for the contemporary art ride. And the third group was one of 'others' who were there, for the most part, for the fresh air and the free trip to France. By and large, the literary bods were interested in the text itself, and the light that could be shone on it. While for the art crowd, context was everything.

All three groups contributed to the in-trip entertainment. One of the 'others' presented a slide-show about pigeon fancying and organised an on-board bingo session. A Professor of twentieth-century literature gave a lucid talk on the theme of time in Proust. And if I remember the gist of that, which I like to think I do, I recall with just as much enthusiasm a video made by Nina Pepys and Karen G that was played to us on the coach's overhead monitors. It was played at least once on each side of the English Channel and involved our host artists reading to each other. Nina stood outside an English country house in Gloucestershire quoting what Evelyn Waugh had to say to Nancy Mitford in 1948 about Marcel Proust. (That he was a mental defective with no sense of humour.) Then Karen, standing on a smart Parisian boulevard, read Nancy Mitford's reply. (That it was a shame that Evelyn, of all people, was reading Proust in English because there wasn't a single joke in the fourteen volumes of Scott-Moncrieff's translation, whereas when reading in the original French one laughed from the stomach as one did when reading Evelyn.)

Karen G and Nina Pepys, then: what can I say to sum them up? 'Oh little Miss Rabbit, and little Miss Bear, I really do think, They're a nice little pair...' The whole trip was fantastic fun. A group of ten passengers bonded so well that just a few weeks after our return a reunion has been arranged in central London for a forthcoming Saturday night. At the reunion I will make a point of mentioning I have embarked on an investigation into the prolific children's author. Yes, Enid was by her own reckoning a 10,000-words-a-day girl, and the books are there to prove it. Most of the individuals at the Proust reunion will be familiar with reading Blyton as a child, and have anecdotes to share. Blyton was a million-readers-per-book writer. And that sort of person doesn't just leave behind her the books. Her gift to the world is a shared cultural heritage.

That seems clear to me. But I'm glad I don't have to explain it all to Gillian Baverstock who is now in her seventies (to me she remains the wide-eyed daughter for whom Enid wrote some of her stories). For Gillian's part she may feel she doesn't have the *time* or the *energy* to get her head around a contemporary art perspective or whatever else it is I feel I may be offering. She may prefer to leave her mother's reputation as a person and as a writer well alone.

All too easily, I can bring to mind an exchange at a forthcoming meeting of the Enid Blyton Society:

Gillian: 'Let me get this straight, young man. You want to organise a coach trip between the main sites of my mother's life?'

Me: 'Not exactly. In order to write a meaningful book about your mother, someone who has had a profound and largely unacknowledged impact on me and so many other readers, I feel I must take advantage of whatever literary skills I have, along with my art world experience.'

Gillian: 'The best of both worlds, eh?'

Me: 'The best of both beautiful worlds… Oh, and I rather hope there'll be as much going on creatively as there will be of a critical and analytical nature.'

But I've lost her full attention. She's glancing towards some older members of the Society who she no doubt recognises from long association. I can tell she's on the point of pulling the plug on our exchange. Time for a bit of lateral action:

Me (imitating Enid's pellucid voice): 'Oh, please do listen, Gillian, darling. This is just as much for you as for anyone else.'

Suddenly Gillian is wide-eyed again. After all these years. Is she wondering what I'm going to say next? For the moment, that's all I could hope for.

CHAPTER ONE

IN BEACONSFIELD

1

Here's Kate at last, looking bright-eyed and bushy-haired. A quick kiss on the lips and I tell her how to get a ticket that will save her a couple of quid. Meanwhile I get the coffees I've been so looking forward to and we sit at a table for the minutes we have in hand before our train pulls out of Marylebone Station. Soon we will be exploring Beaconsfield, the town where Enid Blyton lived for the last thirty years of her boundlessly creative life.

I met Kate on the Proust coach trip two months ago. We spent last Friday night together, went to the Proust reunion meal on Saturday, and retreated to our own personal spaces on Sunday. But it feels good to be back together again at the start of a new week. Arm-in-arm, we glide along the platform and into the train that is waiting to transport us to our destination of choice.

In the carriage Kate gets out her reading material. She showed me this book within a few minutes of us meeting on Friday. It's a hardback copy of *Five Fall Into Adventure* which I read recently myself. The striking thing about Kate's book is that it's wrapped in brown paper. It takes me back to my childhood when each year under my mother's supervision I would cover my schoolbooks with brown paper in the same way. Kate's book has its title and the author's name written in earnest capitals on the cover, the words underlined. The sight tells the story of a child who has been taught to take care of *all* her precious books, not just the ones that went in her school-bag.

As a ten-year-old I read the Famous Five stories without any context for them. I now know that from 1940, for twenty years, Blyton went from Beaconsfield to Swanage twice a year for holidays. And for twenty-two years in a row, except 1959, she published a Famous Five title. These books are set in Kirrin. With Kirrin Cottage looking out over Kirrin Bay to crumbling Kirrin Castle set on mysterious Kirrin Island. But for Kirrin, read Swanage, for most intents and purposes, and in a month or two I will be renting a cottage there and hope to be filling it with Proust buddies. I like to think of it as a logical progression: from *Fifty Go Off To Balbec* to *Five Go Mad in Dorset*.

Many of the Famous Five stories begin with tomboy George (Georgina), and her dog Timmy, meeting her three cousins Julian, Dick and Anne as they disembark from the London train as it pulls into Kirrin Station. I'm not sure if the Blyton family made the trip from their Beaconsfield home to Swanage by train very often, since they had a family car and undoubtedly used it to tour Dorset. But those opening scenes set in the station give me confidence that Enid knew the journey by train well enough, and loved what it stood for. She would first travel from Beaconsfield to Marylebone. Then she would shoot across London by Bakerloo Line to Waterloo. And then a new train would propel her south only to pull up at end-of-line Swanage. Today we're going in the opposite direction, and not for that whole journey. But it's tremendously exciting for all that. Holiday… freedom… adventure.

At some point during the Proust meal on Saturday, Kate asked me about the ages of the children in the Famous Five books. I confidently told her that Julian was 12, Dick and George 11, and Anne 10 at the beginning of the first book, and that thereafter their ages weren't really mentioned. Kate pursed her lips, pulled *Five Fall Into Adventure* out of her bag, turned over a few pages and read out a sentence which stated unambiguously that Julian was 16. I had to see it myself written in black ink on white page. And it meant I had to spend half an hour yesterday following up the revelation. The first book, *Five on a Treasure Island*, takes place in summer. The second, *Five Go Adventuring Again,* takes place the following winter. *Five Run Away Together* takes place the summer following the treasure-island summer. Thereafter books four, five, six, seven and eight happen during consecutive Easter and summer holidays, which is consistent with Julian being 16 years old in the summer in which the action of the ninth book, *Five Fall Into Adventure*, takes place. However, after that factual statement in the ninth book, Blyton really does stop being overt about the age thing. Her characters exist out of time from then on. Out of time and in timeless character.

I hate to interrupt Kate's reading, especially since she's got a little smile on her face. But I have to know how she's getting on with her book. So I ask her.

'I'm on the beach at Kirrin with ragamuffin Jo!'

Christ, she's only got to the end of chapter two, what has she been playing at? But instead of asking that, I offer more constructively: 'Ragamuffin Jo who the Five take to be a boy?'

'She's just been PUNCHED on the chin by Dick, who thought she was a boy!'

'It's one of the most violent scenes in the whole series. I hate that punch.'

'Dick's told her she can't fight GEORGE, because George is a girl. She'll have to fight HIM. And he's ready to punch her again!'

But Dick – who's fifteen I now have to bear in mind – doesn't get to strike Jo again, as far as I recall. Not at that stage anyway. 'Er… Doesn't Jo tell Dick that she's a girl as well, so she CAN fight George? Then Julian steps in to say there will be no more fighting, and he insults Jo in some way, the result being that poor Jo bursts into tears.'

'Julian tells her to clear off. That's what upsets her. Really she wants to hang out on the beach with the Five.'

'What? – an unwashed little gypsy girl make friends with our clean-cut bunch who are enjoying a well-deserved holiday from their expensive boarding schools? I THINK NOT!'

'Poor ragamuffin Jo, I feel sorry for her,' says Kate, plaintively. 'She doesn't have any books of her own wrapped up in brown paper with her name on them. I bet her nasty gypsy father doesn't even let her go to school. She certainly won't know where her local library is. I bet she can't even read or write.'

And we look at each other as our train rolls along. Counting our blessings then, and our blessings still.

2

Just up from Beaconsfield Station there's a branch of the Red Cross next to an Oxfam shop. The sight of either would pull at my collecting habit. The sight of both of them together sets up a frisson of expectation in the trainspotting sector of my brain. The charity shop is my oyster.

In the Red Cross shop there are a few Blyton books, as I'd expect. I like to spend a minute or two with any new title I come across whether I buy it or not. There's one here called *Bimbo and Topsy*. It's from 1943, so the Famous Five series had just been embarked upon. The book begins with a letter to children – the prospective readers – from a purring Bimbo. And the volume ends on page 157 with a letter to children, which signs off with barks and licks from Topsy. The first page of the book itself tells how one day a new kitten called Bimbo arrived at Green Hedges. Not only is the actual name of Blyton's Beaconsfield house mentioned, so is the name of her older daughter Gillian. The second daughter's name, Imogen, catches my eye when I turn over. The text and illustration both suggest the girls are about 5 years old. In fact, by 1943 Gillian, born in 1931, would have been 12, and at boarding school, and Imogen, born in 1935, would have been 8, and attending the local day school. Enid's girls were growing up fast! But their ageing wasn't so out of control that Super-Enid, in her mind's eye, couldn't put her daughters firmly back in the nursery at Green Hedges to be bowled over by the antics of Bimbo and Topsy.

Would these have been real pets, I wonder. I read the first chapter. A fox-terrier called Bobs is mentioned. Now that was a real dog, Enid's favourite pet when she lived three miles from Beaconsfield in a house called Old Thatch. Bobs became a mythical figure, and wrote a column – a complement to Enid's own longer column – in *Teacher's World*. Indeed when the real Bobs died, Enid didn't allow the chauffeur to mark the dog's grave with a monument, and Bobs' monthly column went on for several years thereafter. Does that seem strange? Not to me. The mortal dog was dead and there was nothing Enid could do about that. But the essential Bobs lived on in the writer's mind, and Enid would keep feeding off her love and affection for the sparky fox-terrier as long as she could.

I keep reading. It's obvious that Topsy and Bimbo were real pets. If only because it seems so odd that Bimbo, the sleek Siamese, is supposed to be the male, and Topsy, the frolicsome puppy, the female. I find it difficult to read the little adventures that way. And I'm sure Enid was only able to maintain their genders in this anti-stereotypical way because Bimbo *was* a boy kitten and Topsy *was* a girl pup. But that simply doesn't work for the reader. Not in the five minutes I've allotted to the book, anyway.

Kate has picked up a Malory Towers paperback. 'I remember reading these. I didn't realise that Enid Blyton wrote them.' As she flicks through the book, I offer the unsolicited information that Blyton wrote one Malory Towers book a year for six years, from 1946, taking the main character from first year to sixth year *à la* J.K. Rowling. The main character is called Darrell Rivers and the boarding school she attends is in Cornwall. Enid's second hus-

band's surname was Darrell Waters. Gillian and Imogen, fruit of
the first marriage, both had their names changed to Darrell Waters,
and the school they both attended to complete their schooling was
also in Cornwall. In 1946, Gillian was 15, and Imogen 10. By the
end of the series in 1952, Gillian was 21, and Imogen 16. So again
Enid was letting things trickle down through her mind for a few
years before opening the literary sluice gates. Kate asks me for the
name of Enid's first husband. Can I remember? She married Hugh
in 1924, when she was 27. But, no, I don't recall Hugh's surname.

'You're not much use as an official Enid Blyton tour guide.'

'*Pollock* – that's it. Hugh Pollock.'

I'm still flicking through *Bimbo and Topsy*. I hope this book is
classed as 'non-fiction', because that's obviously what it is.
Chapters like 'Bimbo and the Trees', 'Fun in the Garden', 'Bobs
Melts Away' are just a straightforward account of what went on at
Green Hedges when Enid was its mistress. The final letter from
Topsy to all the children urges them to come and live next door so
that they – the readers – could tell Topsy and Bimbo what to put in
their next book. Too late for that, too late. But I like both the sentiment, and the suggestion that experience is all. Actually, all the
Blyton books I can see in this Red Cross shop were written at Green
Hedges, though it's not a special display or anything. Such a collection of Enid Blyton's Green Hedges work could be found inside just
about any charity shop in the country.

Next door, the Oxfam branch has a friendly feel to it, several
women talking across the shop account for that. However, the
words 'Famous Five' leap out from the glossy cover of a hardback
volume and attract all my attention.

It's a 500-pager containing three of the twenty-one Five stories.
It's a weird collection because the books are *Five on a Treasure
Island*, *Five Go Adventuring Again* and *Five Go to Billycock Hill*.
That's the first, second and sixteenth book in the series. Why have
they done that? It can't be to do with rights, because Hodder &

Stoughton, now Hodder Headline, are the original publishers of all the Five books, and if they don't actually own the copyright they still get a licence to publish the books. The volume I'm holding is advertised as containing three Famous Five 'Adventures' while there is apparently a companion volume that consists of three Famous Five 'Mysteries'. Can some editor at Hodder's really have gone through the titles from the third one on saying, 'No, that's a mystery rather than an adventure... No, that's a holiday jaunt rather than an adventure...'. Or perhaps one editor said to another: 'Let's bung the first three books in one volume and see if we can shift another ten thousand copies.' And the assistant editor would have said 'Righty-oh', but then made sure that his own personal favourite was included.

I didn't read *Five Go To Billycock Hill* as a child. But as a ten-year-old I wrote in my diary that *Five Go To Finniston Farm* was the best Famous Five book I'd read to date. And I remember linking Finniston Farm to Billycock Hill (Finniston Hill... Billycock Farm... Finnicock Hill... Billystone Farm), and desperately wanting to read the latter. But the books only existed as hardbacks then, which I couldn't afford. And it wasn't among the titles stocked by my local library. So, no Billycock adventure for me. Not until about a month ago.

Billycock Hill is the only Famous Five book I've bought new. It cost me £4.99 from Waterstone's, and is a special edition – first printed in 1997, on the centenary of the author's birth – reproducing part of the dust-cover of the original hardback as the paperback's cover. It includes all of the Eileen Soper line drawings that accompanied the original text. I bought it because the image of fine-featured, tousle-haired George on the cover reminded me of Laura, an artist friend, with whom I was going to spend a couple of days walking along Hadrian's Wall. I got well into the book, alone on the train to Newcastle. And then I left it in my rucksack when I met Laura. But in the middle of our first walking day, a circular route, Laura asked if I'd read her a chapter as we rested up in a wood. So I did. And we enjoyed that. And over the next couple of days I read more chapters. On one occasion, in a youth hostel, I was sitting cross-legged on the end of her top bunk, as she listened while lying on her back, her feet within a few inches of my crotch. I found the conjunction of bodies, book, the said and the unsaid, the done and the undone, decidedly erotic. She fell asleep.

At the next youth hostel the same happened – she bloody well fell asleep in the middle of some slick reading! Though she had a better excuse that time, having just walked sixteen miles that day and then drunk three pints of beer. I'd bought the book with the intention of giving it to Laura, knowing that I'd come across an original hardback, with or without dust-cover, sooner or later. But in the end I held onto the book so as to be able to finish the story on the train back home. I sent Laura an e-mail summarising the last fifty pages in a jokey fashion. But when I spoke to her later, she said she hadn't read the e-mail properly as she hoped to get hold of the book and finish reading it herself. This made me feel guilty about hanging onto what was really her book. Alas, I can't post her the paperback now because of some intimate notes I made on that particular copy. But I'll make sure that she gets the book in some shape or form. Perhaps one day I'll send her the paperback itself, because by then my written comment that 'The cock in Billycock is silent' will no longer mean anything to either of us.

Where am I? In a charity shop in Beaconsfield with Kate. She is talking with the volunteers, talking to them about Enid Blyton. One volunteer – seeing that I am paying attention to their chat now – tells us that Blyton's house on Blyton Close was demolished ages ago.

'Yes, it was knocked down shortly after her death. But we're going to visit the street anyway,' I tell her.

There's a short, possibly significant, silence. We're told that we should come back at lunchtime because the store manager will be in then, and he lives near Blyton Close. I've a hunch this might be worth following up.

'Any more Blyton memorabilia in the town?' asks Kate, chirpily.

A big blonde woman speaks: 'There's the model village. That has a model of Green Hedges. Trouble is, I don't think it's open just now.'

'It's not open until the school holidays,' I confirm.

'Anything else?' asks Kate, on my behalf.

A third woman wanders over from the back of the shop, admires Kate's dramatic hairstyle, and tells us that just across the street there is a metal sculpture tribute thingy to Enid Blyton. 'Noddy and a few other characters. But it's no big deal, really. I'm sure most people passing it on their way to the supermarket don't even know it's there.'

We'll check that out. Our proposed trip to Swanage is mentioned. And Kate is asked which of the Five she will be when we hire our own Kirrin Cottage. 'George?' hazards the woman. 'How did you guess?' replies Kate.

Soon everyone is laughing, and when we stop actually laughing out loud, we're still smiling. The five of us continue to have a conversation about Enid Blyton, all of us no doubt feeling we have a firm foundation in the conversation because of having read the books, two, three, four decades ago. If I was to propose that Kate, myself and the people now present in this Oxfam shop were to stage a Famous Five adventure in Swanage in the spring, I think we'd all sign up for it here and now. The Oxfam Five could live next door to the Proust Five. And I'd float between the two groups as everyone's – not just George's – loyal Timmy.

In the meantime, we're in Blyton Close. There isn't much to see. It's a perfectly ordinary suburban road, a dead-end. There are about a dozen houses here (in Blyton's time there were just two large properties) all with gravel drives and garages, all empty looking. Kate actually walks up the drive of a house called Kirrin

Cottage and rings the bell, but there is no one in. Nor is there any-one in at the new detached house called Green Hedges. So we stand in the middle of the road and imagine what a hell of a job the Proust coach would have trying to turn around here. It would have to go forward into the drive of Kirrin Cottage, then back up into the drive of Green Hedges, then forward into Kirrin Cottage, then back into Green Hedges... Kirrin Cottage... Green Hedges... Our driver was making twenty-one-point turns throughout the French trip. And a twenty-one-point turn is what we imagine he would have to do to turn around in Blyton Close. Any resident gazing out from behind net curtains would be wondering what on earth the 'IN REMEMBRANCE OF THINGS PAST' coach was playing at.

Kate asks to be reminded when Blyton lived here. She lived here from 1938, when she was 41, to her death thirty years later. Was she married during that time? Yes, she was married. First, to Hugh Pollock, though the marriage broke up when he was absent a lot at the beginning of the Second World War. In any case, Hugh had reverted to the problems he had with alcohol while she was becom-ing more confident in herself through her increasing – but not yet astonishing – success as a writer. In 1941, at about the time when Hugh embarked on a relationship with someone else, Enid began to see Kenneth Darrell Waters, a man several years older than her. Darrell Waters, a 50-year-old surgeon, was to become her second husband.

'Was the second marriage happy?'

'It seems so. They got on well physically, just as Hugh and Enid had.'

'How do you know, Dunc?'

'Oh, it's what her biographer and her daughter think. I admit I wasn't actually in their bedroom when they got it on. But I've seen the odd quote from Enid. Yes, she loved Hugh for a good ten years. And she loved Kenneth too, for the rest of their life together.'

'What about this number two husband, then?'

'He provided solid emotional support and devoted companionship. Enid had as much respect for his photographic memory as he did for her energy, intelligence and clear writing. And although he was fundamentally an outdoors, sporty person – not an intellectual – so was she, you might say.'

'She was a writer first of all, wasn't she?'

'Oh, yes, I almost forgot. She was a writing phenomenon.'

God, I can't believe that the house isn't still here. When I visited John Ruskin's home in the Lake District, there were special places that allowed the writer's character to be better understood. And I bet Blyton would have surrounded herself with objects and structures that expressed her personality as a writer. For example, the long swing-seat on which she sat outside and wrote in the summer months. I would love to have been able to see that, to sit on it, to get into a Blyton rhythm. She would sit there at 10 a.m., and close her eyes for a minute to let her mind clear. In due course, her characters and their environment would appear in her mind's eye. Then she would open her eyes again and desperately try – by tapping away at a typewriter resting on a board on her knees – to keep up with the flow of images and dialogue emanating from the private cinema screen in her head.

So why isn't the house here? I recall reading in the short biography written by George Greenfield, Enid's literary agent, that her assets were in Darrell Waters Ltd, and that a man called Eric Rogers was the head of that company. Darrell Waters Ltd had been formed in 1949 because Enid hadn't been paying enough tax. Suddenly it became important that the house was in the company's name and she was charged an annual rent, which could be offset against her income. This reduced her annual income tax liability. This was fine, as far as it went. But, according to Greenfield, Eric Rogers was soon running a Bentley, charged to Darrell Waters Ltd, and each weekday lunchtime Rogers would eat and drink at a corner table in the Savoy, charging the bill to Enid's company again. Such expenditure may have been tax-deductible, but all that meant was that Enid Blyton's wealth was reduced by £5, say, for every £10 the pig spent at his high-class trough.

Rogers got himself written into the will of Enid, and of Kenneth too, who predeceased her. So he was due a large slice of the Green Hedges pie on her death. Therefore it became inevitable that – rather than preserve the house as a monument for the millions of readers who had made Enid's (and Eric Rogers') fortune – Green Hedges was sold to developers. In the process, Rogers got his hands on yet more money.

So how did one Eric Rogers, complete philistine, get control of Enid Blyton's empire, which was founded on an imaginative link with children and a literary talent? Eric Rogers and Kenneth Darrell Waters had a mutual interest in sport, and – of all things moronic – horse racing in particular. Kenneth would use his photographic memory in respect of the form and pedigree of race-horses. He would run his name down the runners of a race and his memory would give him more background information than the paper itself.

Enid: 'What happened to the philistine? Reader, I married him!'

Kate and I walk back into town and, as it's not far away, take a slight detour to Bekenscot Model Village. The front gate is heavily padlocked, and there's nothing to see beyond the gate but an approach to out-of-sight buildings. So that's that. But Kate takes hold of the lock and demonstrates that it's not actually in use. It's just draped around both sides of the gate in a decorative manner. Ha! So we push the gate open and walk in. Trespassing is much easier with someone else, particularly a woman. What could be more harmless than the two of us, an eminently respectable-looking pair, strolling along a lane together. I'm utterly relaxed when we come across a man with a wheel-barrow. And after a few sentences of banter he is leading us to the scale model of Green Hedges.

As we walk through it, the model village looks great. There are little houses and churches and a police station on landscaped sites. It's so *Noddy in Toyland*. Indeed this place was in existence when Enid lived at Green Hedges and I've no doubt she strolled among this scale landscape, this green and mini England, when thinking about Noddy stories. Of course, first things first, Blyton was charmed and impressed when she met the Belgian illustrator Harmsen van der Beek in 1949, and their initial meeting – when she saw some preliminary sketches – inspired her to write the first two sixty-pagers. So the publisher had two finished stories in his hands four days after the meeting.

Beek's drawings were the immediate inspiration for Noddy but this undulating Toy Town of Bekenscot must have prompted many a Noddy scene too. Especially after poor Beek died of overwork, just seven books into what became a twenty-four book series. Every cloud has a silver lining though, and the first illustration in the eighth book, the first illustration drawn by an illustrator other than Beek, has Noddy waking up in his Bed-For-One, stretching deliciously and waving his hand at a sunbeam. A great example of an artist letting the joy he or she is feeling from landing a fantastic commission feed straight back into his or her work. Oh, what a big celebration is taking place in little Noddy's striped pyjamas!

We arrive at Green Hedges. The model has been taken away from the hedge-lined base and is lying on its side underneath a lean-to. This protects it from the rain, I suppose. But our guide helps me to turn it the right way up, and we pull it out from some other clutter so that there is space all around the model. I start talking with Kate about the model, the plan of the garden, the photographs pinned to a notice-board on the inside of the lean-to and the workman gets the idea that we might be here for some time. He just leaves us to it! How very obliging of him; now let me try to get my head around Green Hedges.

Actually, I may be able to do just that. I can consider the house from all angles, with the help of recollections of a book called *A Childhood at Green Hedges*. This book was written in the late eighties by Imogen Smallwood, Enid's younger daughter. And I suppose the main impression it gives is that, yes, Enid Blyton had been a generous and brilliant mother to the world's children, to all those who read her books or wrote to her, anyway. But she had been an occasionally cold and consistently unapproachable stranger to her actual children, especially Imogen.

Enid: 'No, Imogen, I cannot "come upstairs to play". It is 11 a.m. and I am working my fingers to the bone, and will be until Daddy gets home.'

A vivid scene from this book comes to mind: that of Enid beating Imogen's bare bottom with the back of a hairbrush, while elsewhere in the lounge, Hugh, dressed in his kilt, appears to be unmoved by Imogen's screams. Strangely enough, in another of Imogen's recollections, she remarks on Hugh having an Ayrshire accent – a small but telling detail – when recalling that he bawled at her for interfering with some special birthday set-up on the lawn at Green Hedges. She goes on to say that she didn't love her poor father very much. All in all, I'd be surprised if Imogen emerged from her childhood with pro-Scottish views, and I pass this impression on to Kate.

Another occasion when Enid meted out corporal punishment was the day when Imogen was visited by her nanny, the woman who had taken care of her when she was first born. The girl got over-excited during the visit and, as far as the working mother sitting at her typewriter downstairs was concerned, she started to make too much noise. Was Enid jealous of the warm relationship that had built up between the nanny and her charge? Well, if she was, it was an isolated incident, because Enid was obviously fulfilled by her daily work, by her vocation, by her 'real' children as she once put it – her books. And it was the urge to get back to writing that made her decide not to breastfeed her second baby;

she handed over total care of her second child to a nanny.

Another vivid scene from Imogen's troubled book: second husband Kenneth is furiously laying into 9-year-old Imogen – verbally, not physically – for being a gigantic pain in her mother's backside. Imogen had just got back home to Green Hedges from her first term at boarding school to find her nanny has been dismissed. Imogen's tantrum was understandable. She realised that there was no longer anyone at home to whom she could pour out her heart.

As well as charting Imogen's emotional ups and downs, the book paints a detailed picture of what went on in the house. And although I didn't pay enough attention to the chapters about the servants' quarters, the upstairs nursery, Enid's part of the house and the gardens, with this architectural model of Green Hedges in my mind I'll only have to revisit the book for that full picture to materialise.

Enid's own autobiography will be good to consult as well in this context. After all *The Story of My Life* might more accurately be called *A Maturity at Green Hedges*, because most of the chapters are set there and the book is full of photographs taken on site. Enid and her second husband walking together… Enid and her teenage daughters laughing together as one happy group… Enid beside the little circular pool she made herself in the middle of the lawn so that she could see birds bathing and drinking when she looked up from her work…

'I'm getting hungry,' says Kate, who probably feels she's been listening to me going on for quite some time. We do need a bit of a break soon, I suppose. In fact, as Kate clarifies, we need 'LUNCH NOW!'. So it's off to a fish-and-chip shop and a sit-down with a mug of tea as we wait for our order. When the fish and chips come, it's a feast for the eyes: big chunks of potatoes, well fried, and two of the largest cod to come out of the North Sea in years. Luckily, we are starving! Luckily, the woman who serves us is willing to fetch some tomato sauce for me. Luckily, she is also happy to go off again and fetch some tartare sauce for Kate. But we don't ask her for anything else – that would be pushing it. Instead we thank the waitress for the wonderful platefuls of food, just as Julian would thank Joan the cook at Kirrin Cottage for a hamper full of sandwiches, hard-boiled eggs, apple tarts and bottles of ginger beer. Just as, in several books, Anne thanks some fat rosy-cheeked farmer's wife for inundating the Five with fresh natural food.

After lunch we sit on a bench and debate whether we should go back to the Oxfam shop now, or later, when we're properly going again. We agree that it would be better to go there before we disappear for a walk. We enter the shop and there's the old boy standing beside the till. Grey suit, reddish face, straight back and an overall impression of backwater conservatism. Or perhaps it's something else. 'Good afternoon, sir,' he says to me, deadpan. 'Good afternoon, madam,' he says to Kate, equally expressionless. 'Can I help you at all?'

I mention that we had called in that morning and... But he knows all about us. He knows that I am a writer and he asks me straight out – but in a perfectly polite way – who I'm writing for. I look at him and blink as I try to get my head round this superficially simple but actually quite complex question.

'Freelance, are you?' he says, finally. I smile back. He turns away from my effort to be friendly. 'And this is your travelling secretary, is it?' He's looking at Kate now, who's surprised to be addressed in this way – once removed. 'Is she competent?' the manager says to me. But I can only stare too, so he turns back to Kate. 'Fishing for compliments, are you, madam?'

Christ, what is this? I pull myself together and ask what I came here to ask. He, however, stonewalls the topic of Blyton Close. Well, no, when I ask a specific question, he does inform me that the Blyton house was on the right-hand side of the street rather than on the left.

The manager goes on talking to us in the most *faux*-respectful way. We have to get out of this shop – it's changed so much since we were here this morning! I ask him if there is a second-hand bookshop in Beaconsfield. He sniffs and tells us there is one along the road, and if we take the number 66 bus we will pass its door. Is it too far to walk? I extract the Ordnance Survey map and open it out. He asks me to lay the map absolutely flat on the table, which I do. He points out with a ruler the curve on the road where the bookshop called 'The Barn' is to be found. It's straight up the main street, I can't miss it. I pick up the map and start to put it away. The manager asks me – very politely, very firmly – to place the map down on the table again, for he has not finished telling me the whereabouts of the shop. So I lay the map down again, just like a soldier would lay down his arms in battle when the enemy had him surrounded and there was a machine-gun pointed at his chest. He has now decided that 'The Barn' is on a different bend in the road, but is very specific about the change of location. 'Go past the garage on the right. Then it's there, on your left.' So that's fine. His every word has still got a weird intensity about it. And I know Kate has turned her back on the guy for the map part of the conversation. However, she's found an old copy of *Mrs Beeton's Cookery Book* and knows just which of her friends would love it. She asks if the manager would be kind enough to put the book aside and she will collect it later on when we return from our afternoon walk.

'The lady wants to pay for the book now and collect it later. Bag please,' shouts our host to no one in particular. The only reason I know he's not talking to me or Kate is that he hasn't finished his request with the word 'sir' or 'madam'. One of the women from this morning comes forward with a smile – for us – and a plastic bag that I know she would like to put over the manager's head.

Seconds later we're outside and have ducked out of sight of the shop window. First, we burst into nervous laughter as we recall everything that the manger said or did inside those four walls.

Second, we work out that what must have intimidated him about us was his briefing by his female staff. Either they'd successfully communicated our sense of freedom and adventure or they'd deliberately wound up the old bloke by making up fake literary credentials for me. But how he was primed for a visit from a WRITER and his COMPANION. The manager had been intent on finding out if this was a real writer that was entering his kingdom, or – oh, God! – just another hopeless fake.

As we walk along the main road out of Beaconsfield towards the second-hand bookshop, an idea comes to me.

'I think we have just met some kind of reincarnation of Mr Goon.'

'Who?'

In order to tell Kate about Goon I have to tell her about Enid's Mystery series, the first of which, *The Mystery of the Burnt Cottage*, was written just a few months after the first Famous Five book. This time there are Five Find-Outers *plus* a dog called Buster. The five in the Mystery books are two sets of brother and sister – Pip and Bets, Larry and Daisy – and it's Fatty who owns the popular Scottie dog called Buster.

'But who is Goon? Tell me that, sir?'

'Hang on – I'll get there. The children operate in Peterswood. Perhaps it's not such a big linguistic leap from "Peter's wood" to "Beacon's field", though Peterswood is mostly based on the village of Bourne End, three miles from Beaconsfield, where Enid lived for nine years with Hugh before moving to Green Hedges. Anyway, what struck me recently was that the Famous Five books were about a group of children on holiday in Kirrin, based on Swanage, which is where Enid went on an annual family holiday. But the Five Find-Outers books were set in the school holidays, at home in Bucks. And the "at home" business gives Enid, or her characters, more confidence in their surroundings, more local characters to focus on, and more opportunity to dig deep.'

'You prefer these books to the Famous Fives, then?' asks Kate.

'They're both very freshly written. Adventures away from home, or on one's doorstep.' I notice that we're passing the garage that the charity shop manager mentioned. All I can see are big isolated houses, typical of what you'd expect on the edge of a well-to-do town. The prospect of a bookshop seems like the remotest of possibilities. We keep walking, with me telling Kate about the second book in the series. It's effectively set at Green Hedges and the adjoining house. Now, in real life Enid's gardener was called Old Tapping (he gets a mention in *A Childhood at Green Hedges*). Apparently, Enid sacked him for stealing vegetables, though she couldn't get rid of him altogether as he went on to become the gardener of the neighbouring property. And in her book, *The Mystery of the Disappearing Cat,* there is a gardener called Old Tupping.

'That was naughty of her.'

'Yeah, well, wait and hear the rest.'

I tell Kate that Old Tupping shouts at his simple-minded but nice assistant, Luke, for giving the little girl who lives in the house next door some strawberry runners that were destined for the bonfire. 'Old Tupping climbs the wall and finds 8-year-old Bets lying on the lawn. (Bear in mind, Imogen would have been the same age at the time of writing.) Old Tupping pulls the girl to her feet, demands to know where the stolen runners are, destroys the neat bit of digging and well-watered planting that little Bets has done in her own patch of lovingly maintained garden. He rips up the strawberry plants and tells the girl she'll go *straight to prison* if she carries on the way she's going. By this time, Bets is in tears but she does manage to reply pluckily that they don't send little girls to prison.'

'*They don't send little girls to prison,*' says Kate, in a suitable voice.

'Old Tupping snarls at her, but having accomplished his search and destroy mission, he storms back to his own territory, the next door garden.'

'What a *horrible* man!' says Kate, hitting the nail on the head.

'Of course, it transpires that it was Old Tupping who stole the valuable Siamese cat from his employer. And Fatty and the rest of the Find-Outers help put him away.'

'Horrible Oxfam Tupping!' says Kate, spot on.

'Peace and tranquillity return to Green Hedges. And with that argumentative, noisy gardener put in his place, Enid can get back to doing her thing.'

'Spinning stories.'

'Standing by the sluice gates, with the handle turned firmly to open.'

It's getting dark now. There's no bookshop here. We get off the main road and sit down in a clearing so that we can watch the sunset. The scene is splendid, but I can't settle for that. 'Can I tell you about the third Mystery?'

'Of course. But you haven't told me about Mr Goon yet.'

'The series evolves quickly. In the first book, conceited Fatty is only tolerated by the other children because of his nice dog, Buster. But by the third book, Frederick Algernon Trotteville – but always Fatty to his peers – has established himself as the undisputed leader of the Find-Outers. Why? Because he's so blooming clever and funny. Not only has he solved the first two mysteries virtually single-handed, not only does he humiliate PC Goon at every opportunity, but he has proved himself to be a master of disguise.'

To convey Fatty's attraction to the rest of the group – his attraction to the reader and to Enid herself – I have to tell Kate about an incident near the beginning of *The Mystery of the Secret Room*. Fatty has been showing off his invisible ink which is actually just orange juice. He writes an insulting letter to PC Goon using it. Larry, Daisy, Bets and Pip can't see the writing until a warm iron is applied and – Hey Presto! – the words appear.

'What did Fatty write?' asks Kate.

'Oh, something along the lines of: "Dear Clear-Orf. Looking forward to the next Mystery. Reckon we'll be solving it first unless

THIS IS HER
FATTY

Julian looked at them in surprise.
This boy was certainly gifted.

your brains get a good oiling in the meantime. Love and kisses from, The Five Find-Outers and Buster".'

'Nice turn of phrase, Fatty's got.'

'Now, Fatty thinks this is such a good letter that he decides to deliver the cooled-down page – seemingly blank again – to Goon. So Fatty disguises himself as a French boy, and when he hands over the sheet of paper in an envelope, Goon doesn't know that he's being handed it by that troublemaker of a fat lad. However, at the next meeting of the Find-Outers, someone points out that if Goon has the wit to apply a warm iron to the apparently blank sheet of paper he'll read the message and will be down on the Find-Outers even harder than before. Fatty sees the sense in this, realises he has been rash, and so writes Goon another letter, an admiring one, praising his well-oiled brains...'

'Well-oiled brains!'

'In disguise as the French boy again, Fatty makes sure he bumps into the policeman. Old Goon is in a furious mood because he has indeed taken a hot iron to the letter and read the insult. He shows the "French boy" the sheet of paper, now blank again, but it is blown out of their hands by a gust of wind, making it an easy matter for Fatty to substitute the second "blank" piece of paper for the first. So when Goon next applies a hot iron to the insulting letter, in the presence of witnesses, it's not insulting at all! And Fatty has run rings around poor old Clear-Orf.'

'So there's quite a lot of messing about in these Mysteries. It's not just straight into the crime and then working through suspects and alibis and all that predictable stuff.'

'Not at all. Enid likes to play with her creations before getting them to put their heads down for a bit.'

'Why is Goon also called Clear-Orf?'

'Because that's what he says every time he sees those nuisance kids. That's what he says every time daft Buster goes for his ankles.'

There is so much more to say about Goon, in particular the link between himself and Hugh and about how certain things that went on in Enid's personal life with her first husband fed into astonishing games she played in her fiction. But I don't want to go into that now. It's a bit late in the day. Besides, I really need to leave that for the Bourne End trip.

So instead I make do with telling Kate a little more about the genius that is Fatty, and how he uses his invisible ink trick to get himself rescued after being taken prisoner in the mysterious secret room of the third Mystery's title. Then I shut up about the Mystery books, and about Enid Blyton, and we have a quiet and companionable quarter-of-an-hour sitting together. Several dog-walkers pass by. Each one of them seems to call out 'Buster!' or 'Timmy!' to their charge, we can't help noticing. It's a bit weird in Beaconsfield.

Eventually, Kate sighs. I ask what's troubling her. She doesn't want to go back to the Oxfam shop to face our Goon or Old Tupping or whoever he is. But I do. Not only has he got Kate's *Mrs Beeton* book, but I must tell him what a lovely walk we've had around the highways and byways of Beaconsfield.

I tell Kate that if he really is a throw-back to Goon, who liked his nosh, he'll have gone through her *Mrs Beeton*, and every time a phrase like steak-and-kidney pie comes up he'll have underlined it in cheap blue biro.

'I'll check it before we leave the shop,' giggles Kate.

So we go in. And we have the chat. I make it clear to Goon that we had a wonderful afternoon, a lovely walk, but that we did not even come close to finding any bookshop. He goes so far as to admit that he perhaps should have told us that the bookshop was in fact just a barn. Not so much 'the' barn as 'a' barn, then? Yes, that's right. Well, fair enough, goodbye, thanks for making our day what it has been – goodbye, goodbye – and we're out of the madhouse.

'Did you notice something?' asks Kate as we trot along the main road.

'He didn't call us sir or madam.'

'Not once, sir.'

'He'd given us such a going over the first time that he felt he didn't need to rise to the occasion when he saw us again.'

'What a pig of a man, *sir*.'

'Goon's the name, *madam*… By the way, have you checked your book?'

Kate takes the hardback out of its plastic bag and reports no underlining of pies of any description. Also, whenever strawberries are mentioned in a recipe, there don't appear to be any comments in the margin about whipping a young girl's bare bottom.

'All that means,' I comment, 'is that Goon isn't as dumb as he looks, and has made his annotations in invisible ink.'

'I'll check that when we get home, Fatty. I'll run a warm iron over *every blooming page*.'

Indeed it is time to go home. The commuters are streaming back into Beaconsfield and we're suddenly exhausted.

But I don't want to go home.

I want to stay right here. In this comfort zone we've carved out for ourselves. I want to stay here with some boys and girls I've known for decades…

3

Four weeks into the school summer holidays and there hadn't been a sniff of a Mystery for the Find-Outers. But Fatty wasn't bothered about that because he was hot on the trail of one now. He was thinking of calling it *The Mystery of Green Hedges* but he didn't have to trouble himself about giving it a name. Not at this stage in the investigation.

The five Find-Outers had agreed to meet in the garden of the Darrell Waters' place by a flowering red rose bush in view of the south aspect of the house. It was midnight and all the children were excited about having successfully crept from their beds and sneaked out of their houses without waking their parents or rousing the Green Hedges household.

'Our mum and dad sleep like logs,' Pip told the others. 'So Bets and I could afford to make the odd creaking noise as we went downstairs. Though Bets shouldn't have giggled as she took a swig from the bottle of lemonade.'

Bets recalled how the lemonade had exploded from her mouth and had splashed onto the lino where it had gone on fizzing. Crikey! She tried not to giggle into the night air as she remembered the scene. It felt strange lying on woollen rugs, late at night, looking towards a dark house in which strangers lived, and the 9-year-old was a bit over-excited by it all. 'Sorry, Pip. But after all, no one did hear us.'

No one had heard Larry and Daisy creep out of their house either. And as Fatty had told them, the double-gate at the end of the drive leading to the big Darrell Waters mansion was open, so that they could just push their bikes through, get off the noisy gravel and onto the silent grass as quickly as possible. They had met the others at the designated spot at exactly the appointed time. Everyone had brought a rug or two, so the five were comfortable enough lying on the lawn.

'So why are we here, Fatty?' asked Larry.

'This is where Enid Blyton lives.'

'Well, we know that!'

'Haven't you heard?' said Fatty, knowing that they hadn't.

'Haven't we heard what?' asked Larry.

'I found out from Goon this afternoon that one of her books has been stolen.'

'Why did he tell *you*?' asked Bets, puzzled.

'He didn't want to, of course,' said Fatty with a superior air. 'But he just couldn't keep the information that he'd been telephoned from Green Hedges to himself. Bursting with self-importance Goon was!'

'So what did you get out of him?' asked Pip.

'Not much more than that,' Fatty had to concede. 'The book has been inscribed and signed.'

'What does "inscribed" mean?' asked Bets.

'On the first blank page is written: "To My Darling Husband, with Love from Enid".'

'Yuck,' said Pip. 'Does that make it more valuable, then?'

'If it was inscribed from any of our mums to our dads, then no, definitely not,' said Fatty. 'But a book of her own, signed by Enid, yes!'

'What book was it?' asked Larry.

Fatty didn't know. 'As soon as Goon realised I was interested, he clammed up. Though I did learn that Enid has told Goon not to investigate the theft for the time being. She's only reported it for insurance purposes.'

An owl hooted.

'Golly, Old Goon is on the case after all. And just to show off, he's doing owl impressions!' said Fatty.

'Where's Buster?' said Bets, suddenly missing the presence of the sparky Scottie dog.

'Can't trust Buster to keep his yappy trap shut at night,' said Fatty. 'So I left him in his basket at home.'

'Oh, poor Buster! He's missing out on all the fun.'

'Missing out on all the fun!' scoffed Fatty. 'He'll be dreaming about snapping at old Clear-Orf's ankles. He'll be chewing regulation issue police trousers all night long. By morning that basket will be a sweat-drenched, hair-matted pit!'

The other children laughed. An owl hooted. 'Those kids

and that public health nuisance of a mutt. CLEAR-ORF!'
translated Fatty. The children laughed again, they were all
glad they'd come out tonight on their odd mission. There
wasn't anywhere they'd rather be than on the case with Fatty.

The moon was shining down on the house, lighting up a
whitewashed, timbered, gable-end set in the middle of the
first floor.

'See that little roofed area?' said Fatty. 'Well, to the left of
it is Enid Blyton's bedroom.'

They all looked.

'For three or four years she slept there with her first husband, Hugh. And for the last eight years she's slept there
with her second husband, Kenneth.'

'Can you do that?' asked Bets.

'Do what?'

'Just change husbands when you want to.'

'Of course you can!' said Fatty, who was 14 going on 40
and a boy of the world. 'You have to divorce one and then
marry the other, but that's just a matter of filling in forms –
you know how adults like to complicate everything. Anyway,
as far as Enid's concerned *nothing has changed* in the last twelve
years or so. She goes to bed early and gets the long sleep that
she needs.

'Why does she need a long sleep?' asked Bets.

'Because her brain is so active during the day! She's a
writer and that means she has to be seeing things and turning those sights into words, for hours on end.'

'A bit like being at school?'

'Except there's not a teacher telling you things. If you're a
writer, you're telling the things to yourself.'

'Do Enid's husbands need long sleeps too?'

'Oh, that's a good question, little Bets,' said Fatty, appre-
ciatively. 'And the answer is yes and yes. *Hugh* needed a long

sleep because every weekday morning he had to get up and go into London where he worked for a publisher. That's how Enid and he met, through him commissioning her to write a book for the company he worked for…'

'What's commissioning?' asked Bets of her friend Fatty. She had come to realise long ago that Fatty knew things that no one else in her world did.

'That's when you promise to pay someone for doing an agreed piece of work.'

'So you could commission me to tidy up your room?' asked Bets.

'Er… yes. Or even better, *you* could get your mum and dad to commission *me* to write up one of our successful mysteries. Your mum and dad would then print up thousands of copies and sell them in bookshops all around the country. Then they would be publishers, just like the company Enid's Hugh worked for.'

'I see,' said Bets who would get Pip to put this idea to their parents at the first occasion they were all sitting round the breakfast table in a spectacularly good mood.

Fatty carried on: 'Of course, Hugh commissioned other authors apart from Enid. He worked with Winston Churchill on his memoirs of the Great War, at a time when Churchill was getting very worried about the possibility of a new war. And Hugh, who had fought and won medals in the First World War, also started to get very worried about the future.'

Larry and Pips frowned. They knew that war was a terrible thing. They expected that they'd have to go and fight in one when they grew up, and hoped they'd be ready for it. But right now they knew they were ready to go over the top wherever Fatty led them.

'Before anyone knew it, Hugh was ill,' continued Fatty. Unfortunately, Fatty wasn't really in a position to say anything about the illness, or about what happened because of it. All he knew was that life changed at Green Hedges.

'As for *Kenneth*, the husband who is lying asleep up there right now. He also needs a lot of sleep.'

'Why?' asked Bets, who was loving the way this new mystery was slowly developing.

'Because he too has to get up early and go into London.'

'Is he a publisher as well?'

'No, he's a surgeon. If Winston Churchill needed an urgent operation then they'd take him to St Stephen's Hospital in the West End, and Kenneth Darrell Waters – Old Magic Fingers himself – would be the man to conduct the operation.'

'Liar!' said Bets, who sometimes knew when Fatty was teasing.

'I'm not kidding about the surgeon bit. Every weekday he's back here by five o'clock and he spends the evening with Enid. They have dinner together just like any other middle-aged couple. She reads him her day's work, which can take quite some time. They wander about the garden and then they go to bed. We could have met at eleven o'clock safely enough; all would have been quiet then. But I thought we should leave it until midnight.'

'Because it feels more mysterious!'

'Exactly, Bets. Because it feels more mysterious.'

The owl hooted. 'Goon again, he probably haunts this place for reasons we know nothing about,' said Fatty. He translated: 'What are those damned kids up to, sticking their noses into other people's private affairs?'

Fatty was young, but already he knew how important it was to really enjoy yourself. And he knew that hardly anyone did when they grew up. Enid did. She was an exception to all sorts of adult rules. And Fatty was going to get to the bottom of how she managed to get older – she was 53 now – and yet stay so young at heart.

'Now the room on the other side of the house on the first floor that we can see: that's the nursery,' said Fatty.

'Are there babies in the house?' asked Bets.

Fatty had to correct himself: 'Or I should say it *was* the nursery when Gillian and Imogen were young. Now Gillian is at university and that's Imogen's bedroom when she's home from school. But turn your attention to the room directly under the main bedroom. That's the library. In summer, Enid sits on the swing-seat in front of it – you can just see something the size of a sofa in between the pillars of the veranda.'

Bets wasn't able to see it in the dark. But she could picture it all right.

Fatty went on: 'In the library, there must be first editions of 300 books – all written by Enid – standing on the shelves. The stolen book could be any one of those.'

'Wow!' said Daisy, wondering if 300 books was a lot for a single writer to have written on her own. And rather thinking it was.

'And of all those books, thirty were published in 1949 alone,' said Fatty. 'And last year wasn't particularly special. She's been writing books at getting on for that rate for a few years now.'

'If she's got so many, I don't know why she should be so bothered about losing one,' said Pip.

'She probably isn't that bothered. But today's theft may have been just the start of something,' said Fatty.

All the Find-Outers were excited about the idea of going inside Green Hedges. And their anticipation was not spoiled by fear, because Fatty made it clear they wouldn't be going inside just yet. All they had to do that night was to look at the house from the garden; to look at the mysterious scene and listen closely to their leader.

They exchanged views about the latest Famous Five book, *Five Get Into Trouble*, which they'd all read and enjoyed.

'The book's good, but *The Mountain of Adventure* is even better,' said Larry, who was a fan of Kiki the parrot who went everywhere with Jack, one of the four children in the Adventure series.

Fatty announced rather pompously: 'This year's *The Rockingdown Mystery* is the first of a new series of Mysteries featuring Barney and his monkey Miranda, to be published by Collins.'

'Oh, Fatty, are you on about publishers again?' said Larry. 'Honestly, who cares?'

'It's important. You see, every major publishing house wants the *kudos* of publishing an Enid Blyton series.'

'What's "*kudos*"?' asked Bets.

'It's Fatty showing off,' answered Pip.

Fatty ignored the flak that was being thrown his way: 'First, Hodder & Stoughton got the Famous Five books. Then Methuen got hold of the Peterswood Mysteries. It's Macmillan who is publishing the Adventure series. And Collins is…'

'You've said that,' scoffed Larry.

'Boring,' said Daisy.

'OK, have it your way. Anyway, as far as *the author herself* is concerned, in order to come up with each new series, she just seems to have to find another niche in her mind. She's effectively set the books at home. She's got the other ones set where she goes on holiday. And then there are those which are set in really exotic places where she can play about with parrot dialogue… "Pop goes the weasel, look you".'

'What was that?' asked Bets, thrown by the peculiar voice.

'That's Fatty trying to sound like the parrot in *The Mountain of Adventure*, which is set in Wales,' said Larry.

'It's Enid succeeding in being funny,' corrected Fatty.

The tawny owl in the grounds of Green Hedges hooted again. And suddenly there was a noisy Welsh parrot sharing the three-acre site:

'Clean your ears, Effans,' said Fatty.

'Too-whit, too-who, look you,' said Fatty.

'Pop goes the weasel, Effans, look you, Boyo, what-effer,' said Fatty.

As the other laughed, Bets threw off her rug and stood up. She had just thought of something.

'Where are you going?' asked Fatty.

Bets skipped off over the lawn. 'Back in a minute,' she chirped. It was cold and dark. No it wasn't, the night was wonderfully cool! And Bets glided across the lawn, skipped across a flower border and skimmed over the drive. In no time she was at her bike and undoing the basket. From somewhere overhead there came a noise that made Bets look up. The sound came again – a vibrating, jarring, churring. What was it? Bets heard the sound a third time – '*Chur-r-r-r-r-r!*' – and knew what it was, thanks to the book now in her hand, her very own Enid Blyton book, a present from her father two birthdays ago and brought with her tonight for good luck. She recalled reading that the nightjar comes out at night and churrs to itself. Bets saw the long-tailed bird fly past, almost swift-like. It wheeled from side to side, hunting for insects. It opened its beak and the sound came again. Bets now thoroughly enjoyed listening to the churring, purring, whirring.

As soon as the nightjar had moved on, Bets did the same. And next thing she was flopping down onto her rug beside the others. She handed Fatty the book. 'What's this?' said Fatty. He switched on a discreet torch and read: *Enid Blyton's Nature Lover's Book*.

Fatty opened it up. He smiled at the title page, which was a thing of beauty. As well as the title of the book at the top, the publisher's name at the bottom, there were a few words written in earnest capitals by a child: 'WILLOW IS MY PUSSY'. Fatty didn't want to embarrass Bets, so he said nothing about her cat, instead remarking dryly:

'I see this book has been published by Evans Brothers, Montague House, Russell Square. You should look them up one day, Bets.'

'Effans, look you, boyo,' said Bets, cheerfully.

'Have I ever told you about the time I went into town and looked up the publisher George Newnes?' asked Fatty. 'He signed my copies of *The Enchanted Wood* and *The Adventures of Sherlock Holmes*, did George. Although I later found out he'd been dead for twenty years.'

The Find-Outers laughed.

'Get old Evans to sign the book for you, Bets,' said Pip.

'Effans, look you, boyo, what-effer, sign underneath my pussy,' said Bets, pleased that she had become as funny as Fatty all of a sudden.

Fatty regarded the contents page. The book was basically a description of walks throughout the year. Fatty's eye was drawn to a June walk 'Ramble at Night'. When Fatty turned to it, he found the word 'Yes' had been carbon-copied onto the facing page.

'This is a work of art, Bets!'

'Read the night ramble, Fatty.'

So Fatty whispered aloud about the full moon, and how the walk started at 8.30 p.m., with the children excited because they'd never been on a night walk before. The long walk, full of highlights, culminated in the children and their uncle crouching beneath a gorse bush listening to the song of the nightingale. They listened in wonder to the astonishing music. And then a clock chimed eleven times. Time to go home if they were to get back by midnight, as their uncle had promised the children's mother.

'Shame they had to go back home so soon,' said Fatty. 'Midnight's when the fun starts!'

Bets replied: 'Perhaps they had to go back because Enid wouldn't have been able to go to bed until the children were safely back home, and she needed her sleep.'

Fatty turned to the very back of the volume. Under a carbon-copied nightingale, in Bets' childish handwriting was written:

'I LOVE ENID BLYTON BOOKS XXXXXXXXXX TRUE!!'

As they took turns to admire the book, Daisy mentioned that she'd just been given *The Upper Fourth at Malory Towers*. She couldn't wait to read it, and to catch up on the school career of Darrell Rivers and all her classmates in the North Tower… Bets broke in to add that she had read *Noddy Goes to Toyland* and *The Secret Seven* in the spring.

Pip was wondering again about the stolen book, when another thought struck him. 'Hang on a minute!' he said, frowning. 'How has *one person* been able to write *all these books* in the last year?'

'*Enid Blyton's Nature Lover's Book* was published five years ago,' said Fatty, a stickler for accuracy.

'Yes, but listen, Fatty!' said Larry, who listed several books they'd already mentioned from 1949, pulling a tuft of grass out from the lawn as he said each favourite's name. 'How has one middle-aged woman been able to write so many brilliant books in so little time?'

'Aha!' said Fatty, triumphantly. 'So you see what the real mystery is?'

And suddenly they did see.

CHAPTER TWO

IN BECKENHAM

1

An hour ago I walked out of the house in Forest Hill where I had lived for fifteen years. The funny thing is that even though I used to go for a walk from that rented base every day, I never made it to Beckenham, which is only four miles away. Why not? After all, I was always looking for new routes along which I could find my muse. Perhaps it was simply because when I walked beside the little brook – along whose course I would occasionally spot the thrilling turquoise flash of a kingfisher – it always seemed that the path fizzled out at Sydenham, forcing me to veer away from my southerly course.

Today, armed with a map, I've discovered that the riverside path carries on after just a few twists through an industrial estate. So I've broken through my old mental barrier and, after a remarkably short time, I am here in the same Beckenham – not Beaconsfield – that Enid Blyton lived in for the first – not last – thirty-odd years of her life.

Indeed, as I step out of the path onto a pavement I'm in sight of Chaffinch Road. Her parents brought her here from East Dulwich, eight miles away, when she was a few months old, and they lived at 95 Chaffinch Road for five years by which time she had a brother. I'm looking at the exact semi-detached house. There is a tiny front garden, but the significant thing about the house (then, and now a century later) is that across the road from it is a railway line leading to central London. On the far side of the road, just in front of the railway fence, is a row of mature trees swishing in the early summer wind. '*Wisha-wisha-wisha*,' go the trees, as they have done for decades, and I take a closer look to see what the toddling Enid may have been especially aware of. It's a lime tree and the bottom of the trunk is a mass of foliage. The shiny grey limbs of the tree, whorled in places like a van Gogh painting, twist as they head up into the tree's main foliage and become topmost branches which are covered in leaves that disappear into blue sky and white cloud. I have to ask the question: 'Is this The Magic Faraway Tree, Enid?' And a clear little voice answers: 'It's just the tree that hit me between the eyes whenever I looked out from my bedroom window.'

I don't stop moving. Instead I walk a hundred yards to the bridge over the railway at Clock House Station. I cross the bridge and walk another hundred yards along Clock House Road to number 35. Enid's second Beckenham home is best remembered by herself, in *The Story of My Life* – the autobiography that she wrote, ostensibly for children – as the place where she came most under her father's influence. In fact, if Green Hedges – as the site and source of Enid's sense of fulfilment – is the first thing about that book, her father's positive influence on her early development is the second.

I stand on the pavement across the road, gazing at the front of the house, and I consider Enid's time here. Apparently, she watched her father gardening round the back and was inspired to request her own little plot. He told her that if she wanted something badly she would have to work hard for it. So in return for Enid cleaning his bike – a good clean, it had to be – she was given a small square of land and a sixpence so that she could buy penny bags of seeds. Enid tended those seeds with care, and they flowered. The next year she was given a shilling by an aunt. She bought plants with the money, and soon she had the makings of a lilac bush, among others. The third year she began to grow vegetables, and that autumn her mother and brothers were impressed with the home-grown produce that Enid provided for the family table.

Enid's father, Thomas, worked with his uncle and brothers in their warehousing business at that time. However, he was also a self-educated man of parts. On occasion he would play the banjo to entertain the family and every evening he would perform classical music on the piano for his own enjoyment. His sister was a professional musician, and when Enid herself took easily enough to the piano as a 6-year-old, he hoped his daughter might follow such a career herself.

But Enid was more interested in her father's bookcases than his piano. Thomas had bought hundreds of books during his engagement to Theresa. Enid soon got stuck into the children's encyclopaedias, the children's classics, and the adult books too. Her father had taught himself to read both French and German, and had a number of books in these languages. Enid, with the aid of a dictionary, read her way through first one French book and then the rest of them, and had started on the German literature when her father realised what she was doing. From then on, he locked the bookcases that contained material he deemed unsuitable for a child. But Enid didn't mind too much as it was only the German books she hadn't read through. And she only had to read a page once to be able to recall it more or less perfectly, an attribute she'd inherited, like so much else, from Thomas.

There is a chapter in *The Story of My Life* called 'My Happiest Times' and it describes the walks she took with her father in the countryside around her Clock House Road home. She was never again to meet anyone who knew as much about nature. As they walked, the amateur naturalist/astronomer/musician/photographer/painter talked to his child. And not just on one level. He quoted poetry, and passed on stories about leprechauns that he had been told in his own childhood. As they walked on, they would entertain each other with jokes, stories, rhymes and anything else that came bubbling up into their clever heads.

Enid devoted another chapter in her autobiography to 'How I Began', by which she meant how she began to write. And the answer was that when she went to bed in this house she would be visited by night stories before going to sleep. These stories just came to her out of her imagination, as her subconscious dealt with all the input she was getting from her father and from life in general, thrilling and scaring the growing child. They weren't dreams – she was awake when the stories came to her, and they had a beginning, a middle and an end. But they were like dreams in that she had no idea what was coming next. One part of her mind invented the story, another lapped it up in wide-eyed surprise. She thought all children had such night stories. But not all children did – and don't – have their own private cinema screen showing films starring and directed by themselves, with a programme that changes every night.

I stand there looking back and forth between the front door of the right-hand house of a pair of semi-detached houses and the front door of the right-hand house of the very next pair of houses. Why? Because a funny thing happened when Enid was 11. The family moved from 35 to 31 Clock House Road. Presumably a five-year lease ran out and couldn't be extended for the same property. How strange it must have been for Enid, though, who had just moved from the primary school thirty yards from her house to St Christopher's School for Girls in Beckenham, to find that she now lived at number 31 rather than at number 35. There was the same piano to practise on, the same bookcases containing the world's literature and the same fields, woods, rivers and animals. Above all, the same stream of night stories. But there were differences too. She had to start again with her garden: and perhaps this gave her an opportunity to compare what she could achieve as an older and wiser gardener. But any progress on that score would have been swamped by the realisation that in the new house the relationship between her domestic mother and her fabulous father was breaking down. Nightly rows were listened to by Enid and the elder of her two younger brothers on the upstairs landing. Enid's beloved father left the family when Enid was nearly 13. The rejected woman swore the children to secrecy, and indeed Enid never told the teachers or girls at St Christopher's of the dark hole that had opened up in her life. In her autobiography she doesn't say what effect the departure of her father had on her night stories and subsequently on her output as a writer. But I'll be bearing that question in mind.

I keep walking, with the facts of Enid's young life as described in Barbara Stoney's biography at the forefront of my mind. When Enid's father left, setting up what turned out to be a successful wholesale clothing business, his guilt offering to the family was the rental of a three-storey, detached house in nearby Elm Road. Here, he expected Theresa, the rejected wife, to make sure Enid carried on with her piano practice, an hour a day. The house is impressive, with climbing plants of various sorts decorating the front. For Enid, the big room to herself on the first floor at the back of the house overlooking the garden – her third garden – was the main attraction. There she wrote her first poems and stories and began to forge an independent outlook. She kept a diary and was mortified when she discovered that her mother had been reading it. She needed a lock for the door of her room then, and a system of communicating with her friends in code. She told Mary Attenborough, her friend at St Christopher's, that the reason for the code was to baffle the postman. But the person she wanted to keep in the dark was surely the mother who didn't understand Enid's bookish ways and was frustrated that the girl wouldn't help her about the house. There's a postcard from Enid to a school-friend reproduced in Stoney's biography. It looks like an array of incomplete boxes, each with a dot in it. That's exactly what it is, but each different 'box' stands for a

THIS IS HER
BETS

She tore down the hillside.

group of three letters. For instance, right hand vertical and bottom horizontal of an implied box is the code for A, B and C. And the positioning of a dot towards the left edge, the middle, or the right edge of the 'box' indicates whether it's the first, second or third letter in the group: in this case A, B or C. Writing such messages would be a bit like texting on a mobile. And I dare say Enid and her friends became just as fast with the seemingly awkward way of communicating as today's children are with their mobiles. The translation of the reproduced postcard in the biography is something like:

'Dear Mary, It is simply glorious in France. The French are awfully greedy here. I can't eat half the stuff. Write to me soon. Love from Enid.'

I wonder if her mother was more baffled by the postcards in dotted-box code or the self-addressed envelopes returning Enid's early compositions from magazine editors. Actually, the mother wasn't confused by these envelopes; they came in dozens each month and proved that this writing lark was a complete waste of time and money. Enid could cope with the rejections, because she'd learned a few ways to protect herself. And as I walk along on the sunny side of these relatively unchanged Beckenham streets, listening to a chaffinch – whose song I've only learned this year to recognise due to a nature book of Enid's – I sing my own version of one of her coded songs:

'Dear Mary. It is simply horrible having a philistine for a mother. All she does is cook and eat. I won't be able to stand it for much longer. Don't stop writing. Never stop writing. Love from Enid.'

I'm approaching the Blyton family's next house, which they moved to when Enid was 18. It's considerably smaller, a two-storey semi-detached, implying that Thomas Blyton's own business wasn't doing as well as it had been, and Enid had to have a much smaller room and less privacy in this house. I don't stop at 13 Westfield Road, because Enid herself didn't stay here for any length of time. By then she was Head Girl at her school, captain of the lacrosse team, rubbish at arithmetic, a tennis champion and had made an impact on the teachers with her imaginative written work. Why else would the headmistress have said in assembly:

'There is a girl currently at this school who will set the Thames on fire one day.'

Set the Thames on fire! What prescience. Though I imagine all it brought to Enid's mind at the time was the kingfisher shooting along the little brook that she'd known all her life.

Enid's best friend Mary was also top of her form, but three years younger. However Mary's aunt Mabel – twenty years older than Enid – took a keen interest in the youngster, who was by then effectively living at the Attenboroughs' mansion on Oakwood Avenue. I'm sitting opposite the place now in a patch of shade, admiring the bulk of the multi-gabled house. A young woman could get lost in a house like that. Or, with Mabel's help, she could more quickly find herself.

Enid left school with the intention of studying music, as her absent father still wished. But in the period of intense practice before going to music school, she became uncomfortably aware that this plan wasn't right for her. She enjoyed playing other people's music, up to a point, but it was the composition of her own stories that she found both easy and satisfying. She wanted to be a professional writer. How to go about it, that was the problem. A summer holiday in Suffolk with friends of the Attenboroughs allowed her to experience some teaching, as an assistant at a Sunday school. She found it easy to remember stories from the Bible and to put them over in a way that her young audience soaked up. And she realised that some kind of teaching of children was the next move for her. Perhaps the longest and most vivid scene in *The Story of My Life* concerns the phone call that Enid made to her father in order to get his permission – which was necessary in these days – to become a teacher, and thereby give up her music. In the end, he was won over, chuckling down the phone in acknowledgement of his daughter's single-mindedness.

Enid was free to find out what made young minds tick. She embarked on a two-year course of Froebel Training at Ipswich. This involved listening to lectures on a range of subjects, teaching children in classrooms, and spending her free time writing. Of course, she excelled. Her passing out testimonial mentions her enthusiasm and energy on the one hand, and her unusual ability to interest children on the other.

Next step was a year at a school in Bickley, Kent. She was in charge of six boys aged between 6 and 8, although she taught English to a class of older children as well. She took them on long walks, passing on to them the same love of nature that had been given to her by her own great teacher, her father. But that year, and for several more, she had no contact with her mother or brothers, despite the fact that in the holidays she kept coming back to Beckenham, to the Attenboroughs' house at Oakwood Avenue. Well, perhaps just the odd coded postcard home:

'Dear Mother. I love Beckenham and always will. But it's Dad's Beckenham I love, not yours. Though I know you will never be able to get your head round the difference. Love from Enid.'

Next step for Enid was to establish a small school of her own to teach the four kids of an architect cousin of Mabel's, based in Surbiton, Surrey. The class was a success, and, when word got around locally, its numbers swelled to fourteen pupils, whose ages ranged from 4 to 10. Two of the original kids went on to be gardeners, claiming that it was Enid's clear and enthusiastic nature lessons that pushed them into their vocation. So she was an inspirational teacher, then. The kids loved her, listened to her, and hung onto her every word. But at the same time, Enid's writing for children was beginning to be accepted by publishers, thanks in part to her being in close proximity to children and realising both how their minds worked and understanding what they did and didn't like. She could write any kind of children's story, so she might as well give the kids what stimulated them! Actually, the kids wanted her, in person, teaching them. But through seven years of teaching experience, Enid hadn't forgotten what it was she wanted for herself. She was a born writer. And as soon as she could and, it seems, without looking back for one moment, she gave up the teaching job and the children she loved, in order to concentrate on writing full time. Single-mindedness? I think her father had it dead right there.

Actually, there's a book that she wrote in 1951 while living at Green Hedges. It's called *The Six Bad Boys* and it deals with the subject of broken homes and the influence of this on the development of the child. The book focuses on three houses next door to each other on the same street, and I realise from today's walk that the houses were, in effect, households that Enid experienced. The Berkeley family move into a house called Summerhayes. The mother is selfish, always moaning at her family and making the two girls take her side against her good-natured but weak husband. The third child, a boy, is caught in the middle, and when the father leaves home the atmosphere in the house falls apart altogether and the boy begins to go bad. Now a lot of that applies to what was going on in the Blyton household at 31 Clock House Road. In fact, when researching her biography, Barbara Stoney brought this particular book to the attention of one of Enid's younger brothers. When he, Hanly, read the scenes of the parents rowing and the children huddled at the top of the stairs, he recognised it from real life and was moved to tears. I think Barbara Stoney rather regretted pushing her research as far as she did on that occasion.

The second family in *Six Bad Boys* is composed of Mrs Kent and her son Bob. They have come to live in Hawthorn Cottage following the death of Mrs Kent's husband. He is a loyal boy, anxious to do what he can for his mother. But his mother finds him rather a nuisance and when she gets a full-time job – which involves her leaving the house before Bob goes to school, and not getting back home until after six o'clock – Bob feels rejected and homeless. He too begins to go bad. Clearly the relationship between the boy and his mother parallels that between Enid and her mother, post-Thomas in the house on Elm Road. (Not that Enid's mother went out to work.) If so, Enid was a big-hearted child with much love to give but in need of the love of at least one parent, which she didn't get. The portrayal of Mrs Kent – who is aware of the distance growing between herself and her child but consciously chooses her own comfort and welfare above the child's clear needs – is chilling.

The two 'going-bad' boys hook up with four others and form a gang, which soon gets them into trouble with the police. But not before they've set up a touching little home-from-home where the six poor castaways read comics and live in a surrogate family world of their own. Such surrogate families haunt much of Enid's best writing. When the children get dealt with by the police and court, one of them, Bob, is effectively adopted by the stable, loving Mackenzie family who live in between the other two houses, in Barlings Cottage. The young Mackenzie girl adores Bob and won't believe the bad stories about him, while Mrs Mackenzie loves Bob as if he were her own child. This must surely echo the relationship between Enid and the Attenboroughs, Mary and Mabel. Grown-up Enid has wrapped her childhood round her little finger and spun a story that takes into account much first-hand experience, and in so doing has fed off her emotional ups and downs. Yes, it's a belter! And it's one of about a dozen full-length books she published that year, the year of *Five on a Hike Together*; *The Mystery of the Vanished Prince*; *Well Done, Secret Seven*; *Last Term at Malory Towers* and *The Buttercup Farm Family*. She probably wrote that last story for the feel-good factor after having put herself through the emotional roller-coaster of *The Six Bad Boys* for which I feel a better title would be *The One Sad Girl*.

Where am I? Or, rather, where have I got to with Enid now that she's left the difficulties of childhood behind and embarked upon her adult life? At a garden party at the Attenboroughs' house she met the 36-year-old Hugh Pollock, the books editor at Newnes, a major publisher in these days. And at the age of 27, with her writing career established, she allowed herself to fall in love. Hugh had won the DSO while serving in the First World War. Indeed he'd been involved in many of the major battles. No doubt he was as charmed by the innocent and effervescent young woman, whose life had hardly been touched by outside events, as she was flattered by the attention of the sophisticated and mature older man. They married, took a flat in Chelsea for a year, but neither was happy living in town. So it was back to the countryside she loved, back to Beckenham to find a house which peeped out at Enid from behind a chestnut tree. Elfin Cottage is the only house I've looked at this morning that has a plaque. I must sit on the wall and gaze at it, 'cos I'm tired after my long walk south to Beckenham, then east and past one... two-three... four... five... six... seven Blyton houses.

By the time she was installed in this house with the garden that Hugh and she designed together, she was happy. At her instigation, Hugh called her his Little Bunny and she called him her Bun. Perhaps there was a bit of father-daughter in their relationship. After all, at the time of their marriage Hugh was the same age as Thomas had been when Enid had been most under his spell.

But, primarily, Hugh was Enid's first lover. *The Adventures of Binkle and Flip* came out at this time, though the original Newnes title was *Enid Blyton's Book of Bunnies*. It has a great scene in it with Flip lying in bed and Binkle taking off a black boot in readiness for getting into the same bed. Binkle – who I think of as Enid because he's the ideas bunny – solemnly says to the usually supportive Flip:

'What about being good for the rest of our lives?'

And Flip, knowing how irrepressible Binkle is, replies:

'Don't try to be funny!'

Binkle doesn't have to try to be funny. He is just full of the mischievous joys of spring. A few chapters start with Flip and

Binkle lying in bed (no other Blyton book is anything like as bed-orientated). One day Binkle rudely awakens his companion to inform him that he's just had this dream in which he'd painted a wonderful picture. Flip asks Binkle what the picture was like, and Binkle says that's the funny thing. Because although everyone else loved the picture, as far as Binkle was concerned it was a blank canvas! This is the beginning of Binkle's scheme to get Wily Weasel, Dinky Dormouse and the rest of the animals of Oak Tree Town to pay for a blank canvas supposedly painted by Binkle.

I can't contain my enthusiasm for this book! In another chapter, Flip comes back from a walk to find his other half in the kitchen of Heather Cottage with a towel wrapped around his head. Flip thinks Binkle has hurt himself, but in fact the towel is to help Binkle concentrate on writing poetry. Again, everyone in the village loves Binkle's poems. But he is in danger of blowing it when the king comes to Oak Tree Town, and Binkle writes a special poem to commemorate the occasion. The early verses recklessly insult the town's citizens and then the poem concludes boldly:

> 'The only persons in this town
> Who're really worth your trip
> Are Binkle, with his whiskers fine
> And naughty little Flip.'

I conjure up a scene with one bunny lying in bed in Elfin Cottage, Oak Tree Town, snuggling up to the other bunny and saying: 'There is a rabbit currently in this bed who will set the Thames on fire one day.'

Set the Thames on fire! No mention yet that it would be the stretch of river just a few miles upstream from Maidenhead.

2

Bromley Library is only a mile away from Elfin Cottage, pushing me still further east. That's where I'm sitting now, having digested a vegetable pastie and a punnet of Kent strawberries.

Where do I start? This is the only library in Britain that subscribes to the *Enid Blyton Society Journal*, so I need to get stuck into that at some point today. But the library is open until 8 p.m. so there is no rush. No mad rush, just a mild tingle of anticipation.

I approach the desk, and stand there waiting for the librarian to attend to me. I try not to move from foot to foot in impatience, but the man continues to look at his computer screen, which is at right angles to me. Does he know I'm here? I shuffle to my left, but he still doesn't register my presence. Perhaps he's doing an urgent bit of librarianship. Surely his main job when sitting in that seat is to attend to the users of the library? Perhaps he's looking something up for another library user. But there is no one else in the local studies department just now, and he doesn't appear to be on the phone, which is lying there inert. What *is* he doing?

'Shall I come back later?' I say, studiously polite.

Turning round, he says very quietly that he didn't see me there, and that I should have announced my presence earlier. He knew I was there all right, but was playing some kind of power game. Anyway, I've got his attention now. He's wearing a badge that says 'Busy Bee' on it. Let's just smile sweetly and get to work. I ask for the item, giving him the reference. He tells me it's in storage on another floor, and that he cannot fetch it just now because he's on his own in the department. He tells me I'll have to wait until two o'clock when a colleague will be reporting for afternoon duty.

I wander away from his big desk and sit at a smaller desk of my own, thinking things over. It's not long until two o'clock. The trouble is, what happens if no one turns up then, giving the Busy Bee an excuse to remain on his backside and do nothing to help me? Me, the world's keenest Enid Blyton scholar! Well, let's cross that bridge when I come to it, and let's just see what other books this library has in its collection.

As one might expect, the library has a fair sprinkling of books that Enid wrote early in her career. I can fetch them myself from the shelves on this floor, so that's what I do. *Real Fairies*. This was published in 1923, when its author was 26 and teaching full time. It's a slim volume of poems in the same format as Enid's first publication *Child Whispers*, which came out the year before. I sample a double-page. I wonder if the librarian would mind if I read 'A Morning Call' aloud. It begins:

> 'When we were having cups of milk
> At just eleven o'clock
> Upon the nursery door we heard
> A tiny little knock.'

Well, no, I shouldn't read it aloud! The librarian would be sure to think I was taking the mickey. The tiny little knock comes from a fairy, of course, and the second and third verses tell how the fairy stays for a glass of milk but is then scared off by the crying of the baby. Charming. I wish I did have the guts to read it aloud. Or perhaps I should read aloud the first verse of the facing poem: 'Lonely'. In this, the poet goes out into the garden, as lonely as can be, and finds a fairy sitting there, beneath a chestnut tree. Would that have been the chestnut tree at Elfin Cottage? Anyway, tears were rolling down the fairy's cheeks because he was lonely too. So the poet played bat and ball with him and they had a lovely time together. Eventually the poet's healthy appetite meant she had to go in for tea. She walked indoors, conscious that the fairy at the bottom of the garden was much happier now that he had got a friend like her. Charming, once again! I have to think of some such similar strategy for getting on the right side of my fairy librarian come two o'clock.

The next book is a thumping great volume called *Teacher's Treasury*, volume 1 of 3. I can see straight away from the navy blue cover – which has patterned indentations, ornate and classical and is finished with gold lettering on the front cover and spine – that this book has been made to closely resemble Arthur Mee's *Children's Encyclopaedia*. And why not? Enid read the set of ten volumes when she lived on Clock House Road. She read them twice, all the way through, according to her autobiography. Shall we say once at number 35 and once at number 31? Moreover, when she was living in the big house in Elm Road, at the age of 14, Arthur Mee accepted and published one of her poems. What joy! – especially in retrospect, as the teenage Enid logged her zillionth subsequent rejection.

The name 'Newnes' is proudly embossed at the foot of the spine. I wonder if Hugh was the editor of the book. The 250 big pages have been printed on what appear to be giant, white marshmallows, pressed flat and squared off, which makes for as bulky a book as one of Arthur Mee's 750-pagers. But despite this equivalence in terms of cubic volume, Enid may have been miserable at the thought that she'd only managed to write *three* volumes while Mee's encyclopaedia ran to *nine* volumes and an equally weighty index. Perhaps the lazy author of *Teacher's Treasury* needed to be consoled by her bedfellow:

Hugh: 'Little Bun, you've got to understand that Arthur Mee didn't write these encyclopaedias on his own. The fact is, he had a huge team of writers and researchers helping him.'

Enid: 'Really, Bun? You're not just saying that to cheer me up?'

Hugh: 'Oh, Binkle! The truth is, Fat Arthur didn't write a word himself! He just sat in his library – sorry, his office – eating buns and fairy cakes all day. You know, like Jumbo the elephant we saw at Regent's Park Zoo.'

I'm glad that Hugh has put it like that, because it takes my curious hands straight to *The Zoo Book*, of which he certainly was the editor. Indeed *The Zoo Book* and the marriage between Enid and Hugh are entwined, date-wise. They met at his office on 1 February 1924, to discuss the proposition that Enid should write a book for children about the zoo. They met again the next day at Victoria, visited Regent's Park Zoo itself, then went to a restaurant and talked about themselves until six o'clock. By April they were engaged. *The Zoo Book* was written by the beginning of July. Enid and Hugh were married in August. *The Zoo Book* was published in October. So is there anything in *The Zoo Book* which reflects what was going on in Enid's private life at the time? Chapters such as 'How Animals are Caught', 'Apes and Monkeys', 'Big Bears and Little Bears' suggest that perhaps there might be. But it's in the chapter called 'Secrets of the Keepers' that I come across a paragraph about a male polar bear who had a wife who irritated him dreadfully. Papa Bear used to stand it as long as he could, then he would suddenly turn on Mama Bear and push her into the water. There he sat on her head until he thought she had been punished enough. But one day he sat too long on her head, and when he climbed out of the pond he found she did not follow him. She was drowned.

Hugh (in bed): 'Oh, such a bad bear! I'll be nothing like him!'

Enid (in that same bed): 'Let me tell you about the monkeys, Bun. They're much worse!'

The cover of *The Zoo Book* shows a chimpanzee wearing a soft hat and a jacket. Not my idea of how a book about the zoo would present its animals in this, the twenty-first century. But times change, and Enid knew her own time well enough:

Enid (considering her book's cover): 'Bun, couldn't you find a stetson to fit the monkey?'

Hugh: 'He wouldn't wear it, Little Bun. Nor would he put up with the gun-belt, holster and six-shooter we tried to tie around his hairy little belly.'

Page 53 of the book is a black-and-white photograph of an

African elephant in his compound at the zoo. Under the photo, Enid – naturalist *extraordinaire* – has written simply: 'Look at his great ears.'

Hugh: (turning the page of the book until he comes across the elephant): 'Look at his great ears!'

Enid: 'We'd soon nibble those great lettucey things down to size. Wouldn't we, Bun?'

Back to the *Teacher's Treasury* of 1926. I love handling this huge book. The contents pages show the volume is divided into three parts: One, Stories; Two, Rhythm and the Dance; Three, Nature Notes. After flicking through the middle section and taking in the musical notation and the tunes ('Hey, Johnny Cope'… 'A-hunting we will go'… 'Ride a Cock horse'… 'Pop goes the weasel'… 'Sing a song of sixpence'…), which I can see are designed to be played on the piano, I understand what we have here. Enid's *Teacher's Treasury* basically contains the lessons taught to her by her own great teacher, her father. My eye goes down the list of nature lessons: winter buds, the snowdrop, the frog, sweet violet, the cuckoo, primrose, rabbit, snake, gnat, dog, butterfly, dandelion, kingfisher, wild rose, poppy, house-fly, spider, shells, heather, when the leaves fall, seed dispersal, migration, the squirrel, winter preparations, cat, robin… It's like a poem. But then nature is like a beautiful rhyming poem which takes me back to the listing for section two and 'Pawing, High-stepping and Galloping Movements'. I flick further back and into section one where we have 'The Princess who wanted the Moon' and 'The Disobedient Bunny'. I wonder if the Princess and the Bunny were one and the same person – Daddy's girl?

Enid: 'Have I set the Thames on fire yet, Bun?'

Hugh: 'No, Little Bun. But can't you feel the heat in this bed?'

The frontispiece of the book is a reproduction of a colour painting of a kingfisher. The turquoise beauty is perched on a tree-stump, watching and waiting. Is it the same kingfisher I saw this morning? Of course it is, watching and waiting for the Moon to appear in the brook. Is it the same kingfisher that Enid saw all those years ago along the little brook that flows from Beckenham to Forest Hill? Of course it is. Many a time Enid would creep up to those quiet spots on the river where she knew the kingfisher liked to perch, out of sight. Her presence would scare the shy bird, so that her father would only have to be looking in vaguely the right direction to be rewarded by one of the most thrilling sights in nature: the flying diamond, the fairy express, the frozen librarian.

It's two o'clock. No sign of any assistant librarian so I wander once more to the bookshelves. A book called *Enid Blyton and the Mystery of Children's Literature* catches my eye. This is a 2001 title, written by David Rudd. It's a PhD thesis, and I see that Macmillan charged £40 for what looks like a standard-issue hardback. Obviously the publishers didn't think they'd be selling many copies of such an overtly academic work. Perhaps this is the only copy they did sell. Anyway, I take advantage of the opportunity to flick through it.

The introduction tells us that the author was a fan of Famous Five books when he was a child. But the day came when he was reading a Five, and he decided that he simply didn't want to know what happened to Julian, Dick, Anne, George and Timmy this time around. So he abandoned the Five, mid-story. Rudd also tells us that when coming back to the books as an adult, he found them boring. What a strange way to set out your stall as the author of a book on Enid Blyton! He gets around that, in a way, by making it clear that he's aiming his book at sorting out the mystery of why Enid Blyton appeals to child readers. But what happened to the child in David Rudd? Did he just disappear? Enid Blyton books are ageless and lucid fantasies. There are so many of them that it is inevitable that the child reader will grow out of them long before he has read all of her work. 'Grow out of them' in the sense that an adolescent has to learn about the world from different angles, and in particular must work at building an understanding of adult life. But, that done, the books written by Blyton are there to be enjoyed in the leisure of one's maturity, alongside Proust, Waugh and all the other unstoppable originals.

Rudd gives detailed readings of three sets of books. Famous Five, Noddy and Malory Towers. Fair enough, but that omits the Mysteries. I turn to the index to find one fleeting reference to Fatty in the whole book, and I begin to have serious doubts about the author's sensibility. Still, a flick through the chapter on Enid's biographical background comes up with the fact that eight of the nineteen chapters in Enid's *The Story of My Life* are about her writing life as opposed to her 'real' life and that throughout the autobiography there are one hundred references to her father compared with only seven to her mother.

The Rudd book is mainly concerned with the questionnaires that the author gives out to children to fill in on the subject of why they enjoy Blyton books, and with interviews he conducts with them himself. (This reminds me of all the indirect research that Enid herself did, while she was teaching children at her own and at other people's schools.) From this data, Rudd concludes that Blyton is best thought of as part of an oral tradition (yeah, sure). The final chapter is called 'Is Blyton Bad For You?' Such a set-up reminds me of all the times I have been asked, in reference to contemporary art, whether it is really art, and if so, whether it is good or bad art. For me, whether the Blyton books (or the contemporary art) is good or bad is not the issue. What's there is either interesting to the receiver or it's not. And if it's interesting you get stuck into it. If it's really interesting you get sucked into it, body and soul.

It's two-thirty. Surely, I don't have to wait any longer for those *Enid Blyton Society Journals*. As I approach the desk, I suddenly realise how I can butter this librarian up. When I arrived in Beckenham this morning, I knew the street names where Enid Blyton had lived, but not the house numbers. Perhaps I thought there would be plaques on each of the houses, or that it would be enough just to be in the vicinity of the Blyton homes. But the lack of a specific object to focus on soon became frustrating. And by the time I got to Elm Road, Enid's fourth home, I asked a postman if he knew which the actual house was. He didn't, but he stood there and we talked about Blyton for twenty minutes before the helpful man directed me to Beckenham Library, which he felt would have the addresses I was after. Sure enough, in the branch library I was handed a booklet written by Geoffrey Flock from the local studies department of Bromley Library, and thanks to this booklet I was able to begin my Blyton circuit again, and properly, from 95 Chaffinch Road.

Now, I've no reason to suppose that my librarian is the same man who was interested enough in Blyton to have put together the booklet that traced her progress through Beckenham. But you never know! And even if my librarian isn't the booklet's author, then at least I will have communicated that my interest in Blyton overlaps with the interests of Bromley Library local studies department.

'Are you... er... Geoffrey Flock?'

He is. So I am able to tell him how useful his booklet has been to me. But – and I find this hard to comprehend – he doesn't warm to me, or to my project. It's as if I'm intruding, first, into his personal space, and, now, into his speciality subject. I sit down again, a little nonplussed, having been told that I will have to wait longer still for the *Society Journals*.

The Enid Blyton Society is run by Tony Summerfield. Recently, I asked him about Enid's letters and diaries. He was, I suppose, as helpful as he could be in the circumstances. Basically, Enid's second husband destroyed her diaries from 1941 onwards, shortly before he died. Tony doesn't know where the earlier diaries are now, but he had a look at them about ten years ago. The best work-related entry that he could find from his perusal of the cursory entries was 'finished book for Birns' which I had to agree was pretty mundane, though 'finished book for Macmillan in five days' would have been a revelation, so thank goodness for the letters to Peter McKellar that are reproduced in the Barbara Stoney biography. These letters also tell us about the 'night stories' of Enid's childhood and her way of mining her visionary gift as an adult. As to letters in general, Tony reckons they're boring, repetitive and widely scattered, and so far no one has felt motivated enough to collect them together. That job needs to be done. Not by me, though.

OK, I'm ready for action now. Letters from Enid – I want to bloody well read a few! And I know there is one printed in most of the early issues of the *EBS Journal*. Taking my courage in my hands I approach the Busy Bee sitting behind his desk.

'Er...' I begin, unpromisingly.

The librarian looks up from his computer screen and smiles. He nods in the direction of my table. I turn around and there is a trolley with a box on it. T-T-Tony's journal!

'My colleague has arrived. Sorry for the delay.'

And I sit down at my desk in a daze.

The *Journal* started in summer 1996 and in the first issue – long out of print – an article by David Cook points out that the Peterswood of the Mysteries is really Bourne End. I photocopy it for later. In issue six, Imogen has a feature called 'Our Books are Facets of Ourselves', and I take a copy of that too. But I sit there and read the article in issue three that Tony Summerfield himself wrote, a piece on books published by Birns Brothers in the 1920s. These were only small books, booklets even. And Birns often didn't include the author's name on the cover or the title page. Nor did they lodge copies of the books with the British Library. They're only being discovered as part of Enid's *oeuvre* now, partly with the help of an old work-book that covers the years 1923-6. Apparently, Enid meticulously recorded when she wrote a story or article, as well as who published it, and how much she was paid for the transaction. Later work-books were destroyed by her second husband along with Enid's diaries. I can see from what Summerfield says that Barbara Stoney's list of 600 published Blyton books is going to have to be updated in any future edition of the biography.

There have been three issues of the *EBS Journal* a year since the late nineties, and I go through them all up until my own subscription started in 2004, copying an average of one article per stapled booklet. That done, I can concentrate on the 'Letter from Enid Blyton' which is printed in each issue. What a feast of early Blyton I'm in for now!

Alas, by the time I've gone through the older issues, I discover there's only one letter that's pre-Green Hedges. But what do I mean 'only'? I have a genuine letter here that's introduced, transcribed and reproduced in facsimile. Let the feast begin!

The letter was written from the flat in Chelsea where Hugh and Enid lived for a year. It's dated Boxing day, 1925. Not much more than a year into the marriage, what does Enid have to say to Ina – a contemporary of Enid's at St Christopher's – and her sister Margaret?

Enid thanks them for the 'dear wee hankies' they have sent her. Enid was delighted when she opened the parcel and shook them out onto her lap. Enid hopes the pair had a lovely Christmas. She did! Her 'extravagant husband' presented her with twenty-four gay parcels on Christmas morning, each with a gorgeous present inside. The nicest of all was all his medals, beautifully mounted. And the second nicest was a red Spanish shawl which she had always wanted.

The main paragraph of the letter explains that by next Christmas, Enid and Hugh will have moved to the dear little house they've bought in Beckenham. For the fourth time in the letter Enid uses the word 'GORGEOUS', this time in capitals, and this time referring to the time that she and her husband have had fun buying furniture for the new house. The house is described as having a big, pink chestnut tree by the front gates. Enid and Hugh have been having a heavenly time planning the garden. They want to make it old-fashioned, with lavender and hollyhocks, foxgloves and violets, primroses and bluebells.

Enid leaves it at that. She has heaps of letters to write that Boxing Day, to all the school-children who have written to her over the festive season. Enid hopes to see Ina and Margaret in 1926, and sends much love.

I lean back. 1926 was the year she published the *Teacher's Treasury* volumes. Also the year she began writing *Sunny Stories for Little Folks*, as the magazine-cum-book which came out irregularly was first called. So perhaps, when it came to it, she would have been too busy to encourage house calls from the girls she had once known at St Christopher's.

But I'll stay with the joy of Boxing Day, 1925, for a while, if I can. I don't suppose the happy couple got up that day. Enid could write her letters in bed. And after writing each letter she would come back to her presents, her 24-carat gold presents:

Enid: 'What did you get these medals for, again, Bun?'

Hugh: 'You know, I don't think I can remember, Little Bunny. Something that happened in another world.'

Enid: 'Oh, I know what you got them for, Bun! It was for feeding the animals at the zoo.'

Hugh: ' I do believe you're right.'

Enid: 'Of course, I'm right! Is this gold one with the pretty red ribbon what you got for feeding the penguins?'

Hugh: 'If you say so, Little Bunny.'

Enid: 'And this cross with the yellow ribbon. That must have been for feeding a very special animal. Jumbo the elephant?'

Hugh: 'No, Little Bunny. It was for feeding a far more special animal than Jumbo. It was for feeding fat Arthur in the Newnes enclosure.'

Enid: 'Fat Arthur must have taken a lot of stuffing.'

'Have you got everything you want?'

'What?' Oh, it's the librarian.

'My colleague is manning the desk now, so I thought I'd come and see if you needed any assistance.'

'No, not really.' Christ, I've got to pull myself together. 'Em... I've just been reading this Enid Blyton letter in the *Society Journal*. It was written when she was living in a flat in Chelsea but very much looking forward to moving back to this area. Moving back to the last house I visited this morning with the help of your guide, in fact. Elfin Cottage.'

Geoffrey Flock glances at the letter and I get the impression that he's familiar with it. He tells me that by February of 1926 Enid and Hugh had indeed moved into their idyllic new house.

'By Valentine's Day?' I venture.

'Actually, not until the end of February. But I'm sure it was a romantic occasion.'

'Not just romantic, Enid was going home to her roots.'

'Well, she does seem to have been reluctant to move away from Beckenham,' admits my suddenly chatty helper. 'Her father was dead by this time, of course. And she never visited her mother. So she wasn't coming home, exactly. Life for Enid for the three years she stayed at Elfin Cottage revolved around her husband and writing for *Sunny Stories* and *Teacher's World*.'

I ask where I might be able to see the relevant old issues of *Sunny Stories* and *Teacher's World*. Bromley Library has a run of *Sunny Stories* from 1944 to 1950, 172 issues in all. But for pre-Green Hedges issues, the British Library at Colindale would be my best bet. That's where I'd need to go for *Teacher's World* as well, the publication that would provide most info about early Enid.

I suppose I could go to Colindale tomorrow, if I really had to. Anyway, back to the happy couple. I have a feeling Geoffrey could be a fund of information about this period in Blyton's life, so I must make suitable enquiries while he's in helpful mode. 'What do you reckon everyday life was like for them at Elfin Cottage? I mean apart from the writing.'

'Well, they both learned to drive while they were there. They bought a car the number plate of which began with the letters Y.E. Young Enid, according to some.' Brightest of bright young things!

'It should have been L.B.,' I suggest.

'L.B.?' asks Geoffrey.

'Little Bunny. Hugh's nickname for her.'

Geoffrey has another pair of initials for me. He tells me that an H.A. interviewed Enid for *Teacher's World*. The interview took place in the garden of Elfin Cottage. H.A. described Enid as a slim, graceful, childlike figure with a head of closely cropped hair. His final question to her was, 'Why did she keep writing when she had a husband, a home and happiness?'

I guess, correctly, that H.A. is Hugh. Alexander was Hugh's middle name, I'm told. Good. But I have to ask: 'So how did Enid answer H.A.'s final question?'

'Oh, she said something like, as long as one child told her that her work brought him pleasure, then she would go on writing.'

'A more honest reply might have been that she simply couldn't stop the stuff pouring out of her.'

Geoffrey likes this. He tells me that it was while at Elfin Cottage that Hugh persuaded Enid to take typing lessons. Her husband was very important to her early development as a writer in this kind of way. Typing slowed her up to begin with, but in 1927 she wrote in her diary that she'd typed 6,000 words in a single day. And at the time this was a record for her. It's great to find someone else willing to talk in terms of words per day, so that is what Geoffrey and I do for a few minutes. But then we move on, trying to visualise a typical working day for Enid during this period. She would have breakfast at eight and see Hugh off to the station. She would feed her pets, give instructions for the day to her maid and settle down to write. Apart from a short break for lunch, she'd work until four – in the garden if the weather allowed – then she'd drive or walk down the long straight road to Shortlands Station to pick up Hugh. And they'd spend the evening in each other's company.

Geoffrey tells me: 'It was in August of 1926 that Enid made a diary entry to the effect that she was so glad she'd married Hugh, and that she wouldn't be unmarried for words. She called him "a perfect dear".'

I get the impression that Geoffrey has read the Barbara Stoney biography just as closely as I have.

'And on Christmas Day, a year after that letter you read, she records in her diary that she received forty-two presents from Hugh.'

'From twenty-four to forty-two presents in one year. Do you think it was a linear progression?'

Geoffrey doesn't answer. Instead he says: 'Of course, the one present Hugh couldn't seem to give Enid at this time was a child of her own. And that, I suspect, was what Enid really wanted.'

'She was 30 in 1927, so she would be getting anxious about that side of things.'

'Old for a first-time mother in those days,' Geoffrey agrees. 'And so there came about the famous visit to the Harley Street gynaecologist and the discovery that Enid had an unusually under-developed uterus.'

That phrase is definitely lifted from the official biography, though Barbara Stoney in turn probably lifted it from a medical report. '"The uterus of a 12 or 13-year-old girl",' I respond, playing the same game.

My colleague seems unsure of what to say next. I could move the conversation back to less sexually charged territory, but I don't think I will. I could do with being left on my own again for a while to mull over some of this crucial stuff.

After a short silence, it's Geoffrey who steers the conversation away from the state of Enid's reproductive organs. But I'm not really listening any more. An imaginative faculty is stirring within me, and the vigour of my engagement with the librarian falls away. Perhaps he notices this, because he wanders off, though not before giving me a friendly nod.

My thoughts are my own again! Enid and Hugh are lying in bed in Elfin Cottage. It's their last Christmas in that bed, because if they haven't heard the news that a new arterial road is going to be built through their beloved Beckenham countryside, they will be hearing such news soon. They are going to have to move. But not for a few months, and certainly not until Enid's had a chance to open her Christmas presents.

Enid: 'Oh, Bun. It's your gorgeous medals all freshly polished. Didn't you give me a present of them last year? And the year before that?'

Hugh: 'These are brand new medals, Little Bun.'

Enid: 'You've been feeding the animals again. Oh, you darling. But you know the present I really want.'

Hugh: 'A fully developed uterus, Little Bunny?'

Enid: 'Oh, it wouldn't have to be a *fully* developed one. Not an arterial road running right through me! But perhaps I could wish for the uterus of an 18-year-old girl. Do you think that would be too much to ask for?'

Hugh: 'Perhaps we should let the doctor have a poke around.'

Enid: 'Oh, Bun… Your paws are…'

'Are you OK there?'

I take a deep breath: 'Sorry, Geoffrey, I was miles away. Yes, I think I have all I need for now.'

'Good. By the way, I've checked and I think you will have to go to the British Library if you wish to consult *Teacher's World*. It's not a terribly easy place to get the most out of, if it's your first visit. This booklet should tell you everything you need to know.'

'Thanks,' I say, adding the leaflet to my pile of papers.

Geoffrey nods. I think he's pleased to know that my research is running along such solid lines.

3

It was Mrs Hilton who'd answered the phone when Fatty rang from London. She'd passed on the message to Bets who had rounded up Pip, Larry, Daisy and Buster who were all on the platform at Peterswood Station as the train drew in.

'There he is!' said Bets, pointing to an elderly, frail, bald man alighting from the train. The man in question simply could not have been Fatty. But so successfully had Fatty disguised himself in the past that no one felt they could ridicule the notion. As the four children peered at the bald man from different angles, a younger, sprightlier, heavier figure stepped down from the train. Buster knew the real Fatty when he saw him, and the Scottie barked his joy at once more being in the presence of his fair-minded keeper.

'Whoa, Buster! At least *you* recognise me. No one else seems to,' said Fatty, patting the excited dog as it jumped up all around him in an effort to get a clean lick.

The others abandoned their scrutiny of the bald man and turned towards their much-loved friend and leader. 'Fatty, Fatty, Fatty!' said Bets, admiringly.

'Pleased to see you too, Bets.'

'How'd you get on in London?' asked Larry.

'Ah, good question. I will bring you all up to date as we stride towards the next stage in our mystery.'

'The Mystery of the Missing Books!' said Pip. He had read in the local paper that special copies of *The Enchanted Wood* and *Adventures of the Wishing-Chair* had disappeared from Green Hedges.

'Well, I prefer to say "The Mystery of Old Thatch", for now,' said Fatty. 'That's the name of Enid's home when she used to live in PetTerswood and wrote about the wishing-chair and the enchanted wood.'

'You mean she used to live here in the village?' asked Daisy.

'Shush, not so loud!' said Larry, looking around them at the quiet streets. 'Goon will hear us.'

'Actually,' said Fatty, 'Mr Goon saw me on the way to the station this morning. He walked alongside, pushing his bike, and – in his transparent way – engaged me in conversation in order to try and work out whether or not we were on the case!'

'You didn't tell him anything?'

'Well, I did say that we were on the trail of something spicy, just to stir him up a bit. But when I mentioned Enid Blyton, he pretended to lose interest. "Beaconsfield is not in my jurisdiction," he said, though that is a lie. And even when I teased him with the fact that she used to live in Petterswood, he pretended he still wasn't interested, though his face had gone the colour of beetroot.'

'How long is it since she lived here?' asked Pip.

'Twenty-one years since she came here from Beckenham. Twelve years since she left for Beaconsfield.'

'Golly!' said Daisy

'Ages ago!' said Pip.

'Isn't that out of *our* juris-whatsit?' asked Bets. 'After all I wasn't even born then. And you three would have been babies.'

'Jurisdiction is a movable feast, Bets.'

'Pardon.'

'I feel the case *is* very much in our patch,' said Fatty, who had decided to read copies of any and all books stolen from

Green Hedges. Sooner or later, such precise knowledge would lead him to the thief. Of course it would! And so what if it didn't?

The Find-Outers had taken the road that leads to the river, rather than walk along the High Street, to avoid passing the house in which Goon lived on his own. And as they sauntered along beside the river, their leader filled them in. Fatty had spent the day with *Teacher's World* in the British Library. But first he had had to get a reader's ticket. That had taken a full hour, but after that hour he had access to what was called 'The Reading Room of the British Museum' for the rest of his life.

'What does "not transferable" mean?' asked Bets, frowning at the blue card she'd been handed.

'That means only I, Frederick Algernon Trotteville, can use the Reading Room. If you or Theophilus Goon want to do your own research into Enid Blyton's books, you blooming well have to get cards of your own.'

'Goon wouldn't know what to do with a book,' said Pip.

'And why would I want to sit in a gloomy old library reading dusty old books all day when you've already done it for me?' asked Bets.

'Exactly!' said Fatty, smiling, and pleased to be back in Peterswood with his friends again, as the library had indeed proven to be a bit on the dull side. Dull and wearisome until the bound volumes of *Teacher's World* had arrived on his desk, that is to say.

'Now listen, everyone, and I'll tell you where we've got to with the investigation.'

Bets stopped skipping so as to be able to concentrate fully on what Fatty was going to tell them. Larry was a bit puzzled why they had to know anything about *Teacher's World*. Some tramp had probably just nipped into Enid Blyton's house, picked up the books at random and, when he'd taken a proper look at his haul, thrown them into a field as valueless! That's what they should be doing – scouring the countryside around Green Hedges. But Fatty had proved to be an inspirational leader lately. So Larry, like the others, was content to follow wherever he led, no questions asked.

First Fatty had to describe *Teacher's World*. It was a weekly, with three densely written columns studded with the odd grey picture throughout its big pages, which were not quite as big as those of a newspaper.

'Something in between *Sunny Stories* and Dad's morning paper?' asked Bets.

But *Sunny Stories* is tiny and *The Times* is huge,' objected Pip.

However, Fatty was happy enough with Bets' description. 'Exactly so, Bets,' he said, as pleased with her as ever.

It was Fatty's mother that had first been able to tell him something about the publication, telling him at the breakfast table that in her own childhood, Enid Blyton's contributions had been of great influence at her school, and at schools generally. Apparently, her teacher had read out Enid's weekly *Letter to Children*. And she seemed to remember that there was also a programme of nature study that her class had followed. Mrs Trotteville was surprised to be told that Fatty didn't know anything about *Teacher's World*, since Enid Blyton had certainly written for it until recently. Did she not still do so?

At the Reading Room, Fatty had discovered that Enid had first written for *Teacher's World* in 1922, and had stopped writing for the educational paper in 1945. So his was the first generation of children for twenty-odd years *not* to have had Enid's words of wisdom read out for them in class. Fatty had never thought of himself as having led a particularly deprived childhood, after all he had his own personal copy of *Sunny Stories* delivered every fortnight. But a proper, big letter from Enid Blyton every week – plus stories, poems and nature lessons – now *that* really would have been something!

Wouldn't it? Fatty had been determined to find out exactly what he'd been missing. So he'd started at the beginning. The first mention of Enid in *Teacher's World* had been in 1922, so he'd dug that up – a story for children about fairies and a broken magic dish. In 1923, there were about a hundred different items in the pages of the weekly, most of them stories to be read out in class. But what had really caught Fatty's attention was the first of Enid Blyton's 'From My Window' articles. These essays, which were written for the teachers themselves, took up a whole column and dealt with a variety of subjects. The very first one was about what children and geniuses had in common: a curiosity about life. Enid's column wondered why – in 99 cases out of 100 – a child would lose this curiosity as he or she got older. Fatty had read the piece with great interest, knowing full well that he was that 1-in-a-100 child who would never lose his curiosity about life.

'Me too,' said Bets.

'And me,' said Pip, Daisy and Larry together.

'Ha!' said Fatty, trying to work out the odds against 5 out of 5 children each being a 1-in-a-100 kid. Actually, that may have been the very point that Enid Blyton was trying to make. Today, society is moving quickly towards a time when grown-ups will live their lives to full potential.

But what was great about the 'From My Window' articles, as far as Fatty was concerned, was that they hinted at what was going on in the author's life. Sometimes the hints were direct, and sometimes not quite so direct. In the middle of 1924 when, week after week, she started coming out with purple prose, Fatty got the distinct impression that something special was happening, between the lines.

'How do you mean?' asked Larry.

Fatty took out his notebook. 'This is from the summer of that year. She and her companion had set off for a walk in the countryside. The birds were singing of "a wonderful, wonderful day". And here is just one of her actual sentences.' Fatty read the sentence about a blackbird which ran to forty scintillating words.

'Say that end bit again,' requested Bets.

'"... the lightsome, lilting, dancing, heart of the sweet Springtime",' repeated Fatty, as Bets resumed her skipping.

'I wonder who the companion was she spoke of,' asked Daisy.

'Aha! Well, a few weeks after the walk in the country, an announcement was made in *Teacher's World* that their Enid was getting married. And shortly after that, her husband does get a passing mention in "From My Window".'

'That's not the man currently at Green Hedges, is it?' wondered Larry.

'No. It's not Kenneth. It's Hugh. Her first husband.'

'The lightsome... lilting... dancing... heart... of the sweet... Springtime,' muttered Bets, making the rhythm of words match her hopscotch movements.

'Here she is writing a piece on "Happiness".' And Fatty read out an exquisite sentence, giving emphasis to all the right places and then pausing at the end of the quotation to let it sink into the minds of his fellow Find-Outers.

Fatty then went on with his report. Enid wrote her 'From My Window' letters for four years. And they covered her move, in 1926, to Elfin Cottage, Beckenham. (Fatty was very impressed with himself for remembering all the dates and places.) Her column changed to the 'Letter to Children' that his own mother had told him about. But then, after a couple of years of that, and after she had moved to Old Thatch in 1929, Enid was given a whole page every week.

Bets wanted to know about this move. 'Where is Beckenham? Why did she move from such a nice-sounding home as Elfin Cottage? Had she been sad to leave, do you think?'

Fatty explained that Beckenham had been a leafy suburb of London when Enid was growing up. But as the century wore on, it had been swallowed up by the expansion of urban London. Enid and Hugh had had to move in order to keep living in the English countryside they so loved. Enid *had* been sad to leave the garden that she and Hugh had made together, but she'd been excited about having a new garden to transform into one of their very own.

Bets seemed satisfied with this information. It quietened her anyway, so that Fatty could carry on: 'Enid's whole page in *Teacher's World* was called… can anyone guess?'

'Just tell us,' said Larry.

'*Enid Blyton's Children's Page*,' said Fatty. 'Each week there was still a letter to the children from Enid, but also a letter to the children from Enid's dog, and a short story written by Enid or by Bobs the dog.'

'Hear that, Buster?' said Pip. 'A dog just like you getting his own column in *Teacher's World*. Can't compete with that, can you?'

'Woof!' said Buster.

'Buster's quite willing to write a column for any magazine that asks him,' said Fatty. 'But I can tell you that whoever he wrote it for – be it *Trainspotters' Weekly* or *Nurses' Monthly* – Buster's column would be about smelly bones every time.'

'And long walks beside the river,' added Daisy.

'As it happens,' said Fatty, lifting his notebook again,

'Buster's already writing a column for *The Daily Express*. You can find it on the same page as the Rupert Bear strip. And let me tell you that Buster's first column was about Dog Happiness.' Fatty found that he only needed to glance at his notebook as he went on. 'Buster's column began: "I've been looking for it straight ahead all my life and I've always found it. I don't mean a nice smelly bone – though that is a very lovely thing – but real, proper, exultant happiness that makes you want to bark, and gives that lift to the heart which is so well known in puppyhood at the thought of some delightful treat!"'

'Woof!' said Buster.

'Yes, I *do* think you're a good writer, Buster,' said Bets.

'Almost as good as Enid,' said Pip.

'Actually, tell a lie,' said Fatty, warming to his theme and turning back a page in his notes so that he had the blackbird quote. 'That was Buster's *second* column. His first included this wonderful bit of canine wisdom: "A Scottie dog took up the tale, and like a born poet, he wove the sunshine and the spring, the budding trees and the starry celandines into a silvery enchantment of yapping – a yapping that came oh, surely not from a Scottie but from the lightsome, lilting, dancing heart of the rolling river".'

'Woof-woof!' said Buster.

'Woof-woof!' echoed Bets, Pip, Larry and Daisy, so that it sounded as if a pack of very happy young dogs was making its carefree way along the river in a westerly direction.

'OK, we're nearly there,' said Fatty.

What Fatty meant was they were at the junction of the riverside path and Haycock Lane. They turned right and after a minute came to a huge inn. There was a house just beyond the inn but you could hardly see it, it was so well shielded by trees and bushes. The 'For Sale' sign was clear

enough, though, and after pointing to it, Fatty led the Find-
Outers through the front gate and into the front garden.

'This is Old Thatch. I've been to the estate agents about
it. The house is empty now and I suppose it will be until it's
bought by someone else.'

When Fatty had found out that the former residence of
Enid Blyton was again up for sale he'd rushed over to view
the property. The house was splendid with its thick roof of
thatch. And although it was mostly just a ground floor
(except the bedroom that Enid had had built on), it was a

proper house rather than a cottage. He'd told his parents
about Old Thatch and had urged them to buy it. Fatty's
father had explained to him that the family couldn't afford
two houses. But Fatty had meant that they should sell their
ordinary house and buy this wonderful one in which Enid
Blyton had written so many books. Too far from the station,
reckoned Mr Trotteville, who had to get up to London and
back every day. And so that was that.

As Fatty talked about the house, he walked straight past
it and into the middle of the garden. The Find-Outers
passed through a rose walk in single file, and then they
found themselves looking at a patchy lawn overhung by
the branches of a beech tree, in a secluded corner of the
garden.

'This is where the play-house used to be,' said Fatty, pointing to marks on the ground.

'Was it a real little house?' asked Bets.

'It had a front door with a knocker, a door-knob and a
lock,' said Fatty. 'The walls were made of brick, half-tim-
bered, with a gable end over the door and a ridge roof with
a proper chimney.' What else could Fatty remember about
the house? 'Oh, and it had leaded windows.'

'Why is it not here any more?' asked Daisy.

'The last family who lived in Old Thatch – the people who bought the house from Enid and Hugh – didn't have young children,' said Fatty. 'They probably thought it didn't look grown-up enough.'

Pip would have liked to peer though the leaded windows to see if there was a fireplace to go with the chimney. 'Pity it's gone now. I would love to have opened the door and gone inside.'

'Well, we can still get inside,' said Fatty, taking a step forward and sitting down on the lawn. 'Easiest thing in the world!' He pointed out a vague ground plan of the old play-house and invited the others inside as well. Soon, the Find-Outers were sitting in a square with straight backs against where the walls might once have been.

'She mentioned this place in *Teacher's World*,' said Fatty, flicking through his notebook. 'But first, in 1931, nineteen years ago, she announced that a lovely new pet had arrived at Old Thatch, and that it was a baby girl called Gillian.' Fatty lowered his book and spoke to the solemn faces around him. 'Actually, I read quite a lot about walks taken by Enid in the lanes around here, with Gillian in the pram. Then, when Enid and Hugh had an extension put on the house, there were enough building materials left over to build this play-house for Gillian.'

'Did you say that Enid described this play-house as it was in its heyday?' asked Larry.

'Yes, this is what she said about it… Close your eyes so that you get a clear picture.' The children closed their eyes, except for Fatty who had to read his notes: 'The house was furnished with a blue rug, a round table, two stools, a blue tea-set, two pictures on the walls, a little lamp hanging from the ceiling and a tiny carpet sweeper.'

'Wait a minute. A blue rug… a round table… two stools…

a blue tea-set... two pictures on the walls... and what else?'
asked Bets.

'A little lamp hanging from the ceiling,' said Larry.

'And a tiny carpet sweeper,' said Daisy.

'It's a bit like Noddy's House-For-One,' said Pip, with his
eyes shut tight.

'Except this place was used by two, not one,' said Fatty.
'Gillian's little sister Imogen was born four years later. The
arrival of another new pet being duly recorded on Enid's
Children's Page.'

'Would Imogen have used the play-house as well, then?'
asked Daisy.

'She was 3 years old when the move to Green Hedges took
place, a move much talked about in *Teacher's World* both
before and after it took place. So, yes, little Imogen would
have played here with Gillian.'

Fatty realised he was listening to a thrush singing from the
chimney-top of Old Thatch. A clear two-piece note sounded. Then the same two-piece was twice repeated.

'Can you hear it?' he asked his friends, excited.

'Hear what?' asked Pip.

'"I know him, February's thrush,"' said Fatty, quoting a
poem from George Meredith, one that reading *Enid Blyton's
Nature Lover's Book* had prompted him to track down. Or was
it her *Round the Year* book? Or was it *Enid Blyton's Nature
Lessons*? Anyway, the first two lines were magic:

> 'I know him, February's thrush,
> And loud at eve he *val-en-tines*.'

Old Thatch's thrush sang on. Fatty had read enough of
Enid's writings about nature to know that the most musical
garden songbirds were the blackbird and the thrush. And

although Fatty – and Enid – put the blackbird's liquid flow in top spot, the thrush's repertoire of repetitions constituted a feast for the ear too. Fatty listened:

'Pretty Dick, Pretty Dick, Pretty Dick… Why did you do it? Why did you do it?… Wit, wit, wit, wit, wit… Fat-ty, Fat-ty, Fat-ty!'

What could Fatty do but take up the bird's challenge:

> 'I know him, April's thrush,
> And loud at eve he *East-er eggs*.'

Suddenly Bets was seeing not just what Fatty had been telling them, but a whole lot more besides. 'Shut your eyes again, everyone,' she said, keeping her own eyes half-open to make sure that Fatty did as he was told.

'OK, they're shut.'

'You know what I'm seeing now, don't you?' said an excited Bets.

'What are you seeing?' asked Pip.

'I'm seeing the playroom at the bottom of Mollie and Peter's garden!'

'Oh, yes! Where they kept the wishing-chair!' said Pip.

'I can see it too!' said Larry. 'Sort of. What does the chair look like, again?'

'Just a chair,' said Bets. 'Quite fancy legs, I suppose. Not just straight up and down, but with curves.'

'I can't remember if the chair grew two wings or four,' said Daisy.

'Two, I think. They grew from the outsides of the front legs,' said Pip.

'There were *four* little red wings!' corrected Bets. 'Otherwise the chair wouldn't have been properly balanced as it flew out of the playroom and into whatever magical fairy land was waiting for Mollie and Peter.' Bets could clearly remember colouring in the illustrations in her copy of the book.

Only Fatty was aware of the fact that *The Adventures of the Wishing-Chair* had been published as a book by Newnes in 1937. The year before the magic faraway tree made its first appearance in *The Enchanted Wood*, serialised in *Sunny Stories*, also a Newnes publication. Fatty had little doubt that the original magic faraway tree wasn't so far away from where they sat now, just a little jump over a nearby stream. But the wishing-chair was enough for his imagination to be going on with.

Everyone still had their eyes shut. Larry spoke: 'I remember reading the first chapter with Daisy in our nursery. How we loved those pictures of Peter and Mollie with their legs up on the old chair, scared of the fox that was running loose around the antique shop.'

Daisy knew exactly what her brother was talking about: 'Then Mollie and Peter were scared of the old man with the beard trailing all the way down to the ground who ordered them to help him and his assistant to catch the fox.' Daisy's eyes were shining as she went on: 'But Mollie was afraid of getting bitten so she pulled her legs further up the chair…'

'Peter wished they were safe at home,' said Larry. 'And the next thing was, the chair grew a pair of red wings from each of its legs and it flew straight out of the shop and over the town and home to the children's playroom… '

'Here!' said Bets.

'Yes, here,' said Pip. 'At the end of each adventure, the chair would fly them back to the playroom at the bottom of the garden and the children would leave the chair there with the other toys and go back into the house for their tea, or to sleep.'

'You mean, the chair would fly them back to the play-house at the bottom of the garden to blend in with a blue tea-set, a blue rug, a round table, two stools and the tiny carpet sweeper,' said Bets, making a fair fist of combining the play-house that had once existed at the bottom of Old Thatch with the one that Enid had preserved in words for posterity.

'Lovely,' said Daisy.

'Do you remember the Snoogle?' asked Pip.

'A creature with the head of a duck, the body of a dragon and the tail of a cat,' said Fatty.

'The Snoogle was supposed to be a monster, and he trapped Peter, Mollie, Chinky and the Wishing-Chair in his castle… but you couldn't be scared when you read about it.'

'No, you couldn't be scared,' said Daisy. 'The worst thing the Snoogle did was to show them where the castle's tea-making equipment was, and demand that when they made a pot of tea for themselves, they also made a separate pot of tea for him, and served it up with a plate of cakes.'

The others smiled.

'Yes,' said Pip. 'And his beaky mouth gobbled all the cakes up in a trice and then the Snoogle went to sleep in his chair, which gave the others a chance to escape.'

Their smiles widened. Fatty announced: 'A cup of tea and some cakes *would* be quite nice.'

'Mollie put the kettle on…' sang Bets.

Immediately the others joined in: 'Mollie put the kettle on… Mollie put the kettle on… Mollie put the kettle on… THE SNOOGLE WANTS TEA!'

At that moment Mr Goon was coming along the lane on a bicycle. He saw the group of children sitting as large as life in the middle of the lawn, clearly up to something. He stopped his bike and approached the gate.

That afternoon, the policeman had cycled to Beaconsfield where he'd had a very unsatisfactory interview with Mrs Darrell Waters (how he hated that name). She had been in the middle of writing a new adventure story for children, and would not be distracted from it in order to talk with him about missing books from the library at Green Hedges. And nor did she want him of all people blundering about the place, as she put it. So Goon had taken a quick look in the library and left it at that. But as he'd made his way back to the village, he'd remembered that Enid had once lived at the cottage where a few years earlier the outhouse had burned down. So here he was, ready to assess just how much she had gone up in the world through the writing of all these ridiculous books. Goon felt a bit queasy. Nevertheless, he had work to do. He leant his bicycle against a bush and peered over the gate into the garden. As he'd already surmised, it was the Trotteville boy and his gang of interfering kids. What were they up to?

As soon as the policeman announced his presence with a shout, Buster went wild, racing about the garden, barking his head off. 'Relax,' Fatty told him. He got up and sauntered about the garden, a pose calculated to infuriate Goon.

'Oi! That's private property,' shouted the policeman. 'What are you lot doing there? Clear-orf, I tell you!'

'Ah, Mr Goon,' said Fatty, giving the impression that it was a pleasure to see him. After quietening Buster, he continued. 'We are here with the express permission of the estate agent. Please *do* feel free to check with him at his High Street premises first thing in the morning. And join us now for an hour of exquisite poetry and modern dance. Welcome to our performance of *Round the Year with Enid Blyton*.' Having said as much, Fatty turned aside from the policeman and stretched both arms out towards the thrush still perched atop

Old Thatch. He recited:

> 'I know him, September's thrush,
> And soft at eve he *aut-umn leaves.*'

As Fatty said 'autumn leaves' he fell in slow motion onto the lawn. The others giggled. But Fatty was straight back up on his feet and on with his performance, which Bets, Larry, Daisy and Pip listened to with relish:

> 'I know him, October's thrush,
> And soft at eve he *mush-room picks.*'

This time all the children fell as one onto their hands and knees, peering at the ground. Even Buster seemed to join in. Goon watched as they crawled about, laughing and giggling. Not one ounce of respect for his authority between the lot of 'em! Still, he might as well try and get some help from the brats. 'Come across any old books lying around in your travels? You'll know the ones I mean, because it'll say: "To My Darling Husband", on the inside.'

'Oh, Mr Goon. I didn't even realise you were married,' said Fatty, starting up the laughter again. 'Who's the lucky lady?'

Goon blushed purple. He knew he shouldn't have tried to be nice to them. His first instinct had been the right one. 'Didn't I tell you children to clear-orf?'

Fatty wasn't going to be pushed around by Goon. Not when he really did have every right to be there. So he stood up, put his hands on his hips and coolly went on with his business. And his business was the one of thoroughly enjoying himself:

'I know him, November's thrush
And soft at eve he *bi-cycle wheels*.'

This impertinence was too much for Goon. He suspected the fat boy probably did have permission to view the property from the estate agent, because there was nothing the toad liked better than to wander into a proper shop and talk man-to-man with professionals, just as if he was an adult himself. So there was nothing to be gained from trying to tell him to clear off. And if he tried to chase them, they'd just split up and run wild round the house and the garden, which was huge. Besides, why should he waste any more of his time? He was off-duty, and it was getting time for his evening meal-for-one. In as dignified a manner as he could muster, Goon pulled his bicycle out from the bush, remounted it, and pedalled off down the lane. He did not deign to say goodnight. Say goodnight! Why should he bother his head about those young nuisances?

Soon the Find-Outers left Old Thatch as well. When they were nearly home, and the policeman had long disappeared from view, Fatty tried to get a perspective on his day's research. How far had he gone towards solving the mystery of Enid Blyton? Some way, surely. He felt he had a strong handle on her background and early writing. But of all the articles he'd read in *Teacher's World*, what stuck in his mind was the ode to happiness Enid had written not long after marrying Hugh. How did it go again?

'I've been looking for it straight ahead all my life and I've always found it… Real, proper, exultant happiness that makes you want to sing, and gives that lift to the heart which is so well known in childhood…'

'Fatty?' said Bets, suddenly. 'Would you mind reciting the poem all the way through? Not just the beginning.'

'The poem?' said Fatty.

'"February's Thrush". Or whatever it's called.'

Fatty wondered if he could remember its three verses in full. He reckoned the words would probably come to him as he went along:

> 'I know him, February's thrush,
> And loud at eve he valentines
> On sprays that paw the naked bush
> Where soon will sprout the thorns and bines…'

Bets didn't really hear the second verse because she was following up the first in her mind. On Valentine's Day earlier that year, she had sent Fatty a card with a big red heart on it. She'd written a silly poem on the card, which was best forgotten even though the sentiment behind it could never be. Fatty had been very nice about the whole thing, thanking her for the card and the poem. But he hadn't sent her one in return. And the way Fatty had thanked her meant that she was pretty sure Fatty wouldn't be sending her a Valentine's Day card next year either. The exchange had made her sad for a whole week. It made her sad still, when she thought about it.

Anyway, back to the third verse. Bets was once again listening to Fatty's clear, strong voice as they walked along the High Street and into the middle of Peterswood:

> 'He sings me out of Winter's throat
> The young time with the life ahead;
> And my young time his leaping note
> Recalls to spirit-mirth from dead.'

Bets felt like sobbing. She was only a child and yet she completely understood what the poet was saying. Her own young time was that time before Fatty had accidentally made her feel rejected. Of course, Bets knew that her young time wasn't finished yet, she wasn't stupid after all. And she still loved and admired Fatty. But all the same, her point was that *she knew* what the old poet was thinking about when he wrote the wonderful-but-sad poem.

'All right, Bets?'

'Yes, Fatty. Just a bit tired, you know.'

'Sure. We'll soon be home, though.'

'Let me hear the wonderful poem again.'

'Oh, Bets! I don't know if that's such a good idea,' said Fatty, who had been a bit slow to cotton on to what must be going through Bets' mind.

'Right from the very beginning, because I missed the second verse last time around.'

Fatty smiled a melancholy smile. He was tired after his long, long day researching into the ordinary life and astonishing work of Enid Blyton. But Bets wanted to hear the poem once more, so that was that.

'Right from the beginning it is, then, Little Bunny.'

CHAPTER THREE

IN BOURNE END

1

It is early afternoon by the time the train from Paddington drops Kate and me at tiny Bourne End station. We've got camping gear, but we haven't got time to tramp out to a campsite, so instead we take our packs with us to Old Thatch. The white cottage is half a mile along the river, then a stroll up Coldmoorholme Lane. Just as it's been for 400 years, never mind the few decades since Enid lived here.

After the trips to Beckenham and Beaconsfield, it feels right to be exploring at last a house and garden in which Enid Blyton lived. The pair who now own Old Thatch have opened it up as a tourist attraction on Fridays and Saturdays from May to August. They are professional gardeners, or at least Jacky Hawthorne is, and it seems to me that the majority of visitors today are here to enjoy the rose arbour, terraces, borders, formal and cottage gardens of Old Thatch. Our host tells me that she gets a fair number of visitors who turn up, like us, because of the Blyton connection. 'Have you been here before?' she asks me, in response to a comment I make about the grounds. Only in my imagination, I assure her.

We leave our bags with Jacky who is in the front garden selling tickets and guide-books. She knows a lot about Enid's time here, and tells us that in her day the garden was much emptier and wilder, with larger lawns. I forget to ask her when the little house made specially for Gillian was removed. But I don't forget to ask about the cellar in which Hugh used to drink on his own. The present owner's fast-blinking silence tells me that I must do my own research on that one.

Kate and I walk all round the garden together. We particularly enjoy ambling down the trellised rose walk. It's a feature that Enid had built in the garden of Green Hedges too, becoming one of the places where, over the years, she chose to be photographed with her husband. However, Kate and I would prefer to get our photograph taken around what now seems like the back of the house given the way Old Thatch is arranged today. Enid refers to this area as the front of the house in quotations in the guide-book. The highlight of this publication must be the facsimile of a page from *Teacher's World*. It's not just any old page but the first *Enid Blyton's Children's Page*, which came out a month after she moved here in 1929. There's actually a line drawing of Old Thatch across the top of the historic page, showing that this building may well be a cottage but it does cover a lot of ground. Also on the facsimile page is a photograph of Bobs, the dog who made the trip from Elfin Cottage in Beckenham with Enid and Hugh. Enid's column runs down the left column of the page, while Bobs' column runs down the right. Share and share alike.

Kate points out that further on in the booklet there is a grainy photograph of Enid sitting outside Old Thatch with a typewriter on her knees. The photograph illustrates thatch and wallflower for the main part, but, yes, that might be a typewriter on her knees. We sit down on a bench near where Enid sat tip-tapping away. Kate persuades a fellow visitor to take hold of our camera and point it at us. 'Now just press the button on the top,' instructs my companion. And seconds later we are looking at a truly iconic image: Fatty and Bets sitting outside Old Thatch, surrounded by a wealth of Home County shrubbery.

What about an up-to-date photo of Bobs? No; no dogs are

allowed in the garden these days, so we have to be content with the snap of him in the booklet, alongside a letter of his that appeared in Enid's *Teacher's World* page. The letter explains that Enid has asked Bobs to keep his letter short as his story already takes up so much of the page that week. According to Bobs, it took him a whole week to think of the story. Bob finishes his short letter by telling his readers that he'd like to find treasure at Old Thatch, but his Mistress would rather he didn't try. Seventy-five years later I would like to find treasure at Old Thatch, in the form of Hugh's cellar. But I've already poked around and it's no good: the former cellar has been blocked off. Kate wants to know what I know about the cellar, but she can wait for a few minutes to find out, surely.

The only public access to the house is to a wide central room where coffee and postcards are sold, but from there you can get a good idea of the whole building. Basically, Old Thatch is a single-storey building. It was made more substantial when Enid had an en suite bedroom built at the top of a low flight of stairs at one end. This was so that Enid and Hugh didn't have to walk to the other end of the long building at night, where the rooms of the children and the maid were located.

I bring two coffees to a table outside the shop, between the old well, much pictured in Enid's time, and a circular pond, which Enid had built to bird-friendly proportions. Kate, having read the booklet from end to end, asks me what really happened to Enid in her Old Thatch years. Not as a householder and a gardener, but as a wife and a writer. And, in such relaxing circumstances, it seems the easiest and most natural thing in the world to fill her in on the details, most of which come from the biography written by Barbara Stoney.

'Enid left Beckenham and came to Bourne End with Hugh in August 1929, when she was 32.'

I feel like I've said that before. But perhaps I haven't, or at least not to Kate.

'She'd just been given the whole page to fill in *Teacher's World* each week. She was writing and editing *Sunny Stories* as and when it came out. And she was publishing other books into the bargain. Her post-bag was so big that there had to be a special delivery for Old Thatch. One of the things she asked her child readers to do was to send in silver paper, and she had a team of people here to fill sacks and to forward them to London where the Great Ormond Street Hospital converted the raw material into funds.'

'A bit like *Blue Peter*,' suggests Kate.

'Sure. Before TV, Enid was a one-woman *Blue Peter*.'

'And Hugh?'

'Well, I don't know what Hugh was up to in his first years at Bourne End, except that a promotion at Newnes meant extra responsibility and longer hours, so he occasionally returned to Old Thatch late at night. That was to be significant later. But first, out of the blue…'

'A beautiful baby!'

'Yes, several years after a course of hormone injections, Enid became pregnant without resort to any further gynaecology. Gillian was born in 1931, so there was much happiness at that time for Hugh and Enid.'

'What effect did that have on her writing?'

'Ha! The year that Gillian was born Enid didn't publish a single book.'

'Couldn't she write when she was pregnant?'

'I didn't say she didn't write *anything*. She still wrote a great deal of stuff for *Sunny Stories for Little Folk* and for *Teacher's World*. But she wrote nothing over and above those commitments.'

'I expect she got into her stride the next year.'

'Well, no, motherhood held her back. She didn't publish a single book in 1932 either and in 1933 her only publications were *Five-Minute Tales*, a collection of sixty stories that had already appeared in *Sunny Stories*, and some little books intended to help very young children to read, none of which would have taken her more than a day or so to write at her usual pace.'

'And Hugh?'

I keep forgetting about her other half. But it is important to bear him in mind given the way things turned out.

'Early in 1933, when Hugh was particularly busy and making trips to Chartwell to meet Winston Churchill, whose book *The World Crisis* was being published by Newnes in monthly parts, he seems to have buckled under the strain. At a time when Churchill was getting concerned about the possibility of a new war, Hugh, who had won medals for bravery in the First World War, also started to brood. The prospect of renewed devastation turned Hugh to the bottle. That's the accepted theory. Secret drinking in times of stress was an old failing of his.'

'I don't suppose Enid would have been much help to him either, deeply involved as she was in her own very different view of the world.'

'I'm not sure. Remember that by 1933 she still wasn't back up to speed with her writing. I guess a lot of her attention was directed towards the baby. It surprises me that Hugh wouldn't have been similarly engrossed. Anyway, he began to regularly return late from London, the worse for drink. The trusty chauffeur, Dick Hughes, was the first to know what was happening, but eventually Enid became aware of the situation too. In fact, as she acknowledged in her diary, Hugh was sick and needed taking care of. They took a long holiday together in Scotland and when they got back, Enid bought Hugh a drum-kit – which was a strange present for someone who hated noise to give to the person with whom she shared a house.'

'I thought Enid liked music.'

'As a child she played the piano, and listened to her father play Bach, Beethoven and Mozart every night on that same piano. But as an adult she doesn't seem to have listened to music, classical or otherwise.'

'So what happened next in this splendid house?'

'First and foremost, Enid wrote. In 1934, the company responsible for *Five-Minute Tales* published a book of thirty longer stories, called *Ten-Minute Tales*. Also published that year was *The Enid Blyton Poetry Book*, *The Red Pixie Book*, three volumes of *World History Retold*, several volumes of short stories under the title of *The Old Thatch Series* and *Round the Year with Enid Blyton* in four volumes – nature books about spring, summer, autumn and winter.'

'A lot of writing,' says Kate.

'It's nothing compared to the amount that she went on to write later. And remember that *The Red Pixie Book* consists of material first published in *Teacher's World* or in *Sunny Stories for Little Folk*.'

'And what about Hugh?'

'Hugh's problems hadn't entirely gone away. But then there was a miscarriage for them both to contend with, and then, in 1935, the arrival of a second baby to celebrate. However, Imogen was given straight to a nurse so that Enid could bomb on with the writing. In 1935 she published several books all right: *The Children's Garden*, which showed children how to go about making their own garden; *The Green Goblin Book*, a series of tales involving three goblins; *Hedgerow Tales*, imaginative stories involving the real creatures you might find along the waysides of Britain; and *Six Enid Blyton Plays*.'

'Good for her,' says Kate.

'But that's still nothing compared to the amounts she went on to write at Green Hedges.'

'In 1936?' asks Kate.

'In 1936 she published *Fifteen-Minute Tales*. I haven't seen that book but I guess it'll contain twenty or so stories one-and-a-half times as long as the stories in the *Ten-Minute* book.'

'Either that, or fifteen minutes was how long it took her to write them.'

'Yeah, true. She also published *The Yellow Fairy Book*, in which two children, Peter and Mary, visit strange lands including the Land of Stupids. And she edited and introduced a book of British birds.'

'Did she really?'

I'm pleased with my research on this particular book, so I trot some of it out: 'An ornithologist called T.A. Coward published a book of British birds in three illustrated volumes. A few years later, it was Enid's job to cut the descriptions down so that the material could all go into a single volume, second edition. A task not made any easier by the fact that she herself had much to say about the kingfisher, cuckoo, swallow, blackbird, robin, and so on. As far as I can tell from comparing the three-volume work with Enid's compressed volume, she resisted the temptation to add to the words in the main section of the book. However, her job of condensing three volumes into one must have been made more difficult by the fact that she wrote a forty-page introduction telling the readers all about birds from another point of view: her own.'

'How do you mean?'

'Among other things, Enid tells you how to attract them into your garden.'

'This garden, for example?'

I look around. Yes, perhaps her bird-watching from the windows of Old Thatch motivated her to write the book. Since we've been sitting at this table a spotted flycatcher has been making forays from the roof, catching insects above the pond.

'How do you know it's a whatchamacallit?' asks Kate.

'Well, it's a flycatcher, obviously. And the only kinds you get in the UK are pied flycatchers, which are black and white, and spotted flycatchers, which are a nondescript brown, like this one.'

'Have you been sneaking a look at Enid's bird book?' says my partner, ticking me off.

Well, I have actually. And I'd like to say more about both

Enid's interest in birds and mine in bird books. But we have to move swiftly on. Just as Enid did.

'From the beginning of 1937, *Sunny Stories* dropped the *"for Little Folk"* part of its title and went weekly. Before that it came out sporadically, and if you'd gone into a newsagent in the early thirties you might have found several on the shelf at any one time. The new regular appearance of what had become a magazine as we now know it allowed Enid to try her hand at serials alongside self-contained stories, like *Adventures of the Wishing-Chair, The Secret Island* and *Mr Galliano's Circus*. God, she was flying! *The Enchanted Wood* was also serialised from 1938 and I'm glad to have it confirmed by our site visit that the enchanted wood – as described in that book – is just a jump over the brook that runs through the back of the garden of Old Thatch. Just as the outhouse in which the two children stored the wishing-chair was surely Gillian's house in a corner of this very garden, though we haven't managed to track it down.'

'I can easily believe all that,' says Kate, who loves the atmosphere and the spaciousness of Old Thatch as much as I do. 'It seems so obvious when you're here.'

'Unfortunately, things were not going so well for Hugh. The outbreak of the Spanish Civil War confirmed his belief in Churchill's warnings that big trouble was brewing in Europe. He took to the bottle again, though this time he took pains that Enid shouldn't find out about the return of what she probably interpreted as his weakness.'

'What did he do? Stay overnight in London?'

'That might have been sensible. But what he did instead was set up a little drinking den in the cellar of this house.'

'Oh, dear.'

'Hugh could only access the cellar from the parlourmaid's bathroom.' I point to the back of Old Thatch where I suspect that room was. 'I dare say this might have been tricky on evenings when the

THIS IS HER
HUGH

The man at the table jumped violently.

maid had turned in early. Or perhaps not. Perhaps Hugh didn't wake the sleeping maid as he quietly entered the room adjoining her bedroom and raised the cellar door and walked down the stairs into his parlour. That's roughly how the process is described in the Barbara Stoney biography. The only person who knew about the cellar's sordid use was Dick Hughes, who was entrusted with the keys every now and again so that he could get rid of the empties. Perhaps he polished Hugh's medals while he was at it. God, you've got to laugh.'

But neither Kate nor I are laughing. After a pause for reflection, I go on:

'So while there was great stuff happening for Enid, creatively and professionally, suddenly she finds out that Hugh has been drinking himself into oblivion in the cellar. The Not-So-Faraway Bar. That's where Hugh's wishing-chair was located. Right next to a bottle of whisky, a glass tumbler and some medals.'

'Poor man.'

'In the summer of 1938, Hugh was hospitalised with pneumonia, which he'd contracted through working hard while being rundown. Enid discovered the bottles in the cellar, and Dick Hughes, in the best interests of his joint employers, had to admit what was going on. Enid's reaction was a complicated one. It's recorded in the Barbara Stoney biography how, during Hugh's hospitalisation, Dick asked Enid how her husband was getting on. He was surprised when the normally imperturbable lady buried her head in her hands and in between sobs admitted that she was frightened and did not know what to do. She didn't want to lose Hugh.'

'She loved him?'

'I'm sure she did, for most of their married life. But he was also an important part of the writing factory she'd turned Old Thatch into. Hugh was an intelligent man, remember. In the early days of their marriage he'd guided Enid's career very effectively. Tony Summerfield has told me that there's no comparison between the professionalism of the work that was published by Newnes and, for example, the little books that Birns churned out in 1933.'

Kate looks thoughtful. I carry on: 'Anyway, Hugh recovered from the self-inflicted illness that nearly killed him. Enid took stock of her idyllic surroundings and wrote a tribute to them in her column in *Teacher's World*. Nevertheless, with this second crisis, Enid decided on a clean break, not from Hugh but from Hugh's temptation: the cellar. As early as the autumn of 1938 – in other words only months after the hospitalisation – the family moved to Green Hedges. Hugh, being extremely fond of the unspoiled surroundings of Old Thatch, was decidedly against the move. But it was on the cards anyway, so that the family could have a bigger house with more staff in residence.'

Kate looks around her and takes in all that Enid was prepared to leave behind. There is just no comparison between this rural paradise and semi-suburban Beaconsfield, lovely mansion though Green Hedges undoubtedly was.

'In the new house, I'm sure Enid worked hard at making things better between Hugh and herself. But the war started, and Hugh insisted on joining up despite his age, and so was away a great deal. Enid couldn't understand why Hugh felt he had to leave both his job and his family.'

'Did she just ignore the war?'

'She didn't like her writing routine being disturbed, that's for sure. But she wasn't a fool either. Her *Teacher's World* column contained a mature perspective on what was happening as a result of the war. Everyone would have to make adjustments to their normal routine, as she put it. She used her pages to try and help children and teachers who had been evacuated from cities to the countryside adjust to their change of surroundings. Hugh joined his old regiment – the Royal Scots Fusiliers – and was posted to Dorking in Surrey where he was put in charge of training the Home Guard. From there he was able to return home once a week. But that's not much when a partnership is on shaky ground. And the marriage seems to have broken down completely in the spring of 1941.'

'How old would the children have been?'

'Gillian would have been 10 and Imogen 6.'

'That wouldn't have pleased Enid, given what had happened to her as a child. Was it Hugh who left Enid?'

'That's hard to say. Apparently, when Hugh was away on duty, Enid began to entertain a few of the able-bodied men who were still kicking around Bourne End. But also, in mid-1940, Hugh had come across Ida Crowe on a visit to the War Office. She'd been a novelist who he'd worked with at Newnes, and as he was in the process of recruiting staff for his new operation he persuaded her to go with him to Dorking. Obviously there was something going on there, since they ended up marrying. But it's not clear whether Enid, or Hugh, was the first to commit adultery.'

'And then?'

'Within a year or so they both had new partners. And a further year or two down the line, Enid was going full tilt at the writing again despite the war. Of course, she had never stopped. However, the Famous Five books and the Mysteries represented a fresh flowering of her talent, even when all hell was breaking loose in Europe. By this time she was in her creative cocoon once more and had perhaps come to think differently about what had happened here at Old Thatch. The first book in the Mystery series, *The Mystery of the Burnt Cottage*, isn't about the burning down of a cottage a mile to the west of Peterswood. But it nearly is. It's about the burning down of a workroom *in the garden* of such a cottage. And Dick Hughes lived with his wife in a small house in the grounds of Old Thatch. But if that was a sort of revenge in print, it was just the start of Enid's literary vengeance.'

'How do you mean?' asks Kate, looking curious.

'Ostensibly, the Mysteries are about the solving of mysteries by the five Find-Outers and Dog. To a large degree, the books are really about the ridiculing of Goon. And I have to say that many examples of Mr Goon's humiliation are extremely funny. There is the chapter in *The Mystery of the Strange Bundle* when Fatty's skill as a ventriloquist has Goon believing that there is a dog, a pig and a man shouting for his aunty in a house that is actually empty except for one small kitten.'

Kate smiles at this example of Goon's gullibility. I go on: 'Or again in *The Mystery of the Secret Room* where – all through the book – Goon is pursued by red-headed delivery boys on bikes. A telegram boy and a butcher's boy in particular: both Fatty in disguise. A disguised Fatty running rings around poor old Goon.'

I pause for a minute, before going on: 'So the question I put to myself at some point while reading the Mystery books was "Why the relentless and spirited humiliation of Goon?"'

'Why, Dunc, why?' echoes Kate.

'Well, I'll tell you,' I say calmly. After all, I'm very sure of my material. 'It's Enid punishing Hugh.'

I place on the table a sheet of paper. In the top half of the page is a rough circle made up of the letters of Goon's full name. THEOPHILUS GOON. Below the jumble of letters are some crossings out as well as several underlined phrases – anagrams that I intend to read now to Kate, in the garden of Old Thatch, where they are most appropriate:

'HUGH OPENS TO OIL... O LET HUGH POISON... O HUGH SPOILT ONE.'

'Is it a coincidence?' asks Kate.

'Might be. But remember that Enid was famous for her practical jokes at school. And as a teenager she was responsible for postcards being sent between herself and her friends written in code. You know, that box and dot business I told you about: a different box and dot combination for each letter of the alphabet.'

'Dear Mary, The French are all gluttons.'

'That's it. Also bear in mind that in the first book of the

Mysteries, Enid has fun with Fatty's name, Pip pointing out that the initials of Frederick Algernon Trotteville spell FAT. In the second book, Enid has a go at Mr Tupping aka Old Tapping the gardener. It's also in *The Mystery of the Disappearing Cat* that the name Theophilus crops up for the first time. Goon is referred to as plain "Goon" or "Mr Goon" until Fatty, who has climbed a tree, overhears a conversation between Goon and Tupping where Goon utters a line which finishes: "If I don't force a confession out of him, my name's not Theophilus Goon!"

'Fatty overhears this from his vantage point in the tree. He chuckles to himself, ostensibly about the fact that Tupping and Goon are falling for all the false clues that the Find-Outers have planted on the scene, but I can't help thinking it's Enid laughing at her own private joke.'

'That is very strange,' says Kate.

'The name doesn't crop up again until the third book, *The Mystery of the Secret Room*, where again it occurs just once, in a sentence that ends: "If I don't sniff something out, my name's not Theophilus Goon."'

'Could she really be so devious?'

'Anyone who has a photographic memory and can write 10,000 words a day can pretty well do what he or she likes. I suspect that when she first came up with "Theophilus Goon", she was aware of its anagram qualities, and these amused her. She may not have given it another conscious thought, but I think the name was working away at the back of her mind when she came up with the climax of the third book in the series.'

Before Kate can respond, I continue:

'Perhaps that's going too far. It's important to bear in mind certain letters to the psychologist – Peter McKellar – that Barbara Stoney reproduces at the back of her biography. In these, Enid admits that in her books she doesn't use anything that she hasn't seen or experienced herself. She uses the phrase "our books are facets of ourselves". But she does emphasise that when she's writing she doesn't know what's going to happen next. It's all her conscious mind can do to keep up with the words and images that her "under-mind" comes up with.

'However she does mention, both in these letters to the psychologist and in her autobiography, that there was a mental blank as far as surnames were concerned. The Christian names of her child characters came from her subconscious along with almost everything else, but she used a telephone directory when she needed to give the children a surname. So I suppose it's possible that in the case of the adult Goon, it was his surname that came from her subconscious and that when she eventually gave him a Christian name she had to resort to some other tactic. Which would help to explain the anagram. Of course, she was quite able to let her conscious mind take control. And when she did she still wrote extremely quickly. Her autobiography and her nature books are not written by her under-mind, but are consciously constructed.'

'So...'

'After writing the first Mystery, she probably realised that Goon and Hugh were linked in her under-mind. And while writing the second one she got involved with the Tupping = Tapping business. She wanted to get the Hugh = Goon equation in there as well, but she knew she'd have to be subtle about it. She also knew that she was committed to the Goon surname. GOON gives the G needed in HUGH. So what forename makes use of the letters H, U and H? Not many. In fact, the only other I've come up with is HUMPHREY.'

'Humphrey Goon! I quite like that, it suggests Humpty-Dumpty. And Goon was always heading for a fall.'

'Humphrey would have given Enid "ME OR PONY HUGH". Or she could have had "OH, HUG MY PEN OR..." But there was much more to be had from the other option.'

'Theophilus it is then.'

I return our attention to the sheet of paper:

'HUGH OPENS TO OIL... O LET HUGH POISON... O HUGH SPOILT ONE.'

Kate takes the paper from me, checking that these really are anagrams, I suppose. Well, they are. And now I have to explain how this leads us straight back to Hugh/Goon in the cellar.

'Listen to this little résumé of *The Mystery of the Secret Room* which was published in 1945. The story focuses on a house in Peterswood that Pip discovers has a secret room... Might even have been Old Thatch... . You have to imagine Goon chasing Pip up the lane there and Pip climbing a tree to escape Goon's notice. Once Goon has blundered off further down the lane, Pip realises the upper room of the house is immaculately kept and lived in, in a house that is otherwise empty and has been so for a long time. The Find-Outers investigate. Fatty gets locked up in the special room, but he escapes thanks to his usual ingenuity. After doing so, he looks around the rest of the house, eventually making his way into the cellar. Bear in mind, he's in disguise. He notices someone else coming down into the *cellar*. Fatty, thinking the man is one of the villains, jumps on him. It's actually Goon. Theophilus Goon. Or, if you believe me: "O Hugh spoilt one".'

I glance at Kate just to make sure she's getting all this.

'Goon is knocked to the dirty ground, and although he manages to shine a torch up to Fatty making his way out of the coal hole, all he sees is another blasted boy in a red wig, one of the red-headed boys that have been plaguing him throughout the Mystery. Fatty rolls a barrel of water on top of the entrance to the cellar and that's that. Well, that's that until the next day when the Chief Inspector arrives and Fatty is congratulated on his latest glorious success (the actual culprits of the case have been rounded up and locked in the secret room upstairs). But who's this damp and black and thoroughly miserable figure who has to be let out of the cellar? Why, it's Theophilus Goon (O soil on Hugh pet). And the poor man is sniffling (Hugh opens to oil) and snivelling (Til Hugh poos one) because he's caught a cold, perhaps even pneumonia (O let Hugh poison)!'

I think Kate is following my analysis. I think she agrees with me that basically it was Enid's subconscious that first came up with the goods, but that once it was down on paper she gradually became aware of what she'd written and why, so that by the third book she was really going for it. Anyway, there's no stopping me now: 'And I can see why Enid did this. I can see why deep down she was so mad, several years after the event. Hugh and she had had it all when they'd been living in this house in the mid-thirties. Health, children, careers in writing and publishing, wealth in the best sense of that word. More than that, *she loved him*. Was her love not enough? What more did he want? Were their two lovely daughters not enough?'

I can't keep still, I have to walk around the garden. Round and round the little circular pond. 'O Hugh spoilt one,' I say aloud, and to the garden at large.

Kate joins me and we walk out of Old Thatch, hand-in-hand. I can't speak for my companion, but I'm thinking: 'Hugh, how could you? How could you let yourself get so spooked by a combination of Churchill and Hitler that you threw all this away?'

'You great Theophilus Goon!' I shout, as we walk through the rose trellis. And I mean every word.

2

Kate and I don't get very far with our camping gear. There is a pub right next to Old Thatch, and Kate would like to have a drink there. After all it's six o'clock, and our exploration of Bourne End proper – or rather Bourne End aka Peterswood – should really wait until we're fresh again tomorrow morning. Besides, my partner thinks I'm missing something.

We enjoy a drink in silence. Then Kate goes to the bar and buys us each another. She tells me she wants to try and put over the non-writer's perspective. She asks me to picture a tired Hugh coming home to an invariably switched-on Enid, an Enid who goes on and on about her latest story with never-ending energy. Hugh just has to take a break from it.

Well, I suppose so. But on balance my sympathies have to be with Enid. Does Kate not agree? She tells me that if, during these last few days, her own little flat had had a cellar, she would have retreated to it on more than one occasion.

'Why?'

'To get some non-Blyton time!'

'What?... I mean, why?'

'Because you have been going on and on about Enid and her work since I picked you up from the station and I'd just about had enough if it.'

I can't tell if Kate's joking. 'Are you joking?'

'Shut up, Enid. You're doin' ma heid in.'

What's that? What has Kate just said?

'It's the same every night. I get back here after a long day an' I have to sit here an listen tae ALL YER BLETHERIN'. And I'll tell ye this, Enid: I CANNAE STAND IT ANY MORE.'

Oh, I get it. But it seems to me that Hugh has a surprisingly broad regional accent for someone who has been working at senior management level in a well-to-do London publishing company for years. But – hey! – what do I know? After a short pause and a sip of beer, I prompt Kate with some of the Home County English that I know Enid spoke so clearly:

'What are you saying to me, Hugh?'

'I'm just tellin' ye that I'm no listenin' to any more of yer blethers, that's all. So you've been writin' a' day – I ken that! You write every day. Am no' askin' ye tae do utherwise. But I am tellin' ye that I'm no sitting here in my own hoos and listenin' tae yer latest lot o' nonsense.'

'What are you going to do instead?' I reply, cautiously.

'I'll tell ye what I'm goin' tae do. The same as I do every night when ye're doin' ma heid in. Though up to now you've been too full o' yersel' tae notice. I'm GOIN' DOWN TAE THE CELLAR FOR A BEVVY!'

Christ, on one level Kate really might mean this as an attack on my focus. But on another it's just a great extension of it. I must try and keep up my end of the exchange. 'Hugh?' I say, hoping that Kate will stay in character for a bit longer, as it's ramificating like billy-oh in my mind.

'Naw, naw. Don't Hugh me! Ye've asked me whit am doin'. An I've telt ye. I'm takin' ma whisky tae the cellar. Don't try tae stop me. And don't try tae come wae me.'

'Hugh?'

'Aye, that's ma name. Don't wear it oot.'

'Oh, Hugh. I am going to come with you to the cellar. I really want to do that. We can drink the whisky together. And be drunk in each other's arms in the morning.'

Kate narrows her eyes. 'Ah, but ye don't want tae be drunk an' hung-over in the mornin'. Do ye, Enid? That would play merry hell with yer word-count. Yer precious word-count!'

'You're right, Hugh. I thought Churchill was the problem. I thought those damned Nazis were the problem. But I can see now that your problem all along has been me. I've been placing too much emphasis on my work. I'm so sorry, darling. Believe me, our life together means a lot more to me than any number of Wishing-Chairs and Enchanted Woods.'

'Now ye're talking, doll,' says Kate, clapping her hands. 'Now ye're talkin' ma language!'

Kate is buzzing and I'm reeling. What has she really been saying? That I haven't been paying her enough attention since we met up? Well, yes, I suppose it's been a long few days for her. But I'm so glad Kate has put her warm heart and witty soul into her speech. I can see the original Old Thatch scenario more clearly now. At least I can begin to see it from the non-writer's point of view.

3

The tent is up and the sleeping bags are zipped together and we're lying side by side. Not a word have I said about Enid Blyton since we left the pub. Not one word.

'Have you got some bed-time reading for us?' asks Kate, brightly.

Well, of course I have, but does she want to hear it? Anyway, I reply in the affirmative. ('In the affirmative'! Hey, I really am uptight.)

'Is it a Mystery?' asks Kate.

Of course it's a Mystery. But Kate has to persuade me that she really wants to hear it.

'How exciting! Which one?'

'*The Mystery of the Vanished Prince.*' And as I say those magical words I feel myself begin to relax.

'Have you only brought the one?'

'I did have a tent to carry down from Scotland, remember. It would have been nice to have transported my entire Blyton library, but then that would have meant asking GNER to add another carriage to their train.' Sarcasm. I must still be on edge.

Kate has a way of getting me to relax. And so does *The Mystery of the Vanished Prince*. The grey cover of the book appears as if it breathes, its texture echoes the skin of my hand. Are those not pores? Well, perhaps it's just the weave of the linen-backed boards under torchlight. But it looks like skin. The cover is decorated, as are all the Mystery hardbacks, with a magnifying glass and a finger-print motif. I place Kate's thumb on the front board at the appropriate place.

'Yes, that's a good fit.' I tell her. 'Goon has no choice but to add you to his list of suspects.'

'What does he suspect me of?'

'Oh, I don't know… Taking his name in vain, perhaps. But he knows deep down that it's not you he's after. It's Fatty. Always Fatty. That toad of a boy who mocks him from pillar to post.'

Kate asks me why I'm so keen on the Mysteries. Does she really need to ask? The Goon theme aside, joy runs through the books like a river. I remind my partner that Enid wrote all the Mysteries while living in Beaconsfield with Kenneth. There she was, settled and happy in both her work and her personal life. And to celebrate this, she looked back on two happy periods of her life pre-Kenneth. The first period was the time she'd spent exploring the Beckenham countryside with her father, before his leaving brought on great misery. The second was when she had been able to explore the delights of Bourne End, before the needs of her children, her writing career and her troubles with Hugh all began to tie her down. In these books, Enid is thinking about herself as a child – Bets – about her growing children – the Find-Outers en masse – and about the lovely countryside in and around Bourne End, just three miles away from where she sits on her throne at Green Hedges, typing out her JOY!

Kate murmurs something warm and supportive. She wants me to go on with this, I know she does. So I open the book. I've brought it with me not only because it contains a scene that takes place in a campsite between Bourne End and Marlow – that is, on this very spot – but because it is the Mystery that is full of the most intoxicating scenes. The frontispiece gives a flavour of the book. Some of the Find-Outers are dressed in exotic clothes and Ern, Goon's nephew, is holding what is referred to as the State Umbrella (actually a golf umbrella) over a haughty girl whom he believes to be the Princess Bongawee (really Bets with a headscarf and a suntan).

I turn the thick cream pages to the Enid part I want to read out. The Find-Outers are down by the river. Ern is holding the State Umbrella over the Princess's head while he and the Find-Outers eat ice-cream. They spot Mr Goon. The policeman is confused as to who it is that's dressed so exotically. The exchange continues. I read aloud the bit where Goon asks Fatty if the girl is a real princess. Bets pipes up in a cheeky voice that amuses Fatty:

'"Ikky-oola-potty-wickle-tok."

'Goon wants to know what the princess has said. Quick as a flash Fatty tells Goon that she wants to know if he's a real policeman, and asks Goon how he should respond. Goon just glares at him. Bets pipes up again with:

"Ribbly-rookatee, paddly-pool."

'Goon wants to know what that means. Fatty puts on an embarrassed look and tells Goon that he doesn't want to translate, as it's rather a personal remark.'

The sparky humour just goes on and on. I love it. So does Kate, I know she does. And I bet Enid marvelled as she heard the dialogue for the first time too, even as she typed the stuff. Her under-mind had silently worked on what had happened a few years before and had transformed it into such light-hearted mischief. Encouraged, I read a bit more. Bets has gone off in peals of laughter. But she manages to compose herself and say to Goon: 'Wonge-bonga-smelly-fidly-tok.'

More curious than ever, Goon pleads with Fatty to translate what's been said, and even tries to ingratiate himself with Fatty by calling him 'Frederick'. But Fatty insists he couldn't possibly translate the last remark, leaving Goon almost beside himself with curiosity and frustration.

I ask Kate to bear in mind that the triangular relationship that exists between Fatty, Bets and Goon is made up of two distinct pairings. The rapport between Fatty and Bets comes from the loving and mutually stimulating relationship that existed between Enid and her father when she was Bets' age. And so when talking to Bets, Fatty is the all-knowing, all-charming father-figure. But when it's Fatty and Goon locking horns, that's another pairing. It's then that the grown-up Enid – witty and wise like her father – is effectively Fatty, mocking Goon who is always and forever the dimmest of Hughs.

'But Hugh wasn't dim.'

'He wasn't fat either. But that's part of the joke. To have him reduced to a bumbling obese idiot.'

I take up *The Mystery of the Vanished Prince* in my own words:

'Turns out that the day after the "Princess Bongawee" deception, the real Prince Bongawee, whose sister Bets was pretending to be, gets kidnapped. And so as not to have Goon making a total fool of himself with his Inspector, jabbering on about a non-existent sister, Fatty has to tell Goon about the trick the Find-Outers played on him. But Goon refuses to believe Fatty. According to Goon, nobody could "talk foreign" if they didn't know the language. Fatty – and here he is very much Enid herself – assures Goon it is possible. Fatty can "talk foreign" for half an hour at a time. And he pours out a stream of gibberish that leaves Mr Goon in a whirl. Fatty tells Mr Goon that he should have a go himself. All the policeman has to do is "let his tongue go loose".'

Several chapters later, Goon decides to take this advice, so I'm turning over the thick pages, looking for that bit. This is a little harder to do than it might be, because this is one book I've kept free from highlighter marks. What am I saying? I haven't been able to use highlighter on any of the beautiful Methuen hardbacks. Anyway, I've found the right part. So here we go. I advise Kate to have in the back of her mind a picture of Hugh in the cellar when taking these words on board.

Goon is on his own in the kitchen at the back of his house. He is trying to 'let his tongue go free' as Fatty has advised him. 'Abbledy, abbledy, abbledy,' Goon gabbles and then pauses to take stock. He tries to recall the stream of foreign-sounding words that Fatty spouted earlier in the day, but he can't. He thought it would be easy to come up with a stream of nonsense, but it isn't. His tongue just

stopped when it was fed up of saying 'abbledy', and his brain simply would not come up with anything else. He tries reciting a
poem: 'The boy stood on the burning deck, abbledy, gabbledy,
abbledy. No, it's no good.' Goon concedes that he's just not up to it.

In Enid's letters to Peter McKellar, she talks about her writing
technique as 'letting her mind go free'. So here in the Mystery
something similar is happening. Fatty is able to 'let his tongue go
free' and Goon can't. Just as Enid was able to let her mind go free,
and Hugh, presumably, couldn't. Well, of course he couldn't. It was
only Enid who could let her mind go free to the extent of being a
one-person publishing phenomenon.

Kate expresses sympathy for Hugh-Goon. Then she asks me
something about Enid's understanding of her own character. It's
a complex matter, but in letters Enid wrote to Dorothy Richards,
who was Imogen's first nurse and became Enid's only close
female friend in adult life, she spoke about herself in revealing
terms. She admitted to being guilty of intellectual arrogance. She
was scornful of people if she thought them stupid, or capable of
being led by the nose, or at the mercy of their upbringing. She
usually managed to suppress this, with a view to being charitable,
but at times she admitted to being contemptuous of those around
her. She liked to dominate, even though it didn't always appear
that way.

'But Hugh wasn't stupid,' says Kate for the second time. 'Or capable of being led by the nose.'

'Wasn't he? He wasn't blazingly bright like Enid. And wasn't he
led by the nose into the Second World War?'

'Wasn't everybody?'

'No, not everybody. The Mysteries were begun during WW2, and
Enid doesn't deign to mention it.'

Silence in the tent.

'What actually happens in *The Mystery of the Vanished Prince*?'

Good question. 'The prince has been kidnapped. The Find-

Outers discover where he has been taken. At the end, Goon has to be let out of a cow-shed...'

'A sort of cellar?'

'That's right! Goon has to be let out of a *cow-cellar* in which some villains locked him up after rescuing him from a swamp. *(O soil on Hugh pet.)* When he's released, he's in a dishevelled state with straw sticking out between his head and his helmet. *(O Hugh spoilt one.)* Goon is humiliated in front of the Chief Inspector who is at the same time praising Fatty for solving the mystery. Fatty tries to soften Goon's humiliation (Enid was trying to be charitable), but this only leads to the Inspector going into an orgy of Fatty-admiration. I can remember the Superintendent's words, if not his exact rank: "Brains are good, courage is excellent, resourcefulness is rare, but generosity crowns everything".'

'Enid talking about herself!'

'Enid giving herself a – not completely deserved – pat on the back. On the other hand, she's just written a rollicking good book, ostensibly for children but really for the likes of you and me, and it's probably only taken her about a week.'

'Don't you know for sure?'

'The books in which she kept a record of her day-to-day work were destroyed from 1941. As were her diaries, though they don't mention the books.'

Silence in the tent. Is Kate getting tired?

'Does Goon's full name get an airing in *Vanished Prince*?'

'Ha! "Theophilus Goon" crops up precisely once in the book. Can I read out the sentence to you?'

'Oh, yes please,' says Kate, sounding keen.

I find the page. I try not to smile. I just read the words as Enid's tirelessly typing fingers placed them into Goon's mouth:

'I'm in charge, see, and I'll solve this mystery or *my name's not Theophilus Goon*.'

'That's fantastic,' says Kate, with no hint of irony.

'What's really fantastic is that tomorrow is going to be as much of a revelation as today...'

'Enid,' says Kate, in what I strongly suspect is about to turn into a Scottish accent.

'Yes, Hugh.'

'Am sorry aboot what a said earlier. A didnae mean anythin' by it. Ye ken that don't ye?'

'Yes, that's all right, darling. Just promise me one thing.'

'Anythin' doll. Just say the word.'

'Promise me that you'll stay clean tomorrow.'

'Ah, Enid. Ye're a hard woman.'

'Promise?'

'Abbledae, gabbledae.'

'That's not a promise, Hugh. That's gibberish.'

'Abbledae, gabbledae, princess.'

And on that note we call it a day.

4

In the morning, we breakfast at our campsite and walk into Bourne End. Feeling the rain in our faces isn't quite as dispiriting as listening to it pattering against the outside of the tent. All the same, we decide to spend an hour in the library in the hope that the weather will have brightened by the time we really need to be out and about.

Nothing Enid says about Peterswood in the Mysteries is inconsistent with Bourne End being what she had in mind. Marlow is said to be three miles away, which is the case. Maidenhead is said to be down-river, as it is. Indeed, the omnipresence of the river in the books is a key indicator. And the Thames flows past Bourne End, whereas it doesn't go anywhere near Beaconsfield. The only part of Beaconsfield that crops up in Peterswood is Green Hedges, long enough for Enid to get the Old Tapping incident off her chest. But that aberration is the exception that proves the rule. Anyway, this is why I'm excited in spite of the rain: we're walking over the foot-bridge into Fatty's home village! If only the sky would brighten up then I really would be flying.

Inside the village library, Kate and I enter the children's section and find the Blyton shelf. There are only two of the Mysteries, *Strange Messages* and *Hidden House*. Is that really all they have at Bourne End public library? I speak to the young woman librarian, telling her that not only did the world's best-selling children's writer live in the village for nine years, one of her major series was actually set here. The girl knew about Blyton, of course, but didn't know about the local connection for the Mystery series. She consults with her colleague, passing on my comments, and then looks up the catalogue for me. Once she's got Blyton on screen, she invites me to come to her side of the desk to check the library's holdings. Sure enough, the library only has *The Mystery of the Strange Messages* and *The Mystery of the Hidden House*.

I join Kate at a table. She tells me it was funny to see me elbow-ing the two young librarians aside and sitting down at their com-puter. I suppose it could have looked that way from a distance, but I'm too busy flicking through *Hidden House* to give it much thought. This is the book in which Goon's nephew is first intro-duced. Dim, but basically sound, Ern dislikes his uncle and wants to be friendly with the Find-Outers. But to begin with they don't want to know. Indeed they're quite cruel to him. They tell Ern that strange lights have been seen at midnight on top of Christmas Hill. As it happens, the lights are flashed by Larry and Pip, and it's Goon who investigates them. In the cold and dark, Fatty teases Goon (thinking it's Ern) with impressions of a clucking hen, a mooing cow and a wailing baby. The wailing baby freaks Goon out, but as the policeman tries to run off, he trips over a root and Fatty pounces on him. 'Ern' is given a pummelling. Such violent behav-iour from Fatty is totally out of character, unless you accept that

Goon is Hugh and that Fatty is Enid here, temporarily losing control. However, the beating is short-lived because Goon shrugs off his unseen assailant and in so doing regains a little of his self-esteem. Goon feels he has fought off a big, strong, hefty chap – or even a gang of bruisers – when in fact it was only Enid with her remarkably light touch regained.

Meanwhile Ern has followed the wrong branch of the local river and so never gets to Christmas Hill. I'm musing over the local geography when the second of the librarians comes over. She coughs to get my attention, and, with great respect, tells me that the Marlow branch library also has two books. *The Mystery of the Vanished Prince* and *The Mystery of the Secret Room*. If I want, she can ask them to put aside the books for me. And if I want to borrow any of the books from Bourne End or Marlow for the duration of my research trip, then all I need to do is take out a temporary membership. Sure, I'll do that. It would be handy to borrow *Hidden House* and *Strange Messages* rather than continue to skim through them here. And, yes, we just might end up in Marlow today, so it would be good if *Secret Room* – not *Vanished Prince* – could be set aside for me.

'You've got them eating out of your hand,' comments Kate, when the second young librarian has retreated back to her desk to make arrangements.

'They've got no idea who they're dealing with,' I say, haughtily.

Kate laughs.

'I mean Enid. Not me.'

Outside, it is still raining. Passing along the main street, I tell Kate that Enid is always referring to the main street of Peterswood. And this is it. There are benches, flanking the street now, as then. There is a bench that looks onto the post-office and other shops in the middle of the village. Fatty and co. spend a fair time on such benches, on the lookout for clues, sometimes even in disguise. There is one occasion when Fatty is sitting on a bench, disguised as a tramp, next to Goon who is also disguised as a tramp. Tramp Fatty (Enid) knows it's tramp Goon (Hugh), but not vice versa. The other Find-Outers pass by, recognise Goon (not Fatty) and ask him inane questions. And it's all Fatty can do not to burst out laughing. Just as it would have been all Enid could do not to burst out laughing as she typed the scene. I don't think Fatty would have been so amused if it had been raining, though. Come to think of it, I don't think it ever rained on the Find-Outers any more than the Famous Five.

I can't help wondering how Enid felt following the first time she ever wrote about the Find-Outers. Dining three miles from here at Green Hedges, on an evening with Kenneth in late 1942 or early 1943, how would the 46-year-old author have reported her day's work? Perhaps she would have been matter-of-fact. She'd begun a new book, and was excited by its potential. The opening scene involved all the main characters watching a blaze one fine spring evening. An outhouse in the grounds of a cottage, about a mile to the west of Bourne End, was burning down.

Kenneth: 'Isn't that where you used to live with Hugh?'

Enid: 'It is, actually. But, as I say, it's… er… not Old Thatch itself that is ablaze, but an outhouse.'

Kenneth isn't that interested. No, that's not fair. Kenneth always shows an interest in Enid's work. So she would go on to explain how this group of four children – two brother-and-sister pairs – were irresistibly drawn out from their houses in the middle of the village to watch the fire. But there was also a mysterious fat boy with a dog, staying with his parents at the inn, right beside 'Old Thatch'. He wants to be friendly with the local children, but they're not sure of him to begin with, despite his nice dog.

Enid: 'He's called Fatty.'

Kenneth: 'Fatty?'

Enid (with a smile): 'Yes, isn't that a glorious name?'

Enid goes on to explain that there's also a fat policeman in attendance at the fire. He orders the children to clear off even though they're not in the way and have every right to watch if they want to.

Enid: 'Clear-orf, you kids! Clear-orf, the lot of you!'

Kenneth (smiling): 'Sounds as if you're going to get a lot of fun out of him. What's he called? You can't call him Fatty as well.'

Enid (glowing in the light of the fire in her head): 'No, he's my Goon. He's my... er... Mr Goon. Oh, Kenneth, I really think I am going to get a lot of fun out of this whole set-up. By this afternoon, in chapter two, the local children had come to accept Fatty as a friend, thanks largely to Buster the dog. And Bets – she's the younger of the girls – has declared that they're the Five Find-Outers and Dog and that they will solve *The Mystery of the Burnt Cottage* before Mr Goon does!'

Kenneth: 'And will they?'

Enid: 'Oh, I expect so. But we'll have to wait and see, won't we? Now don't ask me any more, darling. I must let it brew in the back of my mind until I can sit down again and let it all stream out in story form, tomorrow.'

It's still raining. We pop into the only café in the village, but it's not a sit-down place, and I have to ask permission for us to stand at a narrow window counter staring out at the bleak scene. 'Perhaps it will dry up by the time we finish our coffee,' says Kate, wistfully. I do hope so. As Enid says in one of her books, it takes twenty minutes to walk from one side of the village to the other. And if we have to retreat to our camp that would really knock us back on our heels. If that does happen, though, perhaps we could follow up the *Hidden House* book by walking to the wood where the action culminates. In fact, following our visit to the library I'm now torn between following up something to the west, to do with *Mystery of the Spiteful Letters,* and researching this *Hidden House* business in other directions. But I can't see us doing either successfully if we get really wet. Getting soaked would switch our minds into neutral and we have to be totally switched on if this exercise is going to work.

The village and its environs were special to Enid. She came here from her beloved rural Beckenham and no doubt found with the passage of time that the countryside around here was exactly the same. Exactly the same seasons, but different seasonal indicators. Exactly the same chaffinches, but a flock of swans on the river instead of a kingfisher. She would have revelled in the similarities and been fascinated by the differences. Dear Beckenham! Dear, dear Bourne End! Especially as she considered them in retrospect, installed in Green Hedges. Just a few miles away but in a third distinct place. Beaconsfield was not quite Bourne End. Just as Bourne End was and wasn't Beckenham.

Kate goes out for a ciggy, smoking it under the awning of a general store across the road. She engages a drenched postman in conversation. Perhaps she's asking him where Frederick Algernon Trotteville lives. And if he looks at her blankly she'll say, 'You know, *Fatty*!' Enid is never specific about where Fatty lived when his parents settled in Peterswood for good, as they do in the second book in the series. But she does move him out of the inn next to the cottage, just to put a bit of distance between her own past and Fatty's present, I suspect. The Hiltons lived next door to the Daykins, and the Trottevilles lived close to those two families but not on the same street.

Actually, I did try and find Fatty's house by scrutinising the beginning of *The Mystery of Holly Lane*. It starts at Peterswood station with the children following a man who they assume to be Fatty in disguise. The man goes off in the direction of Fatty's house, sure enough. But then, in a heavy French accent, he asks the children for directions to 'Grintriss'. The children ignore this and instead take 'Fatty' the short distance to the Trotteville house. Of course it's not Fatty at all, so there is much embarrassment all round. And the house the Frenchman has been asking for is Green Trees (near relation to Green Hedges) on Holly Lane. Green Trees is next door to a house which has been broken into, and so the Mystery is up and

running. *Holly Lane* is fabulous entertainment. The only trouble
with it is that it botches the directions to Fatty's house. All through
that scene I think of Fatty as Enid's French-speaking father. Bets
thinks she knows where he lives but in the end has to accept that
she's got that sadly wrong. Her Fatty eludes her.

I join Kate across the street and we share a bit of body warmth.
'Guess what I'm describing...' I say.

'OK,' says Kate, dreamily.

'Green, blue... red, red, green... orange, grey, red, cream...
yellow, red, blue, light blue, grey, blue.'

'Mmmm... If it wasn't for the green I'd have said it was something to do with the colour of the sky. Perhaps at different times of
day.'

'Cold. It's the colours of the covers of my copies of the original
Methuen hardbacks of the Mysteries – without dust-covers – as I
left them laid out in chronological order over the floor of my room
the night before travelling south this time around.'

Kate snorts. 'OK, I get the idea. My turn. I spy with my little
eye...'

And I wait for Kate to come up with something that will distract
me from what verges on melancholy.

'Black, black, grey... grey, grey, blue... blue, blue, blue, blue,
blue...'

She's right – the sky is clearing! So we get on our way before the
weather has a chance to change its mind. We walk along the High
Street going west, then turn right and walk north for a while, the
hedges sparkling with sunlit rainwater. We're heading for
Sheepridge. I'm pretty sure that's the place in *Mystery of the Spiteful
Letters* that Fatty and the gang go to, because the anonymous letters that have been received by residents of Peterswood bear such
a postmark, and they're always franked on a Monday. On the other
hand, the Find-Outers catch a bus from Peterswood and seem to be
on the bus for a fair time. Each of the Find-Outers sits beside a fel-

low passenger and tries to find out if that person is a regular Monday morning traveller. Poor Daisy has to sit beside Mr Goon who is following up a similar line of enquiry. There is a good feeling on the bus, and Enid clearly enjoyed writing the scene. The bonhomie is epitomised by Pip saying facetiously to the person he's sitting beside: 'Do you see that extraordinarily clever-looking boy sitting at the front of the bus?' Of course, he means Fatty. In this context, I suspect Enid means her father.

The sun shines. We are smiling and laughing. Kate spots a bird of prey and wonders what it is. It's as big as the buzzards that I see regularly in my own backyard, but this bird has different shaped wings and a sharper tail. Actually, it might be a red kite. I seem to recall reading about the species being reintroduced to the Chilterns around Oxford, which is, I suppose, where we are, in the strict non-Blytonian sense.

We go from another westerly path to the minor northerly road that leads to Sheepridge. We plan to buy postcards and to use the same post-box that is used in *Spiteful Letters* to send spiteful postcards of our own. I must send one to Mr Goon at Bourne End police station. What, though? I tell Kate that at the beginning of *The Mystery of the Strange Messages*, Goon receives three anonymous notes at his house on the High Street. He can't make anything of them and he assumes they're a hoax. The notes are found in various parts of the house by Mrs Hicks, the woman who cleans and cooks for Goon. One is left on the coal shovel, another is posted through the letter-box, and a third is stuck to the dustbin lid with sticky tape. But she never sees the person who leaves the notes.

'Is this a "Theophilus Goon" thing?'

'Actually, no. As usual "Theophilus" only comes up once in the book, as far as I'm aware. Not here but rather innocuously when Goon's nephew Ern refers to his Uncle Theophilus.'

'What about these notes then?'

I have to use the library book to jog my memory: 'The notes are in envelopes with two words cut from newspapers pasted onto them, "mr." and "goon".'

'Who leaves the notes?'

'The woman who does for Goon. And as Goon is always and forever Hugh, the person really responsible for the notes is the woman who does for Hugh.'

'Enid!' says Kate. 'What do the notes say?'

I flick through the book, my eye settling on the capital letters on near-consecutive pages. 'The first reads: "TURN HIM OUT OF THE IVIES"; the second: "ASK SMITH WHAT HIS REAL NAME IS" and the third: "CALL YOURSELF A POLICEMAN? BETTER GO AND SEE SMITH".'

Kate smiles. 'What's the context?'

'Goon assumes the notes are from Fatty, fresh home for the holidays. But when he is out interviewing the Find-Outers en masse he gets another note, left in an empty milk-bottle, which he knows can't have come from Fatty or his gang.'

'What does it say?' asks Kate, looking forward to another example of Enid's dry wit.

'It says: "WHY DON'T YOU DO WHAT YOU ARE TOLD, EGG-HEAD?"'

Kate smiles again: 'I'm going to write a spiteful postcard to Enid, care of Old Thatch. And it's going to say: "TELL HUGH WHAT HIS REAL NAME IS."'

Then Kate scraps this dated message and composes a new one, addressed not to Enid but to the local police force in Tayside, where I live. Apparently, it will say: 'MAKE A BUNDLE OF THE BOOKS ON THE FLOOR OF HIS BEDROOM AND CHUCK THEM IN THE RIVER."'

I tell Kate that her latest piece of spite is very *Mystery of the Strange Bundle*. But she hasn't read the book so I have to clarify:

'In that book – *Strange Bundle*, not *Strange Messages* – Fatty witnesses a bundle of stuff being thrown into the river at Peterswood.

For reasons I forget, he throws a bundle into the river as well. Anyway, Goon takes a boat-hook and extracts one strange bundle, only to find that it doesn't contain what he was hoping for. It's a bundle of old clothes some of which he manages to stuff down the back of Fatty's neck.'

'I'm glad to hear that Goon gets the better of him occasionally.'

'Yes, it's a weird scene. Fatty (mature Enid) takes a pummelling, which Bets (young Enid) is very annoyed about. So Goon ends up in the doghouse once again… But you're right, it is good that Goon gets to lay a hand on Fatty.'

'Is Goon portrayed as a violent man?'

'He does bully and strike his nephew. He canes him in at least one book, for going against his authority.'

'Was Hugh violent with the children?'

'I don't think so. In Imogen's memoirs, it's Enid who beats her, while Hugh sits by in his kilt, not interfering.'

Kate gives me a reminder of Hugh's Scottish accent. But she doesn't do so with the same panache as before. That was yesterday's thing, today we've gone beyond that. We're at Sheepridge, to be precise. There's a pub here and nothing else. Three houses, one pub, no post-office, no post-box. So that's that. *Sheepsale!* I suddenly remember. I'm sure Sheepridge is mentioned in the book, but it's Sheepsale where the Monday market is held. Unfortunately there is no Sheepsale marked on my map. I blame Bourne End's inadequate library for this mix-up. If the library had had a copy of *The Mystery of the Spiteful Letters* this wild goose chase would never have happened. But then perhaps that would have been a shame.

We'd better get back to Bourne End. It would be nice to walk to Marlow where the plot of *The Mystery of the Hidden House* thickens. It would have been nice to walk back from Marlow to Bourne End, a circuit that Fatty jogs in an effort to lose weight in *The Mystery of the Missing Man*. But the afternoon is wearing on and we don't want to exhaust ourselves.

As we saunter along a lane, Kate asks: 'What date were these books written again?'

'The earliest of them was published in December, 1943. *Vanished Prince* was published in 1951. The latest would have been *Strange Messages*, from 1957.'

'And in this period, during and after the war, when Goon was being ridiculed, what was happening to the real Hugh?'

'Barbara Stoney doesn't talk about Hugh's later years in her biography of Enid, but she does tell the story in a separate article published in the *Enid Blyton Society Journal*.'

'And?'

'In 1942 he went over to the States to lecture American troops. He was an advisor on "static defense", whatever that is. It involved going on a lecture tour along the states of the eastern seaboard, and he seems to have been very successful in that role.'

'Was he interviewed to get that information?'

'When Stoney was commissioned to do Enid's biography, no one on Enid's side of the family knew what had happened to him or where he was. It was 1971 by the time the biographer tracked him down, seriously ill in Malta. Unfortunately, he died before she could get either his side of what had happened between Enid and himself or his story of what had happened to him post-Enid.'

'I suppose neither Gillian nor Imogen ever got to see their father again.'

'No. Hugh did return to England in 1943 in order to marry Ida Crowe, the novelist who had been working for him when he was serving in the army. And straight away they had a baby of their own. It was Ida and the grown daughter, Rosemary, who were able to tell Barbara Stoney what happened to Hugh in the years after Enid. That's when it emerged that Enid wouldn't let Hugh see Gillian or Imogen, though such access rights had been part of the reason that Enid had been allowed to divorce Hugh, and not vice versa.'

'She may have thought Hugh's visits would upset them.'

'Either that, or she reckoned having Hugh knocking about the place would disturb her writing routine. How could she get on with her latest Mystery with Theophilus himself looking over her shoulder, complicating everything?'

Silence reigns as we plod along the sun-splashed country lane until I take up the story again: 'The job in the States lasted until the end of the war. Hugh was praised to the rafters for his war effort. Generals wrote great things about him. He even got the Legion of Merit, signed by President Truman.'

'Good for Goon,' says Kate.

'But when he came back to England at the end of the war, he couldn't get his old job back with Newnes.'

'Why not?'

'Because that would have upset the publisher's star author. And as it turned out Hugh couldn't get a job with any other publisher. Probably for much the same reason.'

'Because Enid had put the word around that he wasn't reliable?'

'Something like that. It wouldn't have taken much. Anyway, it seems he didn't make a fuss. He just turned to his army contacts and got a job in the Historical Section of the Cabinet Office overseeing the writing of the Normandy Invasion. He met Winston Churchill again.'

'He always got on well with TOP BRASS, didn't he?'

'That editing job lasted until 1950, by which time the first seven Mysteries had been published. But then he got into financial difficulties. Partly because he was out of work, and partly because he was paying for Gillian and Imogen's private schools.'

'Really?'

'Yes, even though he hadn't been allowed to see either of his older children since the divorce, he was made to pay through the nose for their education.'

'Was he paying all the school fees? Or just half?'

'Good point. I don't know. Perhaps Enid was paying her share. Why wouldn't she have been? She was making stacks of royalties by then from the Mysteries, Famous Five, Malory Towers, Noddy and the rest, and she gave lots of money to charity. She wasn't mean in most respects. But come to think of it, she may simply have wanted to punish Hugh.'

'So what happened?'

'What seems to have saved the bloke was that Ida went back to writing novels around 1950, and achieved some success.'

'Good for her.'

'Yeah, Ida was a bit of a goer with the typewriter too. She churned out eight or nine romantic novels a year, and, with Hugh's help, secured contracts with five different publishers. So, between them, Hugh and Ida made a pretty good fist of it.'

'I'm glad.'

'Me too. Barbara Stoney reports that according to Rosemary – Hugh and Ida's daughter – her father was a complex character, a clever, sensitive, witty and courageous man who led a tempestuous life, which is a much more positive summing up-than Imogen's.'

'Rosemary's Hugh doesn't sound *at all* like Enid's Goon.'

'No, he doesn't. Goon is so much less than Hugh was, as a man. But, then, he's so much more as a character. I don't think for one moment that Enid was fair to Hugh, but I do think that turning him into Goon was one of the best ideas – or irresistible urges – she ever had.'

Oh, but this countryside we're walking through is to be enjoyed too. And for the same reason – for its own timeless qualities. As we walk, I can hear a yellowhammer... As we walk on I can hear another... As we persist with the walking-on business, I realise we are heading towards a third yellowhammer – which is singing – and that I can still hear the other two birds to our left and right.

'Can you hear them?' I ask Kate.

'That?' she asks.

'Yes… According to Enid, the song can be rendered in words as: *A little bit of bread and no cheese.*'

Kate: 'Hush. Let me listen… '

'*A little bit of…*'

The bird has become conscious of our approach and isn't finishing its song properly. Or at least that's my hypothesis.

'*A little bit of…*'

'We should just stand still for a minute. And let it relax. Besides, from here we can listen to all three birds:

'*A little bit of bread and no… chee-eese,*' goes the bird away to our left.

'*A little bit of bread and no…*' sings the bird just in front of us, gaining in confidence it would seem. But still not quite there yet.

'*A little bit of bread and no… chee-ee-eese,*' goes the bird away to our right.

'This is making me so hungry,' sings Kate.

'*A little bit of bread and no… **che-ee-ee-ee-ee-ee-ee-eese!**'* says the bird in front of us, to our joy. All of a sudden we're both ravenous.

By the time we get back into the village we're sick of the sound of cheese but are keen on the idea of fish and chips. Alas, we have to wait for two packs of Brownies to get their chips first, herded by two Brown Owls. Actually, it's fun to watch each Brownie in turn detach herself from the neat queue of hungry Brownies waiting outside the shop. Each Brownie solemnly steps forward to accept her bag of chips from Brown Owl, and then slips out of the shop again to sit beside her chip-chomping chums on the pavement.

So, on the one hand, we don't mind waiting, and watching, but, on the other, we are absolutely starving by the time we are sitting on a bench in the middle of Bourne End, scoffing one fish and one portion of chips between us. This eating rough is more of a Famous Five thing than a Find-Outers, I point out. After all, Fatty and the others operate from their home village and so are able to pop back home for meals. Indeed their houses each come complete with cooks. In *The Mystery of the Spiteful Letters*, when the Hiltons' regular cook goes sick, Mrs Hilton gets a temporary replacement (who is eventually found to be the one sending the spiteful letters). Anyway, the fact that there are only four Hiltons – Pip, Bets and their parents – and that they have two other resident servants as well, has no bearing on their need for a temporary cook. As for Mrs Hilton making the meals herself for a week or two – what an outrageous thought! I'm pretty sure that Enid was thinking of her own Green Hedges household whenever she thought of the houses of the Hiltons/Daykins/Trottevilles. And if Enid's cook was incapacitated for a while then clearly she wasn't going to alter her writing pattern to cope with the emergency. Get another bloody cook in! That was Enid's analysis of the situation. Come to think of it, it wasn't Enid who did for Hugh, it was a cook and a housemaid.

What scrumptious fish and chips! I glance at the seated children. There is a book called *Enid Blyton's Book of Brownies*, which I mention aloud. In case I'm confusing Kate, I point out that Enid's Brownies are little fairy creatures, full of charm not chips. Kate suggests the chip-eating Brownies are charming too. I look at them: munch, munch, munch, go the pale Brownies. Indeed, they are charm solemnified. Bets to the nth degree.

Sitting beside me on the bench, Kate asks if I want to know what her favourite memory from the day has been, or what it is that keeps coming back to her, making her smile.

Of course I want to know.

'Something you said when we paused by this bench after coming out of the library. The rain prevented me from savouring the image at the time.'

'What image?'

'Fatty and Goon sitting side by side on this same bench in the High Street, both disguised as tramps.'

The image glows in my mind too. I bring to mind *The Mystery of the Invisible Thief* and flesh out the scene for us: 'The other Find-

Outers walk past and recognise Goon, but fail to recognise Fatty. To tease Goon, first Pip comes back and asks Goon what the time is. Goon tells him. Then Larry approaches the bench and asks Goon if he has change for sixpence. Goon tells him to clear off. Then Daisy approaches and asks Goon if the bus to Sheepridge stops there.'

'Sheepridge!'

'Yes, definitely Sheepridge, not Sheepsale. So we didn't go on a wild goose chase after all.'

'Of course not. So Goon sent her packing?'

'Yes.'

'What did Bets ask?'

'That's right, Bets is the last to approach the bench. When she does, it is to ask Mr Goon if he has seen their little dog, Buster. I can't remember exactly what Goon answers in a fit of temper, but I know that Fatty has to pass off his laughter as a coughing fit.'

Kate stares straight in front of her, pondering what I've described. Then she tells me: 'That's all good. But I think I prefer the simple image of Fatty and Goon sitting side by side, sharing the sense of being on the case.'

I sit there, holding Kate's hand. Then I take up the bench incident myself: 'I hadn't realised it before, but those are two nice moments between Bets and Goon and between Fatty and Goon. If Bets is Enid and Goon is Hugh, then the little dog being referred to could usefully be thought of as Bobs. Bobs was bought by Enid in 1926 when Hugh and she were living at Elfin Cottage in Beckenham. She introduced him to readers of "From My Window" as a rascal that she wouldn't be able to stop loving for as long as he lived. But Bobs really came into his own after the move to Old Thatch, writing his doggy column for *Teacher's World*. In fact, it was Bobs that announced to *Teacher's World* readers that Britain was at war with Germany, after being told by little Gillian.'

'That's Enid letting us know how adult she thinks the war is.'

'Mmmm… The real Bobs had died in 1935, shortly after the

birth of Imogen. But that smooth-haired fox-terrier had so captured Enid's imagination that he lived on in Enid's mind to write a
column that went on for years.'

Kate (wide-eyed): 'Have you seen our little dog, Bobs?'

OK, so Kate is Bets-cum-Enid this time around. So I must be
Hugh. Which is fair enough:

Me (sighing): 'How many times do I hiv tae tell ye, Enid? Bobs is
buried in an unmarked grave in the garden o' Old Thatch.'

Kate: 'Liar.'

Me: 'An unmarked grave, Enid.'

Kate: 'Liar, liar. Tramp on fire.'

That is all good. But in the end I agree with Kate. Best of all is the
simple image of Fatty and Goon sitting side by side on the public
bench, disguised as tramps.

Infinitely complicated human beings. Disguised as tramps.

5

Mr Goon was dozing in his armchair when there came a
clatter and a bump from the front door. That would be the
postman, waking him up as usual. A staggering amount of
mail arrived at Peterswood police station each morning at
about eleven. None of it was ever addressed to him.

The policeman picked up the brown parcel, which had
the words 'THEOPHILUS' and 'GOON' marked boldly in
black ink. For once it looked like it was for him, then. No
stamps: hand-delivered. So it wasn't the post as such. Goon
sat down at the table and tore the wrapping paper into
shreds. What on earth was this? Well, it was a book. Was it
one of the books that had gone missing from Green Hedges?
If it was, then Goon had solved the case on his own and
without any help from those damn children.

The Mystery of the Burnt Cottage it said in white letters near the top of the front cover. And sure enough there was a painting of a cottage on fire. Beneath the burning cottage was a confused-looking policeman writing in a notebook. Mr Goon had no idea what the burly officer was writing, but the words 'ENID' and 'BLYTON' in red capitals were printed close by. All very mysterious so far, but it was only when Goon opened the book that he got annoyed. Over the first blank page, where Goon felt entitled to come across proof that this was indeed a Green Hedges book, there were a lot of meaningless marks. Goon flicked through the volume, paying special attention to the near-blank early pages, but there was no other writing. What did it mean? Goon looked again. Boxes, dots, boxes and dots... Gah! It meant that the book had come from Frederick Trotteville. Would that toad of a boy never be done with wasting police time?

Goon walked upstairs. He didn't want the book messing up his private quarters, so the cell was the only place for it. He opened the door and entered the room, which was in a right old state. Until the fat boy had escaped from here, he'd kept it tidy. Or, rather, he'd kept it empty of objects that a prisoner could make use of in any way. But once the room had been shown to be completely useless as a holding cell, then Goon had to admit he'd let it go to seed. There was a bed in here now. That was sensible enough and indeed it had been used by Ern when Goon had had his nephew staying over in the school holidays.

But a bed had been only the start of it. The room could now be fairly described as his boxes 'n' bottles room, as it was chocker with both. Hadn't Goon told Ern to get rid of the dead soldiers? Nothing worse than clearing away your own empties. Clearly his nephew hadn't paid a blind bit of notice. Goon took a good look round the clutter. He wondered what he'd been thinking of the day he'd gone to his allotment and filled a cardboard box with branches and stones. Another box was full of onions pulled from his allotment in the last fortnight. Each onion was as big as a child's head. Goon could win medals for the onions that he'd grown on his allotment this year. Trouble is, that was just about all he could do with them. Inedible giant onions were coming out of Goon's ears. The kitchen was full of them. The woman who did for him had taken away two bags full, but wouldn't take any more. And still Goon had a worryingly large surplus of onions. He supposed they could just rot in this spare room. Was that the plan? And if that was the best solution for the onions, then the book could rot there with them.

The Mystery of Whatever-it-was had no sooner settled down in the box than Goon thought of a better plan. The book might still have something to do with the valuable ones that had been going missing from Green Hedges. The key might be written right there in code. He would find those children and present the fat boy with the book and insist on getting a translation of the boxes and dots. Goon knocked over an empty bottle with his foot. For a terrible moment, he was struck by a vision that the boxes in the strange message might stand for the cardboard boxes in his spare room, and the dots for stones and onions. But even if that was right, it wasn't a translation in the strict terms that Goon was looking for.

Mr Goon was still feeling harassed as he pushed his bike from the shed to the pavement. But the cares of office dissolved as he peddled through the quiet streets of Peterswood.

6

As Mr Goon cycled past an entrance to the village allotments, he was oblivious to the fact that the five Find-Outers and Dog were there. Why had Fatty asked the others to meet him on Goon's allotment? Larry had asked the question without getting any answer, so now Pip followed up with the same question.

Fatty bent down as if he hadn't heard, and when he stood back up again he was holding what looked like a swede. But it wasn't a swede. Fatty was surrounded by rows of giant onions, some of which had been dug up by Goon and taken away, but most of which lay bulging up from the soil like skulls. Gingerly, Fatty tiptoed to the less Somme-like part of Goon's allotment, where it was just an overgrown mess of weeds. There he made himself comfortable, sitting alongside the others.

'Why, Fatty, why?' asked Bets, following up Pip and Larry's unanswered question about why they were meeting in such an odd place. Fatty emerged from his thoughts long enough to answer: 'You know what Goon's like these days. He's always turning up at our parents' houses looking for us. He knows all about my shed and he'd be searching it on a daily basis if I didn't keep it locked. We wouldn't be safe there this morning. He even found us on the site of the old play-house at Old Thatch, when we really should have been entitled to believe we were beyond his prying eye. It's getting very hard to keep out of sight of old Goon. So I had this idea of hiding here, in the lion's den.'

'Which lion?' said Bets, looking worried.

'That's just a figure of speech, Bets,' said Fatty. 'We're quite safe here, especially from nosy policemen. Goon only works his allotment for a couple of hours on a Sunday as an alternative to going to church. Never at any other time.'

'But why do you think Goon might be looking for us today?' asked Daisy.

'Well, the fact is...' said Fatty, looking sheepish.

'Oh, you haven't sent him another letter written in invisible ink, have you?' asked Bets, rather excited at the thought that Fatty might have done exactly that.

'Not quite. But something just as reckless, I'm afraid.' And Fatty told them about the book and its strange message.

The children were curious as to why Fatty had sent Goon the book in the first place. But much more curious to know what Fatty had written in the code he'd taught them after he'd come back from the British Library

'What I've written translates as follows,' said Fatty, clearing his throat before announcing:

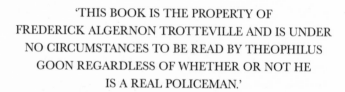

'THIS BOOK IS THE PROPERTY OF
FREDERICK ALGERNON TROTTEVILLE AND IS UNDER
NO CIRCUMSTANCES TO BE READ BY THEOPHILUS
GOON REGARDLESS OF WHETHER OR NOT HE
IS A REAL POLICEMAN.'

'Oh, Fatty!' giggled Bets. 'What if he manages to translate it? He was able to read the invisible writing by applying a hot iron, remember.'

'Mr Goon is not always as stupid as he usually is,' conceded Fatty. 'But when I woke up this morning, a blackbird was singing, and I felt I had to do something that proved I was in just as high spirits as it was. Lying in bed, I could see the cover of the book and the words just came to my mind! Besides, I'd been looking for an excuse to use the code that Enid herself had used as a teenager. And it was so easy to use the diagram, which told me exactly what sides of a box I needed to use for each letter, and where the dot should be placed. Really, I had the sentence written in code in less time than it would have taken to write out the message for Goon in plain English.'

'Surely not,' said Larry.

'Well, in a lot less time than I had imagined, anyway. Otherwise why would I have bothered writing my name and Goon's out in full? Or bothered with the waffly bits?'

Pip made a spluttering noise. 'Sorry. I've just had this picture of Goon getting the parcel this morning... You send him a book, Fatty. You write a message saying that Goon shouldn't read the book. But the message is written in code so that he can't read it. So it's as if there was no message there at all! And yet you know Goon won't read the book because... well, he just won't, will he? So sending the book, and writing the message, were both pointless exercises.'

'I don't know if "pointless" is the word,' said Fatty, pretending to be offended. 'Anyway, there I was this morning in my room, and there was the book with its secret message to Goon. And the next stage of parcelling up the book and delivering it to Goon just seemed to come automatically.'

'If he applies a hot iron to the message will he be able to read it?' asked Bets, before realising the question was silly.

'The only way he'll be able to read the message is if he's got volume one of Arthur Mee's *Children's Encyclopaedia* at home.'

'He probably does have that in the spare room,' suggested Larry. 'I'm sure I saw a full set of encyclopaedias up there when I called on Ern that time.'

This was a joke. And it was followed by others. But eventually the children calmed down and turned their attention towards the morning's main business. Where had they got to in their investigation? Well, the latest book to go missing from Green Hedges was a valuable copy of *Hello, Mr Twiddle*. So the Find-Outers were going to read a battered old copy of the book that Fatty had long owned.

'I wonder what we're in store for this time,' said Pip, as

excited as any of them at the prospect of a new book.

'It's not much to look at,' said Fatty, 'though it *is* a lovely old Newnes volume.' The plain green cover might have been mistaken for that of a book on gardening. In fact, *Hello, Mr Twiddle* was a collection of stories about a muddle-headed old gentleman, each of which had first appeared in *Sunny Stories*.

'Any good?' asked Larry.

'We can all be the judges of that,' said Fatty, preparing to read a story from the middle of the volume.

'OK this is "Mr Twiddle Makes a Muddle".'

'Mr Twiddle Makes a Muddle!' said Daisy, relishing the repetitions.

'Isn't there a Mr Meddle as well?' asked Pip. 'I mean, hasn't Enid written…'

'Yeah, there's a book called *Merry Mr Meddle*,' said Fatty.

'Is there a *Merry Mr Twiddle*?' asked Daisy, hopefully.

'No, but there's a *Mr Meddle's Muddle*,' said Fatty, realising he could field such questions all day. However, Larry broke in to say that he had just remembered something pertinent to the investigation.

'And what is that, pray?' asked Fatty.

Larry reported that Hugh Pollock had been seen creeping about the neighbourhood.

Fatty whistled, and put Twiddle on hold.

'Who?' asked Bets

'Enid's first husband,' said Fatty, thoughtfully.

'Golly,' said Bets.

'Apparently, he's hard up for cash. Perhaps even bankrupt,' said Larry, who'd got all this information from his mum, who had got it in turn from her cook.

'*Bankrupt*,' repeated Pip, relishing the word that seemed to scare grown-ups more than any other. 'Do you think he might have stolen the valuable books from Green Hedges in order to stave off his bankruptcy?'

'Pip, were you listening when we went through all our suspects the other day?' asked Fatty, almost crossly.

'Y-e-s,' said Pip, hesitantly. It wasn't like Fatty to be so cutting.

'Well, in that case you should understand that the one person who certainly *is not* stealing books from Green Hedges is the honourable Mr Hugh Pollock.'

'Enid doesn't trust him,' said Pip.

'Enid has her qualities, we all know that. But would you take her opinion about Hugh's honesty and integrity over those of Winston Churchill and the President of the United States?'

'Yeah, I would,' chirped Pip.

'Oh, Pip,' said Bets with exasperation. 'Hugh is a *hero*. And heroes don't go about stealing other people's books.'

'No matter what the provocation,' agreed Fatty.

'Sorry, you two,' said Pip, sticking to his guns. 'But Enid begs to differ. And I'm with her.'

7

Mr Goon was getting mighty fed up looking for kids who seemed to have disappeared clear off the face of the earth. He'd checked both the Hilton and the Daykins houses. Then he'd cycled the short distance to the Trotteville house and had a good look round the shed that the fat boy and the others used at the bottom of the garden. No trace. Where were those kids? They *were* around, according to the Hilton housekeeper. But if that was true, just where in Peterswood were they?

Goon found himself dismounting from his bicycle back

at the Trotteville house. He knocked on the door as he'd done half an hour earlier. No one answered. However, there was a hand-made sign Sellotaped to the front door that said 'Enid Blyton Library. Please Enter'. So Goon did just that.

'Anybody in?' asked Goon, self-consciously. He reminded himself that he was making enquiries in the line of his official duties, so there was no need to go round on tip toe. 'ANYBODY IN? IT'S THE POLICE!' he boomed.

No flaming answer. So Goon marched upstairs and went straight into the fat boy's bedroom. There were books all across one wall of the room. No point in checking them for the volumes that had gone missing from Green Hedges, he had already done that twice. Instead he let his gaze roam free. It did not look in the least like a normal boy's bedroom – with pictures of footballers and film stars on the walls. But, then, Trotteville was not a normal boy. Goon snorted at the very idea.

There was a desk situated under the main window. And on that desk was a large book open at a page headed: 'LITTLE PROBLEMS FOR CLEVER PEOPLE'. Goon supposed this was the sort of thing that the fat boy would read in order to keep his brains 'well-oiled'. The problems would be child's play for a trained policeman to answer. The question at the top of a column asked: 'How did the sheep stand?' It went on: 'I saw an odd sight the other day. Two sheep were standing in a field one looking due north and the other due south. How do you think that each could see the other without turning round? Can you give the answer?'

Goon sat down at Fatty's desk and thought long and hard about the problem, but all he came up with was that if both sheep bent their heads and looked underneath their bodies they would see the other sheep. He suspected this wasn't the answer the book was looking for, since it was a bit messy. What was the official answer? Turning to the contents page, Goon saw that the volume contained sections that gave answers to general problems such as: 'Can we think without words?... Does the brain need food?... Is the country healthier than the town?... How does a fly walk on the ceiling?... Is it darkest just before dawn?... What makes us hungry?... Why does a glow-worm glow?... Why is a raindrop round?... Is war between nations inevitable?... Is Scotland a real country?... Will frogs and fishes some day turn into animals like horses?'

Mr Goon would have liked to know the answers to some, if not all, of these questions. It was a pity he hadn't been given an encyclopaedia like this when he'd been a lad, because then he would have had the time to learn all about the world. But right now, as a busy policeman, he only had time to look up the answer to the tricky sheep question. He turned to page 502, and read: 'This is what is usually known as a "catch" question; and the answer is that, as the sheep stood, they faced each other, one looking north and the other south.'

Goon pictured the sheep standing staring into each other's eyes. Truth is, he felt a bit of a fool. Yes, yet another blasted book had made Goon feel like a complete idiot! So he turned back to the problem page to pit his wits against another question. However, he noticed that the facing page was headed: 'HOW TO KEEP A SECRET IN WRITING'. And in the middle of the page was a series of boxes and dots just like the message he'd received that morning. There was a little diagram comprising letters of the alphabet and a grid which was the key to the whole thing. So that's how Fatty had turned his words into boxes and dots! Goon realised he would be able to translate the dotted boxes back into words using this diagram. It was just his bad luck that in the end he'd forgotten to bring the damn Enid Blyton book with him. But in the next moment he realised he didn't need the book or the diagram in the encyclopaedia, because the fat boy had been careless enough to write down his message on a sheet of paper and to leave that sheet of paper lying on the desk beside the encyclopaedia!

Mr Goon picked it up and read the message. And he fumed. He read it again. What a pig that boy was! What a little snob! Goon had not had access to books when he was growing up, whereas Master Frederick Trotteville had at least one middle-class parent who knew the advantage of a good education. Didn't the Trotteville boy go to a public school where they even got to play tennis? Didn't he get the best books presented to him on a silver platter? Of course he did. And instead of thanking his lucky stars, Master Frederick spent his time tormenting folk less fortunate than himself.

Goon recalled the time there had been a civic reception in Peterswood for Sir George Newnes. Goon's own Chief Inspector of police had chosen to introduce his lordship to Fatty, a mere schoolboy, and in so doing they had walked right past Goon, ignoring him completely. The Chief had then told Sir George a lot of nonsense about what a great detective in-the-making Fatty was, and what a great future he had in the force when he was old enough to join up.

Goon got madder and madder with Fatty. He approached the bookshelves. There was an enormous section of Enid Blyton books. That name again – Enid *blooming* Blyton! He couldn't find a copy of *The Mystery of the Burnt Cottage*, which made sense as he had dropped it in the box with the onions in his spare room. But there was a book called *The Mystery of the Pantomime Cat* that Goon grabbed hold of. So Goon wasn't allowed to read about the mystery of the burnt cottage, was he? Well, neither would Master Trotteville be reading about any pantomime cats. As Goon marched through to the bathroom with the hardback, he knew he was on shaky ground. But he couldn't stop himself turning on the cold tap at the end of the bath, inserting the plug in the plug hole and, once the water had reached a depth of six inches or so, dropping the book into the water.

As the water continued to pour into the bath, so certain hated words flowed round Goon's mind: 'THIS BOOK IS THE PROPERTY OF FREDERICK ALGERNON TROTTEVILLE...' Goon watched as the jet of water knocked the book away from the plug area '... AND IS UNDER NO CIRCUMSTANCES TO BE READ BY THEOPHILUS GOON...' he watched as the book floated back towards the plughole in the prevailing current '... REGARDLESS OF WHETHER OR NOT HE IS A REAL POLICEMAN.'... Real policeman, real soldier... Back and forth the book bob-bob-bobbed, until Fatty's teasing words were washed right out of Goon's mind. Goon stared at the dust-jacket, which was glistening wet. There was no burnt cottage on the cover of this book, but the policeman was there and in exactly the same posture as on the cover of the other book. The officer was scratching his ear and looking baffled, with his notebook held open in front of him. So the fat boy wasn't sure if Goon was a real officer of the law, was he? And perhaps Enid – high-and-mighty – Blyton wasn't sure, either. Well, Goon would let them know all right. He would teach them respect for the armed forces.

Goon went back into Fatty's room and took hold of about a dozen similar red-covered books. Five this; Five that; Five and the other. Enid, Enid, Enid, Enid, Enid… He carried the job lot through to the bathroom and dropped the books, which fell with a great splash into the fast-filling bath. He fished about in the water for the *Pantomime Cat* book. Opening it, he discovered that only the covers were wet, along with the edges of the paper. So he held open both covers like wings, and he dunked the middle section of paper into the water. Goon pushed it down into the water until it bashed into the other books so that the pages spread apart and water could get into them properly. The churning of the water, its slapping and splashing satisfied him. Satisfying also was how the water got between the pages, coating each with a glossy surface that was the beginning of the end of their easy legibility. Happy about how things were progressing in the bathroom, Goon went back into the bedroom for more fuel. After five minutes all Fatty's Blyton books were waterlogged. Indeed, Goon had to shake off the idea that Enid Darrell Waters herself was lying there, underwater.

Goon sat down for a rest. He was partial to a day-dream at the end of a hard day's work. It was the only time he could ever let his mind go free… Well, well, what's this? The Chief Inspector was arriving in a big car to congratulate Goon on his first-class detective work. Only it wasn't the Chief that got out of the Rolls, it was Winston Churchill. Churchill congratulated Goon on dealing so professionally with the books that had been written by enemy spies. Churchill took a big cigar from his mouth. 'How would you feel about being promoted to Inspector?' asked Sir Winston, passing Goon the cigar. Mr Goon took a puff from it, trying not to think about Enid Darrell Waters in the bath, trying desperately not to think about her lovely children or what he'd recklessly done to the fat boy's books. After a few deep puffs, Goon had his finer feelings under control. He realised that Churchill was still waiting for an answer. So rather than keep the busy man hanging on indefinitely, Goon (puff) answered (puff-puff): 'Chuffed, sir. I'd be absolutely chuffed to bits about that.'

8

It was late in the afternoon by the time that Fatty got back home. Bets was with him, and the first thing they had to do was check out some facts regarding Mr Twiddle, Mr Meddle and Mr Pink-Whistle books. It had been a long day, first out on the allotment and then along by the river, but nevertheless they ran upstairs taking two steps at a time in a shared thirst for knowledge.

'Crikey!' said Fatty when he saw the gap in the bookcases where his Blytons should have been. 'Now *my* books have gone, Bets!'

'Oh, Fatty, they're in here,' said Bets. She was standing looking into the bath. What a horrible sight! Her hand went down and she picked *Five Go Down to the Sea* out of the cold water. It was an empty cover. The pages had been ripped out and must have been part of that huge pile of loose, torn, saturated paper that was bloating the bath. 'Oh, Fatty, they're ruined,' said Bets, starting to cry. 'First, Enid's books stolen and now this.'

'Don't, Bets,' said Fatty, who felt his own distress recede when confronted with that of his young friend. He put his arm around her shoulders. 'They're only books, and it'll be fun to replace them. Though it is the most extraordinary thing.'

'Who could have committed such a beastly crime?' asked
Bets, a tear running down her cheek, though she had
stopped crying fresh ones. 'The same person who is stealing
them from Green Hedges, I expect.'

'I don't think so.' Fatty knew who had destroyed his books
all right, and why. Truth is, Fatty almost admired Goon for
getting his own back so quickly. He told Bets what he reckoned had happened. 'Oh, no!' said Bets, shaking her head.
'How could he be so cruel?'

'Well, I suppose this settles the question as to whether or
not he's a real policeman,' said Fatty, jauntily.

Bets wondered if there was anything that good old Fatty
couldn't make a joke about. But she still couldn't see the
funny side. 'All your precious Enid Blytons are gone, Fatty,'
she said soberly.

'Not quite, Bets,' said Fatty, 'Follow me!'

They went downstairs, Fatty poured them both a glass of
lemonade from the fridge and they took their drinks into the
living room. On Mrs Trotteville's good coffee-table was a
cut-crystal bowl and in the glistening bowl was an Enid
Blyton book.

'It's a bit special, so it's on display. An ornament, really.
Mum loves it, though she's not read it.'

Fatty picked it out of the sparkling bowl and showed it to
Bets. On the cover, it said: 'Enid Blyton invites you to…'
then there was a gap before it stated boldly: 'A Story Party at
Green Hedges'. The author was sitting on a seat surrounded by spellbound listeners. Enid was wearing a pink dress
and her hands were raised slightly from her lap, as if
cradling a book. Though in fact it seemed she was telling a
story without aid of the written word. Fatty turned to the
back cover, which showed a view through a green door into
a dining room, the table covered in cakes and jellies, the

table surrounded by children. Enid was there too with her
back to the reader, holding a cup and saucer. There was a
single empty chair at the far side of the table.

As Fatty flicked through the book, he explained to Bets
that something subtle was going on. In three different places
there was an invitation issued by Enid Blyton to a story-party
at Green Hedges, then a space for the child owner of the
book to fill in his or her own name. Before the child reader
got carried away, Enid did say on the dust-jacket: 'Of
course, I know you can't really come,' which was a bit of a
downer. Nevertheless, Fatty had often imagined his name on
the invitation: 'Frederick Algernon Trotteville'.

Bets took the book and soon got the idea. Thirteen children (plus one) were invited to Green Hedges, and on the first
double-page the illustrator had drawn the lucky children
dressed in coats as they traipsed up to the front door in a long
straggling line. It was a winter scene, or at least there was no
foliage on the trees. The house they approached really was
Green Hedges; Bets recognised the half-timbering and the
roof layout from the Find-Outers visit. Enid had opened the
front door and was welcoming them in.

Bets flicked through the book and picked up the gist of it.
Enid told a story to each child in turn. And after each story
there was a page which contained a bit of chat between Enid
and her listeners – basically a thank-you from one child for
the previous story, and the choosing of a child to receive the
next one. After seven stories, the group moved from the playroom at Green Hedges to the dining-room. And after tea
there was a move back to the playroom, and seven more stories followed.

Bets loved the book and wanted to read a story. But Fatty
took it from her. Bets' disappointment disappeared when she
saw Fatty write 'Bets Hilton' in the invitation box on the

front end-paper. She watched as Fatty turned over a few
pages and prepared to write along the line in a second box:

Enid Blyton
IS GIVING A STORY-PARTY AT
GREEN HEDGES
This invitation is for

_____

Please come if you can

For one dreadful second, Bets thought Fatty was going to
write 'Theophilus Goon' in the box, as a joke. That would
have been just like Fatty! But, no, it was Bets' name that dear
Fatty wrote in the box, and handed the book over. For a
moment the names 'Bets Hilton' and 'Enid Blyton' seemed
to dissolve into each other and become one. But that was just
a mirage.

Bets looked at the back cover. The empty seat around
Green Hedges' dining room table was truly hers then. She
was the fourteenth child invited to the party. Oh, Bets could-
n't wait to get inside Green Hedges for a story-party and tea.
The very words 'Green Hedges' had the same magic indoors
as 'Faraway Tree' had out of doors.

'Fatty, are the Find-Outers going back to Green Hedges
soon?'

'We are indeed, Bets.'

But first he had a task for Bets. Fatty had surreptitiously
taken back the book and made a parcel of it addressed to Mr
Goon, 29 High Street. 'Er… Would you deliver this on your
way home?'

'Oh, Fatty,' said Bets, her heart sinking to her boots. 'What about my invitation to the party?'

'Don't worry about that,' said Fatty, seriously. 'There are lots of crimes that Mr Goon would commit in his own self-interest. But I think I can say that preventing a lovely little girl from attending a party at Green Hedges by withholding what is rightfully hers is not among them… By the way, I've put a note in with the book asking Goon to forward you the price of a party frock.'

Bets felt her eyes filling with tears again. Not because of Goon's generosity, which she found hard to believe in, but because of Fatty's kindness, which crowned everything.

CHAPTER FOUR

IN AND AROUND BLAIRGOWRIE

1

I slip into the study and sit down at my computer. The machine is sleeping, just as I usually am this early in the morning. But at the touch of a key it lights up for me. Typically it would be ten o'clock by the time I'm doing this as a preliminary to getting down to a couple of hours of solid word-processing. But this morning I'm just having a quick check on things before heading out for the day.

Outlook Express makes a deflating 'phut.' No one has tried to communicate with me between midnight and 8 a.m., not even the Enid Blyton Society which automatically tells me when certain topics in the Forum have been active. Or at least it's supposed to do that. Yawning, I log into the Forums section of the EBS website. Sure enough, the last entry under the heading 'The Author' is the posting under my moniker, 'Green Hedges'. The EBS website was set up in January 2005, just as I was getting going with my Blyton research, so I was one of the first to sign on. Since then there has been a steady stream of Enid's readers recognising that this is the place to swap notes on all things Blyton, and the membership is now in the hundreds. However, the interface lets me know that I am the only one surfing the site at the moment. It tells me also that in the three days since Green Hedges posted the topic, twenty-six members or guests have read it, but no responses have been left. Is my question not engaging enough, then? Let me read what I've said under the heading 'The Men in Enid's Life':

Who was the most important man in Enid's life as far as her writing was concerned? I suppose it must be down to one of the following three:

1) Her father. He left Enid when she was twelve years old which is perhaps why so much of her writing is about children who are effectively fatherless. Perhaps the books were partly written for her father who was such an important formative influence on her tastes and whom she loved and missed so much.

2) Her first husband. He published her first books and encouraged the development of her career in its early stages. He was also the father of her two children. Surely the existence of Imogen and Gillian affected what Enid went on to write?

3) Her second husband. No children with him, but the stable relationship he helped provide coincided with Enid's much more prolific period. The Famous Five books, the Noddy titles, the Find-Outers, and most of the other series come from this settled period in her life.

Perhaps there is a fourth man I don't know about who played just an important role? Or perhaps Enid would have written the same number and type of books regardless of the impact any man made on her personal life.

Anyone got any views on this? Love to hear them!

I suppose the trouble is, unless Barbara Stoney surfs the site, or Tony Summerfield decides to get involved in the nitty-gritty of his society's forums, as he does do from time to time, I'm not likely to get a substantial reply. But it's not substance I'm looking for. I know it's down to me to research and write this book alone. However, a bit of encouragement from a fellow enthusiast – young or old, strait-laced or idiosyncratic – wouldn't go amiss.

Back to the e-mail, but there's no joy. Zero e-mail activity through the night and for a while longer is what I would expect. But then Dubai must be two or three hours ahead of UK time, and that's where Kate is at the moment, on holiday with relatives. I've sent her a copy of the first three chapters of my work-in-progress and am waiting to hear if she likes it. She might want anonymity in the book. She might calculate that at 50,000 words the half-book would have taken a full-speed Enid a mere five working days to write. She might even have changed her mind about travelling to Swanage with me next month because I'll just plunder everything that happens for my writing. God, I hope she hasn't changed her mind! The train tickets from London are bought and the hotel room is taking shape in my mind's eye. Though I haven't yet plucked up the élan to e-mail the Grand Hotel to ask for a room at half the advertised rate. 'On what grounds?' I hear the hotelier's voice ask. On the grounds that we're going to be in town researching Enid Blyton, who graced the hotel with her presence for several years in a row in the fifties.

This room is also a library, and before I slip away again I can't help checking out the latest addition to its shelves. It's a large-format art book. On the cover are written the words *Nathalia Edenmont* and *Still About Life*. But Nathalia Edenmont isn't the author of this sumptuous volume, I am. It's published by the Wetterling Gallery in Stockholm, and so many blank pages are used around the artist's full-page colour photographs you could be forgiven for thinking that paper could be picked up for free from giant stacks of the stuff on the outskirts of Swedish forests.

The writing of *Still About Life* distracted me from my main Blyton project for a couple of weeks. But, now that I have a box of the luxurious books, I have to accept that the distraction was worth it. It's my first Enid piece in print. In no way can it compete with the 100-odd Blyton titles I have on shelves elsewhere in the room. But, then, this isn't about competition. The text in *Still About Life* complements these other books, climaxing in a spoof Binkle and Flip adventure. My justification for all the bunny stuff is that the dominant motif of the photographs is the flower with an eye in the centre. Eyes that the artist extracts from rabbits she kills herself. Oh, yes, these flower pictures are not merely decorative! That blue eye staring at me from the middle of a red rose once belonged to a live rabbit. To be honest, I feel I've humanised Edenmont's cold if brilliant work. Certainly, I've Blytonised it. Happily, Nathalia is enthusiastic about our collaboration, as is her gallery. I just hope Enid won't be turning in her grave.

Enid: 'Oh, Bun, look what they've done to my Binkle and Flip!'

Hugh: 'It's all right, Little Bunny. Don't you see that it's still all about you? Still all about us.'

But that art project is done and dusted. Right now I need to get back on the main track. So I leave the study, descend the stairs and grab the car keys. Next thing I know I'm waiting at the road junction on the other side of the property boundary, noticing the foil packet and the can that have been shoved into the body of the evergreen hedge that surrounds my parents' house. Coke and crisps are all the children that attend the secondary school along the road care about; Coke and crisps and undermining the green hedges of the local residents. Still, I wouldn't like to see them humanely put down and their eyes plucked out for use in fine art photography. Good Lord, no! – Enid's ghost really would be upset then.

I need to get back on Enid's track. And I need to restore some balance to my research. Accordingly, my plan is to investigate what underpins the Famous Five books, that most successful of series which was written alongside the Mystery series. Yes, there was a Famous Five story and a Mystery every single year from 1943 to 1954. There was a Five and a Mystery for a few more years after that. And then it was the Mystery series that fizzled out allowing Enid to plough on with the Kirrin quintet.

I drive the five miles to Loch Clunie and park by the handsome, waterside church, now closed. The morning is windless, and a mist hangs over the still water. Two swans glow on the placid surface. They echo the large ghostly slab of white on the far shore, a grand house that is the only property on the long, low hillside above the loch. On my side of the calm water there's an old Iron Age fort, or at least the mound of earthworks that once supported it, and I have to walk around that before I have a view of what I've come here for. A hundred yards from the shore there is an island with an old castle in the centre of it. This is not Kirrin Castle on Kirrin Island overlooked by Kirrin Cottage on the south coast of England. But then even when I travel to Swanage and look out over Swanage Bay, as Enid did repeatedly from 1940, I won't see a ruined castle on an island. And as for finding the island-castle that Enid encountered on holiday with Hugh in the Channel Islands back in 1926, well I don't think there's any need to do that. The scene in front of me is as close as I can get to what was in Enid Blyton's mind's eye when she set out to write her first Famous Five book, or at least it'll do for my present purposes.

The island is covered with trees, which cut down the view of the crumbling ruin to just glimpses. I have to walk a bit further around the shore of the loch before the sun's rays catch the high walls of Clunie Castle and make them burst into warmer colours and three-dimensional life. Although the ruin is called a castle, it looks as if it wasn't ever any more than a fortified house. The most obvious architectural feature left is the gable end of a conventional-enough ridged roof. Above the apex of stone there are tree-tops: coniferous branches that have been made decidedly ragged by cormorant droppings. There are several cormorants perched up there now. And another bird is skimming across the long loch towards the island. I watch it... and watch it... and at the last minute the black bird rises steeply and takes its place on the branches of a tall Scots pine, spreading its wings out to dry. The majestic cross it presents takes me back to Clunie church rather than to the restless jackdaws that dominate Kirrin Castle. But that's all right. I can live with that.

My mind will revert to Kirrin without needing too much external help.

The castle on the island really is the dominant motif of the first Famous Five book, *Five on a Treasure Island*. The island belongs to George, sort of, through her mother, but she is eager to share it with her three cousins. For a while it just has a strong visual presence in the book, but in due course George does row the Five out there. Now I've thought of rowing a boat out to Clunie Island. There is only a single vessel that operates on the loch, and that is the one that I can just see, sticking out from the boat-house on the far bank. The loch is obviously part of Forneth House's estate and chances are that if I found out who lived there and wrote a letter explaining my interest, I might be taken out to the island on that boat. I don't think I'm going to go down that route, though. On balance, it feels awkward to get involved with strangers. It's important for me that it is in a sense *my* island and that I don't have to ask anyone's permission to visit it. Standing here, I am in visual possession of the island, and that's all I require.

When George and the others go out to Kirrin Island from Kirrin Cottage, they have with them a map taken from a boat that's long been shipwrecked on the side of the island which is not visible from the shore. According to the map, there is gold hidden in the dungeons of the castle, so the Five are intent on locating it. They search for an entrance to the dungeon in a castle room, but can't find it. They look in the courtyard for a second entrance, and do locate it thanks to Timmy chasing a rabbit into a gorse bush which causes the dog to fall down a well (the fall is stopped after a few feet by a stone that has wedged itself across the well). The well is marked on the map, close to the second entrance to the dungeons, and that is why the Five soon manage to find the stone with the weed-covered iron ring. With the help of a rope – which they all grasp and pull on together – the entrance stone is lifted. And the Five are able to descend rock stairs into the heart of the island itself.

God, I'm remembering this so clearly! I am helped in part by the wonderful view I have of Clunie Castle in all its metaphoric glory. Get in the boat and row out there with some suspicious landowner at my elbow? Now why would I want to do that? It would be a recipe for remaining on the surface of the island. When what I need is the tools – the vision – to dig deep underground.

The dungeons of Kirrin Castle are extensive. Eventually the Five locate a room with a strong wooden door. They take an axe to the lock, in which process Dick gets a splinter in the face. Dick needs his bleeding cut seen to, so Anne and Julian go with him back up to the surface, leaving George to carry on smashing in the door. Julian is back down the dungeon steps in time to help George explore the room and to find the pile of gold ingots. Treasure! But Timmy is barking. And the reason for this is that there are other treasure hunters on the island, people who have been trying to buy the island from George's parents just so that they can legally own anything found there. George and Julian are soon locked up in the ingot room, and Timmy is given a note to take to Dick and Anne, telling them to come down and see the treasure for themselves. However, George cleverly signs the note she's forced to write: 'Georgina'. So Dick and Anne read the note brought by Timmy, realise something is wrong, and hide. When the treasure-seekers are forced to leave the island to get assistance (they can't move the heavy, gold bars on their own, Enid would have us believe), Dick and Anne go to help Julian and George. But they can't go down the entrance to the cellars, because the men have placed great boulders on top (again, Enid would like us to believe that the men can't carry off the ingots but they can move around boulders so heavy that children can't even budge them).

Never mind, because Dick is brave enough to go down the iron ladder into the well, and then, when the ladder stops, descend further by rope, knowing that there is a hole in the side of the well and that he can crawl into the dungeons that way. He does just that.

Well done, Dick! And he lets George and Julian out from the locked door. Next? Well, they can't flee the island because the trespassers have taken away their oars. So instead they formulate a plan: when the men get back and go underground, Dick will creep up behind them and lock them in the ingot room. Meanwhile Julian, George and Anne will have tried their best to block the entrance to the dungeons so that even if the men do get out of the ingot room they won't be able to get back up to the surface again. Fine. Or, rather, Dick doesn't quite manage to lock the three men in the cellar, though he does escape up the well before they can get their hands on him. The stones the children pile on top of the exit from the dungeons don't hold the men up for long. But they are delayed long enough for the Five to get away in their boat. And so it's a simple matter of reporting the matter to the police on the mainland. The men are imprisoned and the treasure enables George's parents to hold onto the island. And that's the story!

What a lot of doors and passages I can make out in the loch's reflection of Clunie Castle! What a lot of coming and going from surface to cellar in *Five on a Treasure Island*! How determined the children have to be to make their way down, up, down another way, up again, down and all around the cellars. Perhaps the emotional climax of the book is when Dick, having risked his life in coming down the well, flings open the dungeon door of the ingot room to be greeted with cries of joy from Julian and George. What do the children find in the dungeons below Kirrin Castle? They find themselves.

In the third book in the series, *Five Run Away Together*, the ingot room is used by kidnappers who keep a little girl locked up there. The Five use their knowledge of the dungeons to run rings round the villains, and release the little girl and take her back to her parents. What do the children find in the dungeons? Again, they find themselves. But this is a relatively dim echoing of the first book. What isn't in the least bit dim is the sixth book in the series, *Five on*

Kirrin Island Again. This was intended to be the last Famous Five title, and Enid really goes for it. Not consciously, I suppose I have to assume. But her under-mind really goes for gold this time.

I wonder how long that cormorant is going to stand there with its wings out, master of all it surveys. Until his wings are thoroughly dry is the answer! Either that or he is waiting for me to finish airing *my* wings. Identically posed, you could say, it might seem as if we're trying to wing each other out. Well, my wings aren't getting tired, though they're not used to precisely this sort of thing. And I don't suppose for one moment that his wings are tiring. So stalemate for the moment, and let's get back to work.

In the sixth book, George's father has borrowed the island from George – still very much the owner even though from time to time she asserts that her cousins own the island with her. Her father has built a metal tower on the island so that he can perform scientific tests. George is not keen on this. She is even less keen on Timmy staying with her father on the island, but agrees to the arrangement when she realises that some villains are trying to steal her father's work. But she only goes along with it on condition that every day her father signals that he and Timmy are all right. The signals can be seen by Dick and Julian in their room with a sea view at Kirrin Cottage. However, after a day or two the signals stop. George is worried (more about Timmy rather than her father). George rows out to the island without telling the others what she is doing. For psychological reasons, Enid seems to want George to do this on her own, and as the author was a master of plot development, her character's decision to go it alone comes across as perfectly natural. George's first problem is locating her father whose island HQ is underground. The first entrance to the dungeons is blocked up and clearly hasn't been used for the couple of years that have passed since the little girl was locked up down below. So George must try and find the entrance that's within the castle room, though she and her cousins searched for it in the first book without success. This time George gets lucky. While she's in a dark corner, a couple of intruders emerge from the wall in order to go up the metal tower. George takes her courage in both hands, pops through the hole in the wall and climbs down the very steep set of steps cut into the rock itself. She descends much further than the dungeons, and realises that she's then in a tunnel which must run under the sea. The tunnel widens into a large chamber which is subdivided into small chambers, and here she comes across her father who is being held prisoner in his own laboratory. There's a lot of intense dialogue between the two. George says *'Oh, Father'* a few times, while the father cannot believe that it really is George. They are surprised and delighted to see each other. But her father is in despair about his situation, and George is desperate to know the whereabouts of Timmy. George *has* to know that Timmy (her essential animal self) is OK. But, no, according to her father there is one thing more important than that. And George's father makes George listen to him. He is working on a discovery that will allow mankind to get limitless power without using coal or oil. But the idea simply mustn't fall into the hands of these villains who just want to profit personally from it. The free energy is to be for the whole world. It is *essential* that his notebook, which he has so far managed to hide, is taken back to the mainland and given to a certain person for safekeeping. George promises to do this. (But *where* is darling Timmy? she feels like screaming aloud. What does it matter if the world has a new source of limitless energy if there's no Timmy to share it with?) George sticks the notebook, which she sees is full of her father's diagrams and his neat small handwriting, into her mackintosh pocket. She then forgets about it until she finds Timmy and releases him from his cage. ('Oh, Timmy, *Timmy*: you're not hurt.') But Timmy growls, because the men are coming back. George knows she is about to be discovered. She remembers the notebook, and gives it to Timmy who takes it in his mouth. George instructs him to go and hide with it. Timmy can do better than that. Instinct tells him that he is in a tunnel that will eventually lead back to the mainland. So next thing, he's waking up the household at Kirrin Cottage. Timmy delivers the book to Julian who takes it straight to George's mother who puts it in the safe.

Now, what is all this about? Where is all this incredibly urgent and pacey stuff actually coming from? I ask the cormorant still standing majestically in the tree above Clunie Castle with his wings outspread and, if I hear him right, his answer goes something like this...

Enid's father left the week before her thirteenth birthday. Well, I've been through that already. He left Enid's strait-laced mother for another woman, one who shared some of his interests in life. But to Enid – who had always got on marvellously well with her father who shared her artistic temperament and who had taught her so much about nature and culture – the feeling must have been one of personal rejection. Complete and utter rejection by her wise parent. 'Oh, Father.'

I recall it was her dear father who encouraged her to read and provided her with books. It was he who encouraged her talent in music; he who showed her how to enjoy both her own garden and the whole natural world out there. He was an amateur astronomer, with a fine telescope, so Enid would have been given a mind-blowing view of the night sky to stimulate her night stories. What more could a growing consciousness ask for?

In *The Story of My Life*, Enid pays homage to her father in every chapter which is not a tribute to Green Hedges, while all her mother could offer was a brooding resentment that Enid always had her head in a book when she could have been helping with the housework. This was not much good to Enid, who even as a child had ambitions to be a writer. After all, she found it so easy to come up with stories to entertain her father as they walked together in the countryside. But everything was put on ice by the father's sudden decision – impossible for the child to understand – to leave the family home. 'Oh, Father, what have I done wrong? And what can I do to put things right?'

Enid's father was 40 when he left his young daughter. He set up an office in the city where Enid would occasionally go to meet him. She never went round to his house so she could avoid the 'other woman'. And it's probably for the same reason that she didn't attend her father's funeral. Poor Thomas was only 50 when he left his daughter for a second time, this time for good. Enid Blyton's career as a published writer started not long after the funeral. By the time she wrote *Five on Kirrin Island Again*, her father had been in his grave for twenty-seven years. Twenty-seven years! But, in a way, poor Enid had been frozen as a person at the age of 12, going on 13. Many of the characters in the main series of books are of that age.

She did try writing a novel for adults once. It was in 1932, when she was 35 and hadn't begun writing her long books for children yet. She wrote it in a month. A diary entry reads: 'Finished my novel. About 90,000 words. It's called *The Caravan Goes On*.' It was sent back by Watt, a literary agent. Enid doesn't say why, and, according to Barbara Stoney, the book was not mentioned again. Though it was probably revised and is one of the books about circus life that were published for the audience that she did understand: children. In the fifties she had another go at writing for adults, this time a play called *The Summer Storm*. The script was sent to her then regular agent, George Greenfield, who found it banal and theatrical (in the worst sense). Enid *was* able to write for an adult audience, but only by focusing on the emotional landscape of children. The trauma she underwent in adolescence meant that she would never be able to open up in a way that would allow her to write about adult loss, pain, love, sex, death. Her range is enormous, within a pre-adolescent mindset.

I've put my wings down. But the cormorant hasn't. And I can visualise Enid with her arms still hovering above the typewriter, allowing her fingers to dance away on the keys for hours longer. So let's go for one last stretch of my wings.

When Enid Blyton's father went away with another woman, Enid was left to sink or swim. She sank. And at the same time she flew. I can't put it any clearer than that. The majestic one above Clunie Castle has pulled as much analysis out of me as there is to be pulled for now.

Raising an arm from where, all this time, it's been, I salute him – or her; as he – or she – continues to salute me.

2

Forfar is a sleepy town. I don't try and wake it. Instead I make my way to the second-hand bookshop.

Last time I was here there were three old copies of Famous Five books on sale for £1 each. I wasn't collecting then, but I did buy one, *Five Go Off in a Caravan*. I was about to go on the Proust coach trip, so was attracted to this particular book's title. I picked up the red hardback and flicked through it. My attention was grabbed by a couple of full-page illustrations, the first of which showed the Five lying on a hillside watching a procession of circus caravans going past, the lead caravan being pulled by an elephant. Then, a few pages later, there was one of the Five skipping down the hill at the sight of their own holiday caravans arriving – a blue one for the boys and a yellow one for the girls. I read the book the same day. It has a great sense of freedom and adventure. It's the fifth in the series, and – like the fourth, *Five Go To Smuggler's Top* – it showed both to the author and her avid readership that the Five books didn't have to be Kirrin-based. Blyton could have the children going anywhere during their precious school holidays, and as long as their sense of adventure (and Timmy) went with them, things would be fine. Better than fine. Things would be relentlessly *alive*.

Today, there is a single Famous Five book. The copy of *Five on*

Kirrin Island Again is typical of early editions of Five books in that eight full-page illustrations have been given a one colour overlay. The book is 192 pages long; twelve batches of sixteen pages each. A double-page overlaid with luscious red is wrapped around the second batch of pages in the book. So, appearing opposite page 16 is an image of the Five – George and Anne wearing red blazers – looking towards Kirrin Island on which George's father's tower is conspicuous. And, opposite page 32 is an image of George in her red blazer in the glass-walled room at the top of her father's tower. There's a great sense of movement between these two images. It's as if the illustrator is as concerned about the pace and development of the story as the writer.

Red overlaid images are also opposite pages 80 and 96 while four blue pages come later in the book. The last pair of images is fascinating, and I keep flicking from one to the other, the intervening batch of pages turning as one in my hand. Opposite page 144, George has surprised her father in the dungeon under Kirrin Island, so deep underground that bright red has turned into luminous blue. While opposite page 160, her father (blue tie) is handing George (blue blazer) a book (electric blue). At least the single line appearing under the image says: 'George took the precious book'. But the image can just as easily be read as George passing the book to her father. Sub-text I read it as Enid passing a book that she has written to her father. And my caption reads: 'Enid gave the precious book'.

This crumbling copy of *Five on Kirrin Island Again* is old enough to have a frontispiece (it was printed in October 1947, just two months after the fast-selling first edition). The image shows Dick, George, Anne and Julian gazing out towards Kirrin Island. Actually, only George is looking out to sea, and she's doing that with the aid of a telescope. This was the dust-wrapper image as well. But only until 1948, when the image was re-drawn so that it didn't appear as if George was looking down the wrong end of the

THIS IS HER
FATHER

George took the precious book.

telescope. The cover image was changed more radically in 1951, the telescope scene being replaced with a scene of George pushing a rowing boat out to sea. Julian is standing up in the boat, and his oar does exactly the same thing as the telescope in the earlier images: it suggests the course of the tunnel from the mainland to the island. How keen must Eileen Soper have been on her symbolic tunnel motif, to have tried so hard to retain it from one revised cover to the next?

I decide to buy the book, a copy of which I already own, if only to tear it apart for the illustrations when I get home. But I'm not finished with this shop. I pick out old paperback copies of *The Castle of Adventure*, *The Enchanted Wood*, *Secret Seven Adventure*, *Third Year at Malory Towers* and *The Naughtiest Girl Again*, this last being an unpriced Armada reprint from 1980. I take the seven books to the owner of the shop. £2 for the Five; 50p for four paperbacks; with *The Naughtiest Girl Again* thrown in for free.

'Oh, you've made my day,' I tell her.

She smiles tentatively at the grown man buying children's books for peanuts.

'No, you have, honestly.'

I drive for just a few more miles and I reach the coast. Lunan Bay isn't dissimilar to Swanage Bay – at least it looks the same on the map – but Lunan Bay is on the east coast of Scotland rather than on the south coast of England. I plod across the sand until I get to the top of the dunes, then I have to smile. There is Kirrin Island, with that distinctive crumbling castle tower, the one that Eileen Soper captured in so many line-illustrations in the Fives. But the wind blows into my face and the image fades. When the breeze from the sea dies down again, I'm looking at Clunie Island and the fortified house; above is the cormorant standing with his wings outstretched, as before. I stand there gazing at the majestic one until a voice attracts my attention:

'Tee-ee-ee-mmy! Tee-ee-ee-mmy!'

The wind is blowing again; I can hear it scything through the grass on top of the dunes behind me.

'Tee-ee-ee-ee-ee-ee-ee-ee-ee-ee-ee-mmy!'

Timmy comes to heel. George kneels down in the sand and strokes her darling dog's chest. 'Take this book to Father,' she says. And George slips a grotty paperback copy of *The Naughtiest Girl Again* into Timmy's mouth. The book was originally published in 1942 and is an early school story. In the same year as the first Five book, then; the same year that George, Timmy et al made it onto the page and a few months before Fatty, Bets, etc. did.

The dog's teeth make indentations in the cover, but George isn't too worried about that. 'Take it to Fatty,' she whispers. But that is a slip on my part. 'Take it to *Father*,' is what George really says. And Timmy bounds across the sand and into the sea, heading straight for the island. He's heading straight for the castle dungeon where Timmy knows George's father likes to hang out with his bookcase full of *The Children's Encyclopaedia*, dreaming of a better, wiser, more egalitarian world.

'NO, TIMMY, GO BY THE TUNNEL. OTHERWISE THE BOOK WILL GET WATERLOGGED!' shouts George.

Timmy swims out towards the island, the wind blowing his whiskers.

'OH, TIMMY, YOU ARE THE NAUGHTIEST DOG!' shouts George, still hoping to get through to her pet.

Timmy loves swimming in the sea. Simply loves it. The dog feels a strong urge to bark his joy. Unfortunately if he did that he would have to let go of the book. And his beloved George has ordered him to take the grubby thing to her good father's library beneath the ocean waves...

'WOOF!' goes Timmy in uncontrollable over-excitement.

'Oh, Timmy, you are the naughtiest dog... again,' says George, accepting defeat this time around, and acknowledging that this isn't the first time such a book has gone to a watery grave.

The naughtiest dog – no, you can't blame Timmy just for being himself – veers away from the island, and is, I notice in my mind's eye, swimming in the sea to my left as I drive the few miles south to Arbroath.

3

I've never been in this town before, so it feels like an adventure right from the start. I get the car-parking bit right, because as soon as I walk out of the park I'm on an Arbroath street which is chock-full of charity shops.

When did I first get into charity shops? When an artist friend, Matthew Thompson, embarked on a project that involved collecting jigsaws by Philmar. The company went bust in the eighties but there are still plenty of their puzzles kicking around in such shops, the only places you can find them these days. There are various series of puzzle, but most are sets of chocolate-box landscapes. The biggest thrill is when it's written on the cardboard box that there is one piece missing. And when you complete the jigsaw, the missing piece always appears to be in the most significant place. *Philmar*. The trademark appearance of the name has branded its pattern onto my mind, in the same way as the Enid Blyton signature has – two strokes underlining the gap between 'Enid' and 'Blyton'.

I choose a charity shop and go in. They have a number of Blytons, and they're also selling children's books at four for a pound. I pick up a couple of Secret Seven books and a new copy of *The Mystery of the Pantomime Cat* and make my way to the till. An elderly volunteer reminds me that I can have four books for a pound. Well, the only other Blyton is a glossy hardback edition of *The Naughtiest Girl Again*, and as I've got rid of one copy of that book already today, I think I'll stick to the three paperbacks at an average cost of 33p each. But a sudden thought changes my mind and I go back to the bookcase.

The front cover of this *Naughtiest Girl Again* is ghastly, even though the idea was good. A schoolgirl is swinging her school bag around her head. Books and pencils are flying out of her satchel, but does she care? No, not the naughtiest girl! A mouse is emerging from her blazer pocket, as perky as its mistress. And her knees – well, it looks as if she's been kneeling in soot. You just don't get any naughtier than that – not in 1972, which was when Dean & Son published this edition.

Is it by my own definition a 'classic' Dean? I turn it over and there, under a symbol – a black circle with the silhouette of an adult in a top-hat holding the hand of a child and showing him, or her, the way ahead – is a boxed list of forty-eight books by Enid Blyton. This is the same boxed list of forty-eight that appears over and over again on the back of the Dean Blytons published in the seventies. *The Naughtiest Girl Again* is in at number 34. I open the book. Its former owner was one Kirsten Talbot of 12 Abbey Court, Arbroath, who got the book as a birthday present from Aunty Jerrie and Uncle James. When I turn the page I am confronted with:

'KIRSTEN OWNS THIS BOOK AND DON'T FORGET IT!!'

I turn over again and am told:

'IF YOU ARE READING THIS NOTE, THEN GET YOUR FACE OUT OF MY BOOK!!'

I actually look over both shoulders just in case forceful Kirsten is here in the charity shop and taking exception to my trespassing on her property. However, even in the face of such intimidation, I turn the page once more. And in the margin above the first page of the story, Kirsten tells me:

'THIS IS YOUR LAST CHANCE. GET OUT NOW!!'

All of her exclamation marks end, not with dots on the bottom of the vertical lines, but circles. Gives them more impact, I suppose. However, there is no more withering ink from the nastiest girl in Arbroath, until right at the back of the book, where she writes touchingly:

'I GIVE UP. YOU READ THE WHOLE THING.'

There's humour here. Perhaps she's not so nasty after all. Ha! Arrows point to the bottom of the page where the naughtiest, nastiest girl in Arbroath gives it one last blast:

'NOW GET LOST!!!!'

Good idea. Let's get out of his shop before I get arrested for loitering in the kiddies' corner. Loitering with intent to bribe Kirsten's children or grandchildren with books that are timeless and precious, or timeworn and worthless, depending on your point of view.

Back in the car, I drive from the car-park to the sea-front and I crack open a Diet Coke. The injection of caffeine is just what I need. I look out of the window to my left. From here, cliffs rise up from the shore, and there's a path all the way to Lunan Bay. Timmy's here with me again, or rather he's here with George. George calls Timmy to her and gives him a good pat on the back and rubs him all over his chest. Then she tells him to take the book, which she shows him and lets him sniff, to her father. George then slips her friend Kirsten's copy of *The Naughtiest Girl Again* into Timmy's mouth.

'Take it to Father,' says George. She adds, 'Not by the sea route this time, but by the underground tunnel.'

Timmy is tempted to bark his understanding but he knows he really shouldn't while he's holding George's glossy hardback book in his mouth. He has been entrusted with a task by his mistress.

'TUNNEL, TIMMY!'

Timmy hesitates. He always prefers the sea route to the island library if he's given the choice.

'TUNNEL, TIMMY, TUNNEL! And I bloody well mean it this time.'

Timmy runs off. Sure enough, he doesn't go out to sea but rushes straight along the sea-front, then up the path and along the cliff edge.

'Oh, Timmy, you are the best dog in the world!' shouts George.

'And Father will have the best library in the world,' adds George, determination shining out of her cornflower blue eyes. 'He simply must have.'

The best library in the world. Now there's an ambition and a half.

4

I drive to Dundee. But when I get close to the middle of the town I take the Tay Bridge option and cross the great river, thereby heading towards St Andrew's. Why? Because I've already trawled the second-hand bookshops and charity shops of the jute-jam-journalism city for Blyton, whereas the university town is still virgin Enid territory.

Boy, am I hungry for lunch as I park the car. But the feeling goes as I enter the charity shop zone. St Andrew's has a couple of charity shops that deal exclusively in books. I gravitate towards them, but before I get there I've picked up *Those Dreadful Children*. It's a messy little Armada paperback but the book was originally published in 1949, a golden year for Enid, so it could be of special interest to my Find-Outers. My Find-Outers are operating in the summer of 1950. Why? Because I really want the 'in the midst of it all' view from then, as well as the more measured one that's available from 2006. Also, I want the child's eye view as well as the adult's. I certainly don't want to set my whole book in libraries and bookshops. Besides, I love Fatty as much as Enid did, and feel I must pay true homage to her creation.

I buy another paperback from the same shop. It's *The Rat-a-tat Mystery*, the fifth of the six 'R' mysteries, and a book that is heavily criticised in the latest issue of *The Enid Blyton Society Journal*. Apparently, in the fourth book, Barney – the boy who goes about with monkey Miranda for company – is reunited with his father. Thirteen-year-old reunited with father – what joy in the Blyton world! And yet it's presumably this 'happy ending' that rips the guts out of the books which follow, those that emerge from a backdrop of make-believe happiness. You'd better keep your teenage creations effectively fatherless, Enid, for the sake of the *oeuvre*. Keep your teenagers parentless for the sake of your real children – the books. In the Fives it's important that George's father is kept as a pale shadow of a character most of the time, disinterested in the children's activities. This allows them the freedom to take risks and initiatives.

In a specialist book branch of Oxfam I pick up a paperback copy of *The Secret Island*. The book was a forerunner to *Five on a Treasure Island*. It was serialised in *Sunny Stories* in 1937/38 and then published as a book in 1938, only Blyton's third full-length story after *The Adventures of the Wishing-Chair* and *Mr Galliano's Circus*. It's about three children – Mike, Nora and Peggy – who have lost their parents in a plane crash and who have gone to live with their aunt and uncle, who mistreat them. There's a fourth child, Jack, also without parents, also unhappy about the way he is overworked by his grandfather on the old man's farm. Jack knows about this wild island in the middle of a lake that nobody ever visits. So one day the children, who have filled a boat with all they think they'll need to survive, row out to the island meaning to stay there. And that's what they do! In the middle of England!

I recall how Enid goes into delicious and believable detail about how the children deal with food, shelter and all the basics of subsistence. They take with them hens, gather fruits and nuts regularly, fish every day, and eventually Jack even goes back and fetches his cow Daisy from the mainland. The beast is none too happy about swimming all the way to the island behind the rowing boat, but she does it nevertheless, and from then on the children have what they'd sorely missed: fresh milk. I'm seeing this all in terms of Kirrin now. George fetching a cow called Timmy to her island. I'm also seeing it in terms of Enid. What she went through in the months after her father deserted her, leaving her to sink or swim.

But back to the book in my hands as written. The children make a house out of willow trees, and they occupy caves in the winter months. They hide in these caves when adults come searching for them. Then Jack, on a secret trip to buy Christmas presents for the others on the mainland, overhears people talking about the parents of the other three. They haven't died in a plane crash after all! They've been stranded on a desert island themselves for a year or more! Oh, what joy when the family is reconciled. Jack is part of the new family, of course. The children are all a bit sorry to leave the island, because they've been happy there together and they've made it a real home. But the important thing is the love and respect the children show each other. And that won't change just because they are all back living in a house, celebrating Christmas in a traditional way and going to school again. The parents don't stick around for long, though. In *The Secret Mountain* they've disappeared again, allowing the children to get stuck into another memorable adventure on their own.

I put back *The Secret Island*. After all I've already got a paperback edition, and it's a copy that wasn't sacrificed to the water when I was researching Goon's bath scene. Sighing, I pick up the book alongside a Newnes hardback of *The Naughtiest Girl Again*. Yes, I've come to accept that there is no avoiding this title today. Besides, this book is beautifully illustrated and printed on that wonderfully soft white paper that Newnes used. I can't help but smell and touch and read the first page, which is about young Elizabeth's enthusiasm for going back to Whyteleafe School for a second term, winter, just a few months after hating the beginning of her first term, summer. Childhood, a mid-twentieth-century school childhood, seeps from the book's pale blue linen pores.

Next door is another charity shop, and here I come across two Noddy books in dust-covers. *Noddy at the Seaside* and *Noddy Gets into Trouble*. They're both priced at 20p. Are they first editions? No, because the back flap of the ragged jackets list all twenty-four titles in the Noddy series, and so they must have been printed after the last book was published in 1963. But these are old copies, perhaps from the sixties or seventies (the publisher has the annoying habit of only giving the date of the first publication, not the date of reprinting). The books are 'with golliwogs', which is as they should be. I'm collecting Noddy books both 'with gollies', that is, the originals, and 'without gollies', that is, a later edition. In the eighties, due to a witless campaign of political correctness, the lovely black dolls were expunged from the books, and bland white characters put in their place. OK, so in the fourth Noddy book, *Here Comes Noddy Again*, a group of golliwogs strip Noddy and steal his car. But where did Noddy get his wheels in the first place? In the second book in the series, *Hurrah For Little Noddy*, Noddy helps the garage proprietor, Mr Golly, to trace some cars that have been stolen from his garage by a gang of goblins. As a reward the respectable black businessman gives Noddy a little car of his own. But since the PC campaign there have been no black faces in Toyland. Is that supposed to make it a better place? It makes it a less colourful, less joyous place. But don't get me wrong – Toyland rocks, even in the revised edition.

I walk down the street, my bag heavy with Blyton bounty. As I'm thinking about lunch again, I spy a little old bookshop down a back street. 'Ye ken whaur Tam bides?' says one old-timer to another outside the shop. I slide past the pair and inside before I realise what a great line I've just heard. I should have hung about and waited to hear the rest of the exchange. Ye ken whaur Tam bides? The line was spoken with an understated, hard-won innocence. An example of local dialect uncorrupted by eighty years – or whatever it is – of the BBC. But I wasn't altogether wrong to come into the shop, because here is a copy of *The Children's Life of Christ* by Enid Blyton.

The book was first printed 10 June 1943. It was reprinted for the eighth time in 1958. So this copy is nearly 50 years old. The story begins: 'The life of Christ is a wonderful story to tell.' Actually, that's just the start of Enid's foreword, which is dated 1 January 1943. Six months from completed manuscript to date of publication, then. You can learn so much just from picking up each and every single book. 'January 1, 1943', it says. 'Happy New Year, Enid' and, turning to another world altogether: 'Happy New Year, Western Europe'.

I flick back. On the title page it announces that the book has been illustrated by Eileen Soper. Obviously she was flavour of the month, because she'd just illustrated the first book in the Famous Five series and perhaps also the second book by then, as the publication date of that one was also the summer of 1943. The War of the Worlds: 1943. Enid Blyton versus Adolf Hitler. Look at those two heavyweights get stuck into one another! Green Hedges' Famous Five defend freedom of speech against the Third Reich's rival theory of a master race. The FF versus the SS. There could only ever have been one winner. If only Hugh Pollock could have understood that, he would have saved himself a lot of grief.

Obviously Eva Braun... sorry, Eileen Soper... was obsessed with Timmy, because opposite the title page is the colour frontispiece from which I learn that Timmy was present at the Nativity. Yes, there is the Virgin Mary with baby Jesus, present and correct in lamp-lit stable. And there are three wise men wearing Middle Eastern garb admiring the new-born babe. All that is par for the course. But dead centre is Timmy the dog – I'd know that big friendly alert creature anywhere – wondering what all the fuss is about.

'Baby *Jesus*, Timothy.'

'Woof,' barks Timmy.

I flick through the book. It falls open at the last page. Blyton tells the reader that she will end the story the way she thinks Jesus would like her to end it – with the crucial commandment Christ kept all through his life. And what would that be, Enid?

'*LOVE ONE ANOTHER.*'

So strange to think that, within the space of a year, and as well as all her usual books, including a Five and a Mystery, Enid published *The Children's Life of Christ*, *Enid Blyton's Nature Lover's Book* and *Here Comes the Circus*. Love one another, love all the creatures, each of which is special in its own way, and love Mother Earth. Say it again, Enid. 'Love Timmy. Love Fatty. Love Jesus. Love Hugh (sort of). Love Goon (the clown). And love all of our fellow creatures. Amen.'

I'm glad to remind myself of the circus books. For Enid, the circus is an alternative to a normal family. People with special talents gravitate towards Mr Galliano's circus, which features in three early serialised Blyton books. The key to the successful running of the circus is the kindness that emanates from the rather distant but distinctly father-like circus master. For all the talents of the animals and performers, they each have their foibles and their vulnerabilities. In *Mr Galliano's Circus*, an elephant breaks out of the compound during a storm. In panic it runs all through the night, until it drops. Animal down! But little Jimmy, who has a winning way with all God's creatures, tracks big Jumbo through the night, gets him back up on his feet again and leads him back to the Secret Island, I mean to Mr Galliano's Circus.

After a small kebab for lunch (actually a limitless feast), I wander down to the shore leaving footsteps in the drying sand. From my bag I dig out just one of my precious purchases, in fact the most recent one. *The Little Girl at Capernaum* was shelved right next to *The Children's Life of Christ*, but I didn't notice its discreet red spine until I was going out of the shop. And I didn't have the energy to even open the book before returning to the counter to buy it.

It's a bible story. In fact, it's one of the many stories told in *The Children's Life of Christ*, expanded to fill a lavishly illustrated, large-format, sixty-page book. On the one hand, I'm not too sure about reading it on a full stomach; I could do with chilling out. On the other, I have a feeling this book is simply going to be all too easy to read. It's a Blyton, after all.

… Anna has been given a model boat by one of the fishermen. She shows it to her father when he gets home for lunch. Jairus thinks his 12-year-old daughter is the loveliest, merriest child in the whole of Capernaum. He takes the afternoon off from his duties at the church, and he makes a sail for Anna's little boat. They sail the boat on the small pond set in the courtyard of their house, Anna's mother listening to the laughter of father and child as she works indoors. But the next day Anna is ill. When Jairus gets home from work he picks up his daughter but she hardly smiles at him. She is put to bed and the doctor is called. The doctor's prognosis is gloomy. Other doctors are called – money no object – but it seems the little girl is doomed. Jairus has one last desperate idea. 'Listen, wife! Shall I go to this man Jesus?'

He has to explain to his wife who Jesus is. But soon he is on his way to Peter's house, which is where Jesus stays when he is in town. Unfortunately, Jesus has gone fishing with Peter. So Jairus returns to his house where his daughter is dying. It breaks his heart to see her poor pale face. His wife urges Jairus to go out again and look for Jesus. He hates to leave his dying daughter but he does, and he runs to the lake where he looks out for Peter's fishing boat – the one that's so like the little boat he and Anna played with the other day. Finally he spots Peter's boat. A crowd of people are waiting for Jesus on shore, but Jairus pushes through them in his anxiety to be given an audience. Jesus is tired and must rest, but Jairus flings himself down and cries out that his daughter is on the point of death. 'I pray you, come and lay your hands on her that she may be healed.'

Jesus complies. The crowd follows Jesus and Jairus towards the child's sick-bed. However, in the crowd there is a woman who wants to get near Jesus for selfish reasons of her own. According to doctors she is past all hope, but she feels that if she could just look into his face or even simply touch the tassel of his cloak she would recover. She manages to do the latter, and at once feels healing power flow through her. She knows that she is healthy and well again. But Jesus has been drained of his strength. 'Who touched me?' he wants to know. His goodness has been sucked out of him. He insists on knowing who touched him, much to Jairus's distress because he feels that time is short for his precious daughter. The woman kneels before Jesus and admits her guilt. Jesus forgives her. He tells her that she has been cured as a result of her faith. He bids her to go in peace.

The book has an irresistible narrative drive, but I make myself pause at this point to consider some pencil marks in the margin. A previous reader has indicated with arrows and page references that a section from page 35 to 47 can be missed out. True, but I bet Enid would have had something to say about that. I suspect she had reasons of her own for wanting to include the story of the selfish woman who distracted Jesus from helping the 12-year-old girl.

Back to the relentless action: a messenger arrives to tell Jairus the bad news that his daughter has died. However, Jesus turns to the distraught Jairus and tells him not to be afraid, but instead to trust him. They proceed towards Jairus's house. Jesus tells the crowd to wait in the street outside. In the courtyard he chastises the professional mourners who have been paid to wail and grieve. Accompanied by Anna's grief-stricken parents and three disciples, Jesus is shown into the room where Anna lies. She does not breathe. Her dark curls fall over her forehead, and her father is distraught as he sees his daughter lying there so still.

Jesus looks down on the little girl with love and compassion. He puts out his hand and takes the child's cold one in his. Then he speaks lovingly: 'Get up, darling.'

Jairus catches his breath in astonishment, surely Anna's eyelashes were flickering! The little girl opens her eyes. She looks up at her parents and the stranger. Has she been ill? She feels quite well again. She wants to rise. She wants to walk and run! Her mother takes her in her arms, crying tears of happiness. Jairus kneels by his loved one, beside himself with joy. He presses his cheek against Anna's warm rosy one, happier than he has ever been in his life before. 'We will sail your little boat on the lake, my darling,' he says. 'You shall see the wind take her swiftly along. We will be together again, you and I.'

Plink. That is a tear falling from my eye onto the page. I don't know about Jesus, but Enid could draw blood out of a stone. My sight is blurred as I turn over and finish the tale. I pull myself together by bringing to mind some facts. This heartfelt little book – written with remarkable restraint: the tone of the narrator never wobbles – was published in 1948. That's the same year that Enid published two dozen other books including *Five Go Off To Camp*, *The Mystery of the Hidden House*, *Third Year at Malory Towers* and *Come to the Circus*. Jesus, or any other miracle-maker, would have been astonished by her deeds.

According to a foreword written by the publisher, this was the second of eight bible stories Enid had promised to write for Lutterworths. But only a couple more appeared, and then not until 1965. It wouldn't surprise me if these two later tales were judged inferior and so remained unpublished at the time of writing. After all, how could Enid have topped *The Little Girl at Capernaum*? Perhaps also, with the identification between Jesus and her father becoming conscious, she felt she couldn't safely go there again. Perhaps she had the same problem with the Barney books and the Adventure series.

Anyway, this reminds me how powerful an idea 'Jesus' was, just a few decades ago. He was a miracle-maker, yes. But more significantly he was *the* moral force behind society. It seems inevitable that a girl brought up to be a Christian in Enid's day, one who had a clever and kind father, would be bound to link the two during childhood.

And Enid's father was not just kind and clever, he was a story-teller, a musician, the life and soul of family parties, a naturalist, and, I suspect, a strong moral force. That is, he emphasised hard work, honesty and personal freedom. A freedom to live one's life that came with a responsibility for the welfare of others. But more than that: I remember from the Barbara Stoney biography that when Enid was just 3 months old, she had whooping cough and was not expected to survive the cold November night. The story goes that Thomas took little Enid from Theresa and hugged her in his arms all night, willing her to live. He saved her life. She lived, anyway. It was a story Thomas told Enid repeatedly, perhaps at her instigation. And it's there, quivering under the calm surface of *The Little Girl at Capernaum*.

Jairus and Jesus are almost one and the same names, though Enid wasn't responsible for that. Moreover, *The Little Girl at Capernaum* contains both the story of the 12-year-old's loss of a father (which happens off-stage, as it were, leading to her death) and the story – wishful thinking – of the father-figure (dwarfing the actual father) returning to save her. It's a sort of good-cop, bad-cop routine. A stunning literary achievement – though just anoth-er one-off-the-dancing-fingers as far as our Enid is concerned – that has left me emotionally drained.

I need recharging. Time for Noddy? Too right! Perhaps Enid needed similarly recharging because the first Noddy story was written in 1949, the year after the Capernaum book. I delve into my bag for *Noddy at the Seaside*. The first illustration is superb. Noddy and Big-Ears are sitting at the little table in Noddy's House-For-One. Big-Ears is leaning forward excitedly, informing Noddy that he has come to share breakfast with him! Noddy doesn't look too sure how to react to this news, other than to carry on eating his boiled egg and toast. But the fact that the portrait of Big-Ears is pinned to the wall behind them means that Noddy knows how he feels about Big-Ears all right: the old pixie is his best friend and the nearest thing he has to a wise old dad.

Big-Ears has come to suggest that they take a holiday by the sea together. The seaside has got heaps of yellow sand. You dig in that and you paddle in the blue sea! It's lovely! So they get all their money together and Noddy drives them to the seaside. Soon Noddy is successfully paddling in the sea and all is set up for a good old adventure…

I consider the beach here at St Andrew's in the pale afternoon sunshine. A few people are walking on the sand, along that wavy line, forever being re-drawn, where the land meets the sea. My eye pans across the waves, the white horses catching the sun's rays, until I can only see deep, blue sea to the east.

'What's that?' asks Noddy, staring into the distance.

'Kirrin Island,' says Big-Ears.

'Shall we swim out to it?'

'Don't be silly. You can't swim, Noddy! Anyway, the crabs would nip your toes. The best thing would be if I took you out in a boat.'

As Big-Ears is rowing out towards the castle-topped island, he explains about the famous underground library that can only be reached by going down a bucket in a well. Noddy doesn't like the sound of that. But when he gets to the island he stumbles across a proper entrance to the underground library. Big-Ears and he have to pull together on a rope attached to an iron ring before the door will open up for them. Down the steep steps and into the cellars they go. It is too dark for Noddy, and even if the best library in the world was down there in the dungeons, he's not sure he could do much reading in the dark. Big-Ears tells him it is a *proper* library and Noddy will be able to switch on electric lights, or borrow books and read them at home, or read them in the tent in which they are going to live while they're on holiday by the sea. When Noddy and Big-Ears are fully underground, a white-bearded giant called Mr

Big Daddy comes along and closes the door to the underground cellars.

'BOOM!'

Noddy and Big-Ears are trapped. But they decide they might as well check out the library while they're there. They discover a room full of books all right. Noddy opens a book at random and reads what has been written on the first page:

'BIG DADDY OWNS THIS BOOK AND DON'T FORGET IT!!'

Without thinking much about it, Noddy turns over the page:

'IF YOU ARE READING THIS NOTE, THEN GET YOUR FACE OUT OF MY CAPERNAUM GIRL!!'

Noddy feels scared. He doesn't know what to do so he turns over to the next page:

'THIS IS YOUR LAST CHANCE. GET YOUR FACE OUT OF MY CAPERNAUM GIRL NOW!!! Noddy is shaking. He hurries through the pages in a desperate attempt to get his face out of Mr Big Daddy's Capernaum Girl.

'I GIVE UP. YOU'VE BEEN RIGHT THROUGH HER.'

Noddy gives a sigh of relief.

'NOW GET LOST!!!!'

Noddy drops the book in terror and runs out of the library, with Big-Ears hot on his heels having been through exactly the same reading experience with a first edition. However, Big-Ears is a bit more aware than Noddy of who Big Daddy actually is. G-G-G-God!

Big-Ears tries to get up to the surface of the island via the well. But he is too fat to get into the well-shaft, and Noddy is too frightened to even try. But it doesn't matter because in his panic to get out of the dungeon, Noddy finds a tunnel and soon he and Big-Ears are racing along it under the sea. A booming voice pursues them:

'BIG DADDY OWNS THIS TUNNEL AND DON'T FORGET IT!!'

Noddy and Big-Ears run faster:

'IF YOU ARE HEARING THIS MESSAGE, THEN GET YOUR BONNY BUMS OUT OF MY TUNNEL!!'

Noddy actually looks over both shoulders just in case Big Daddy is right there behind them. He's not, but his big booming voice is:

'THIS IS YOUR LAST CHANCE. GET YOUR BONY BUMS OUT NOW!!'

Noddy realises that Big Daddy probably said 'bony' the previous time as well. Though it was a funny thing to say about Big-Ears, who had plenty flesh on his big bones. Noddy sees a light at the tunnel's end. He keeps running and emerges into the summer sun. Sand and sea and little Tessie Bear on the beach in her pretty sun-hat. Big-Ears emerges from the tunnel as well, and as he does they hear Big Daddy's final words:

'I GIVE UP. YOU RAN THE WHOLE WAY.'

Noddy and Big-Ears are out of puff but pleased to be free and above land and admiring Tessie's furry bottom.

'NOW GET LOST!!!!' says a voice from the heavens.

Noddy and Big-Ears jump into Noddy's little car. 'That was a nice holiday by the seaside,' says Noddy. 'But if you don't mind we're going straight home now.'

Big-Ears does not put up an argument for staying at the seaside. 'Drop me at Toadstool House,' is all he asks.

As they drive towards home, Noddy begins to relax. And as he begins to relax he thinks back to his experience in the underground library.

'Big-Ears?'

'YOH!' replies Big-Ears, also beginning to feel much better in himself.

'Did you notice something funny about the books in that library?'

'I'm not sure that I did.'

'Every one of them was called exactly the same thing.'

'Really?'

'Every single one was called *Gnid Blyton*.'

And that tickles old Big-Ears. Fancy little Noddy mistaking the author's name for the title! Fancy Noddy not even getting the author's name right! It tickles Big-Ears into asking Noddy a simple question:

'Ye ken?'

Noddy has no idea what Big-Ears has asked him, or even if it was a proper question. But he laughs.

'Ye ken?' repeats Big-Ears with a blissful smile.

Noddy laughs out loud. Because it is so good to be alive, on holiday with dear old Big-Ears instead of Big Daddy, and going straight home to Toyland with a lot of absolute nonsense ringing in his ears:

'Ye ken whaur Gnid bides?'

5

I don't manage to go straight home after all. I've got one last stop, though there's no way I'm going round the whole circuit of eleven charity shops that I know of in Perth. However, there is just one shop that I really must pop into in order to round off my day. It's a run of the mill branch of Barnardo's. The last time I was here, the shop had several Enid Blyton books on sale at prices only a serious collector would pay, and the frustration of this stopped me from looking properly at the books. Today I am going to have that proper look.

There are three of them, front covers facing out. Each is from the Adventure series starring Kiki the parrot. A Famous Five book and a Mystery were published every single year from 1943 to 1954. However, a Five, a Mystery and an Adventure volume appeared every year from 1946 to 1950, the core years of Enid's super-productive period. Five plus five plus five equals fifteen ultimate titles. Not a dud among them.

These three are standing on a single, make-do shelf, high up the wall and within sight of anyone at the desk. I walk past a wire basket full of ladies' shoes (any pair for £2), pick up a rubber-topped footstool, place it at the base of the wall I'm interested in, and stand on the stool. Straight in front of my chest is a pin-board covered in assorted jewellery, £1 for any item. But above my head, I can just reach the shelf whose contents read, from left to right: *The Island of Adventure*, £20, *The Circus of Adventure*, £40, and *The River of Adventure*, £75. The prices are a joke; no one is going to pay anything like these amounts. If the books were advertised on the net, then it's possible that the books would sell for about half their present asking price, so it's not even worth my while making an offer in the region of £5 per book, which is what they'd be worth to me. It would be nice if the two Blyton parrots standing to attention in my library at home (on a different shelf from *Flaubert's Parrot*, but still very much part of the same collection) could have these three parrots for company, however it's just not going to happen. But let me take that proper look, anyway.

The River of Adventure is a first edition, but the spine leans to one side. The book is in its original dust-jacket, but it is badly torn and has a big chunk missing from the front. Actually, the tearing is getting worse because the price of the book is written on a paper band that encircles the book, and it is rather too tight a fit. Now that I've taken off the band, I won't be able to get it back on without further damaging the cover, so I think I'll leave it off when I'm done.

In the foreword, Blyton tells how she meant to finish the Adventure series at the sixth book, in 1950, with the marriage of Bill Smugs – he often comes to the children's rescue – to the mother of Philip and Dinah. However, the demand for more stories had been such that Enid had felt obliged by the bond that exists between reader and author to write another story. Thus it was that *The Circus of Adventure* (1952) had been written. After this book too she received thousands of letters from children. And so Enid had taken up her portable typewriter once again and came up with *The River of Adventure* (1955). Fair enough, I read what she says.

But what she doesn't say is that it was this precise book that Blyton – in a letter to the psychologist Peter McKellar – admitted that she had begun on Monday and finished on Friday of the same week, making an average of 12,000 words per day. Boom-boom! So while the book might be sub-standard because the adventuresome children have gained Bill Smugs as an overt father-figure, and while it might also be *sub*-sub-standard because it was written in such a dizzy rush, still – and perhaps partly because of these reasons – it is the one particular book I ache to possess in this, its original form. In short, I'd pay a tenner for it – but no more.

I put the book back on the shelf and look round the shop from my high vantage point. A young man asks the woman at the till whether he can have a look at the teddy-bear in the window. A rough-looking, grey-bearded man who has been mumbling to himself now looks towards the young man and says obnoxiously:

'Iz-zit fur yir boy-friend?'

The young man turns away from his questioner with a palpable shudder. I turn back to the books and try to put the encounter out of my mind. Neither *The Island of Adventure* (sixth edition) nor *The Circus of Adventure* (first edition) have dust-covers, but both have Kiki present and correct on the spine. Oh, but I wish I hadn't rattled Kiki's cage again, because I know she could make things difficult for me here.

'Iz-zit?'

It could be Kate talking in her Scottish accent.

'Izzit?… Izzit?… Izzit?… Iz-zat fur yir boyfriend?'

Please don't, Kate. Please don't, Kiki. Don't make me laugh.

I will just stand here, and I won't say or do anything to attract attention to myself, though I don't expect full co-operation in this from a certain feathered fiend.

'Wipe your mouth. Close the door. How many times have I told you to close your boyfriend's mouth?' says Kiki.

The young man has fled without the bear. The tramp (for that's certainly how Enid would have described him) is now asking if there's a toilet in the shop. He has to ask the question a second time before one of the women volunteers tells him firmly that there is no public toilet in the shop, but she adds that there's a very good one in the centre. She means St John's Shopping Centre, which is only about 200 metres from here. So that's good, he can wander off in that direction, leaving me to concentrate on these books.

I still can't get over *The River of Adventure* costing £75. Perhaps I should buy it anyway. But that's not right! Damn, I can't get out of my mind the notion that the homeless chap is going to poke me in the back and say 'How's this for a river of adventure?' I look towards the man, who is now standing by the door looking back into the shop, challenging us, it seems. Our eyes only meet for an instant (I look away), but in that split second I'm forced to change my mind about him. He actually looks quite an elegant figure standing there. His grey beard is respectable enough. True, he doesn't take care about his appearance in the modern way, but he possesses a quiet dignity. I must have misheard what he said earlier.

What if it's Jesus? No, I don't mean that. Let's not go there.

What if it's Enid's father. Yes, that's what gets my mind tripping over itself in a bid to keep up with the implications. Thomas Blyton must have heard I was writing about his daughter and wanted to see whether I was taking liberties with Enid's family background. What would make more sense than for him to emerge from his underground library disguised as a tramp in order to check me out? It's what Fatty would have done. Has Thomas come to put the record straight? 'Oh, Father, is it really you?' I can hear Enid asking from the shelf above my head.

'Izzit?... Izzit?... Izzit?' says Kiki, in lieu of her mistress.

I sense Thomas looking at the books. He is surely proud of his daughter for having written about an Island of Adventure, a Circus of Adventure and a River of Adventure. Perhaps he has heard that there is a Castle, a Valley, a Mountain, a Sea and a Ship as well. What a lot of Adventures! And that's only a fraction of his daughter's literary adventure! If Thomas has any imagination – and he certainly does – he will realise we could be in a proper bookshop, or a public library, its shelves heaving with books written by Enid Blyton and only by Enid Blyton.

Thomas is standing at the door, smiling at me. So he doesn't disapprove of the bookworm standing on the rubber-topped stool. He doesn't want me to leave his daughter on the shelf and exit the shop. He acknowledges I have a right to be there. More than that, although he can see that I'm as easily intimidated as Noddy or Big-Ears, bless their cotton socks, he knows I'm not going anywhere until I'm good and ready. Nothing could stop me carrying on with this project. Just like nothing could stop Thomas's daughter from carrying on with her writing career. Just like nothing could stop Thomas from living his life to the full.

Enid tells an intense little episode in *The Story of My Life*. Her father collected birds' eggs, which he kept in a cabinet of little drawers, neatly arranged and labelled. One of the things Enid had to do to help him was climb trees and insert her hand into holes in branches to see if any bird's nest was there, and to feel for eggs. Perhaps I'm thinking of the story right now because of my own present position relative to collectables.

Anyway, Enid didn't like taking the eggs, even though her father never wanted more than one from each nest. He didn't know how scared she was putting her hand down into those small holes. Once she heard a hissing sound and was sure it was a snake. Her father dismissed that idea, and told his daughter that tits sometimes hissed when they were frightened. He urged her to put her hand in and feel if there were any eggs. Enid did as she was told, and put her hand into the hole, but it was shaking. How she hoped that her father was right. She prayed to God for it not to be an adder! Of course, it wasn't a snake. Her father was right and it was a tit's nest with lots of eggs. They felt warm and sweet under her hand and so did the sitting bird.

'You needn't take an egg,' said her father, bestowing the gift of life on a blue tit or a coal tit or whatever it was. 'Just tell me how many there are in case the number breaks the record of eggs in a tit's nest.'

Life is to be lived, reckoned Thomas Blyton, cut down in his prime at the age of fifty. But at least he lived that life to the full while he had the chance. I bet he was adding to his collection of life experience on the very day he dropped to the earth like a stone.

He's gone from the shop now. I stand rooted to the spot a little above the ground, plumb tuckered out after my long day trailing in the wake of the incredible Enid Blyton.

'Ye ken?'

Oh, God, what's coming now? I'm trembling on the stool like a bird in the hand, with another very different bird at my ear.

'Ye ken?'

If Kiki could only wait until I got home and regrouped.

'Ye ken whaur Enid bides?'

6

Four Find-Outers had been given their instructions. They were to rendezvous at 7 p.m. by the gates of Green Hedges. If Fatty wasn't there to meet them they were not – repeat, not – to wait for him, but to proceed to their destination so as not to waste valuable investigation time. Fatty would join them just as soon as he could.

'He's not here,' said Larry nervously.

'What can be keeping him?' said Daisy.

'Probably just finishing dinner,' suggested Pip. 'You know how much he likes his nosh. And on Thursday evening, Mrs Trotteville always serves shepherd's pie, Fatty's favourite. Shall we give him five minutes to deal with the second portion that he simply won't have been able to resist? Old Fatty wouldn't really want to be left out of a Mystery at this stage.'

'No,' said Bets. 'Fatty gave us our instructions, it's up to us to keep to them, because we've only got so much time.'

Nobody argued. They knew that Bets was right. As a group they walked gingerly towards the house. 'But, oh, where is our leader?' they all wondered. 'Where is marvellous Fatty?' wondered Bets most of all.

They paused on the floorboards when they reached the loggia, and as Larry crept towards the back door, Bets looked at the swing-seat on which Enid did her writing during summer months. But there was no sign of the writing process now. No pages, no typewriter. Perhaps she'd taken all her stuff indoors. After all, she and her husband were out to dinner that evening, so Fatty had reliably informed them. And she wouldn't have left any valuable manuscript outside, at the mercy of the wind, the neighbourhood cats and whatever prowler was stealing her signed first editions. Heavens – Bets was a prowler that night! And didn't it feel exciting.

Larry passed through the back door, which was unlocked, as Fatty had said it would be. He walked a few steps down the red-tiled hall, and passed into the first door on the right. This was Enid's lounge, where she wrote when she wasn't able to write outside. Larry entered the room and stood still. Daisy followed and stood by his side, her gaze taking in the whole room. Pip followed and had to step to the side in order to get a proper view of the place. My goodness there were vases of flowers everywhere, and the scent of roses. What a wonderful place to work! Bets had to push her way between Daisy and Pips before she had a view of the room, and it was then that she realised why the others were still standing so close to the door. A middle-aged woman was sitting in the big seat by the fireplace. She had a sheaf of papers in her hands, and it seemed she must have looked up from them as the group of children had entered the room. She'd visibly put her reading on hold, as she inspected each face in turn with sharp curiosity.

'Well, well, well, well, well! What have we here?' said the woman, slightly disappointing Bets. Because that's exactly what her own mother would have said in the circumstances. She'd somehow expected more from the world's most famous children's author.

'Are you Enid Blyton?' asked Larry, just to get some spurious initiative back. But damn Fatty, he was thinking. Fatty had promised they'd have the place to themselves.

'I am the owner of this private domain, yes. And you are?'

'Er... Larry Daykin.'

Larry left it at that. The imperious woman's eyes moved on to the next scared face.

'I'm Daisy. Larry's sister. We live in Peterswood.' Their host smiled, but her face lost none of the intense curiosity it was displaying. Slowly, the spider's eyes moved to the next fly caught in its web.

'Pip. Pi-pip. I'm... er... Pip,' said Pip.

'Pip or Pip-pip?' asked Enid, loving every moment.

'Pip, just Pi-pi-pip,' said Pip, wishing he could stop Pipping. 'Mrs Hilton's son.'

'Oh, yes, I know Mrs Hilton *very well*,' said Enid. Her eyes moved on to the fourth face, a pretty, younger version of Pip's. 'And you must be little *Bets*.' The woman's eyes lingered on Bets for a full five seconds to her embarrassment. Finally, the householder said to them all: 'I've seen each of you about the village, of course. But one never really *looks*, does one?'

Bets was looking now. Fatty had told her that when on a mystery it was important to keep one's cool in situations and to *really* look and to *really* listen. Enid Blyton was wearing a dark pleated skirt and white blouse and red cardigan, with a turquoise brooch at her neck. The shoes were neat and sensible. The only showy thing about her appearance was her scarlet nail varnish. Bets shivered, because the author's typing hands looked like bloodied claws. At that moment, she raised one talon to her face and scratched her cheek. To Bets surprise, no blood was drawn.

Keep looking, Bets told herself. Enid Blyton's nose was a little bulbous. And her brown eyes, small and alert, were deep-set within unevenly drooping lids. She radiated positive energy, though, and Bets had complete confidence in the essential good nature of the person who sat before them. Suddenly, Bets told Enid that she too wanted to be a writer when she grew up.

'Do you, child? And what makes you think you have the making of a writer in you?'

Bets told Enid that she was always making up stories herself. She would lie in bed every night until a new story had unfolded in her head. She hadn't even told her best friend Fatty about these night stories because she wasn't sure if they were any good.

'You must tell *somebody* your stories sooner or later, because finding an audience other than yourself is what being a writer is mostly about. It is also about persistence in the face of having no one else who will appreciate your work. You will find that many people will tell you that you are not a writer, even if you *have* got the makings of one inside you.'

Bets stared at Enid, soaking up the advice.

'When I was just a few years older than you are now, I was sending out stories every week. And these were always returned to me without any words of encouragement. My family wanted me to become a musician, because I had an aptitude for the piano. Which would have been a fine career for me, except that I couldn't compose music so I would have been trapped playing other people's compositions. And why should I be trapped in such a way when ideas for stories and poems were bubbling out of my head every day?'

'So what did you do?' asked Bets.

'In my reading, which was continual and wide-ranging, I came across a few words of wisdom. These: "We fail! But screw your courage to the sticking-place. And we'll not fail." Do you know who wrote these words?'

'You.'

'No, child,' said Enid, smiling. 'William Shakespeare wrote them. The lines are spoken by Lady MacBeth in the play called simply…

'*MacBeth*,' said Bets.

'Have you read it?'

'Is this a dagger I see before me?'

Enid smiled. 'Read it again as soon as you get the chance. Read anything and everything by Shakespeare, over and over again. Stories came very easily to his mind too. He came up with memorable sayings almost every time he put quill to paper. What a lucky man he was to have such a talent. And courage too. Do you think you have the talent?'

'I don't know,' said Bets, in all seriousness.

'The courage?'

'Oh, yes. At least, I think I've got the kind of courage you mean. Which I'd call stubbornness.'

Their host smiled and stood up. Bets remembered Enid Blyton as a slimmer woman than she was now. But she also remembered that one of the rules of life was that people did get stouter as they got older. Enid still went in a bit at the waist, but then her hips were imposing and her bust was large. The author's wiry hair was very dark brown, just a little flecked with grey. Was that right? Bets had no idea when people started to go grey. At 30… 40… 50 years old? Enid was 53 (Bets knew she simply had to remember the year and add three), so presumably it did make sense that the more Bets looked at the woman's hair, the more she noticed that it was streaked with grey.

Keep looking, thought Bets, as the others babbled away in an effort to explain their presence. Larry was talking about how they'd all been anxious to get her autograph, but didn't know how to go about it. Finally, they'd plucked up the courage to come along to Green Hedges and simply ask. There had been no answer at the front door. So they'd come to the back door, and, finding it unlocked, they'd take the liberty of… of… of… Larry seemed to lose confidence in his own pathetic story.

Suddenly the author bent from the waist, and placed her hands flat on the floor without bending her knees. It seemed she had a very supple body. With her head close to the floor, and her face out of view, Enid fired up the question: 'Do you know anything about a fat boy – your age, Larry – who keeps hanging around my house?'

'A fat boy?' said Larry, looking around at Daisy and Pip, all of whose eyes were suddenly scared on Fatty's behalf as well as their own.

'I believe he's known to the local policeman. When I mentioned to him that this fat boy had been hanging around Green Hedges, disturbing my concentration, he replied at length concerning – and I quote – "that toad of a fat boy". Indeed, he went on in such a torrent of "toad this" and "fat boy that", I wondered if I could make use of such a peculiar policeman in a book. And then I realised that I already *do* make full use of just such a policeman in my Mystery series!'

Enid straightened up, smiling broadly. Her face was red after her exertions. But apparently she wasn't finished doing her stretching exercises. She spread her legs slightly, planting both her feet just as firmly on the carpet of her lounge as before, bent down from the waist again, and this time rested her head on the carpet of the room. It really was the most extraordinary demonstration of suppleness, because the author was by no means short in the leg department. Bets only knew one other person who could rest his head on the floor like that, his back bent at such an angle...

'So none of you can tell me anything about the extraordinarily clever-looking fat boy who haunts Green Hedges?'

'Fatty!' shouted Bets, making the others turn around and stare at her in surprise. Was Bets giving Fatty away?

'It's *you*! Oh, it's *you*!' she went on.

When the others turned back to look at their host, it wasn't the formidable Enid Blyton they were sharing the room with, but Fatty, who was lying on the floor, laughing his head off.

'Oh, thank goodness for that,' he said, when he'd calmed down enough to talk. 'I kept thinking I would burst out laughing at your poor shocked faces. And that hopeless story you were trying to tell me, Larry... That's what all the bending down to the floor was about. It stopped you from seeing my face.'

Pip had sunk to the floor, his face buried in his hands in shock and relief. Larry and Daisy had pounced on Fatty, punching him not all that playfully. Bets was laughing as hard as Fatty, but at the same time was prodding his bosom and hips, investigating Fatty's brilliant disguise.

'The best bit is the nose,' said Fatty, 'although I did put on the putty in a hurry and when I caught sight of myself in the mirror just before you came in, I did feel I might have overdone the effect. What do you think?'

'Fatty you *are* Enid Blyton,' said Bets. 'And we hate you for it.'

'Honestly, Fatty. I nearly died of shame,' said Pip.

'Nonsense. I just woke you up a bit. And now that you are awake, I want you to look at this.'

Bets was skipping around the room. All these flowers! Vases and vases of roses, geraniums, carnations, hyacinths, lilies and types she didn't yet know the name of because she hadn't seen them before. All the blooms of summer, she supposed, from the garden of Green Hedges. Red roses mostly, but blue and yellow and orange and purple flowers also. 'What next, fat Enid?' she said when she'd finished her dance.

'You know the Adventure series?' asked Fatty.

'Kiki!' said Bets.

'I love *The Valley of Adventure*,' said Pip.

'I've read all five books so far,' said Larry.

'Me too,' said Daisy. 'Pity Jack and Philip get to do everything while Dinah and what's-her-name just tag along for the ride. Still, there's Kiki...'

'Shut the door, Pip. Wipe your feet, Pip-Pip. How many times have I told you to wipe your feet? Pip-Pip-Pip,' said Bets, making the others giggle.

'I still love the books,' admitted Daisy. 'Kiki is such a star.'

'Well, well, well, well, well... Pip, Pip, Pip, Pip, Pip,' said Bets skipping round the room again. Suddenly there were four parrots in the lounge of Green Hedges. Four parrots making an awful racket, and Fatty sitting like the Buddha in Enid Blyton's chair.

When his team had let off a little steam, Fatty spoke seriously: 'Now, as you can see if you look on the table, a sixth Adventure book is being written this very week. Title: *The Ship of Adventure*. And if any of you can think of anything more exciting than being in the room with such an unfinished manuscript, then you're a better Find-Outer than I am. If I'm not mistaken, Enid will have finished the book by tomorrow evening.'

Fatty had already been through the pile of paper and identified where the end of each day's writing came. He handed Monday's work to Bets, Tuesday's to Pip, Wednesday's to Daisy and Thursday's to Larry. His idea was that each of the Find-Outers read through a day's work so that they could put the book together later on that night.

'Coo!' said Pip, wondering if that could really be done.

'What about you, Fatty? You haven't got anything to do,' said Bets.

'*Au contraire*, Bets,' said Fatty.

What Fatty had to do was further explore the library next door. Earlier in the evening he'd found vases of red roses whose scent fought with the smell of stale cigar smoke. He'd found a big brown box of a television, which tried unsuccessfully to compete with the colourful array of books that covered the walls. He'd also found several significant gaps in the bookshelves where volumes had disappeared. Fatty had consulted many books, but had paid particular attention to books that had been signed or inscribed. For example, he'd taken a close look at the title page of the latest Five book, which was now committed to his photographic memory:

FIVE GET INTO TROUBLE

By
ENID BLYTON

Illustrated by Eileen Soper

To My Darling Husband
Can't wait to get into trouble with you.
come the summer holidays.

In fact, all the books in the Famous Five series were inscribed 'To My Darling Husband'. And each one was further inscribed in a punning way that had fairly caught Fatty's attention. The Find-Outer had committed these personal messages of Enid to his memory also:

Five on a Treasure Island ('You're welcome to my treasure any day.')

Five Go Adventuring Again ('You and I will go adventuring again come next Swanage.')

Five Run Away Together ('Run away to Swanage with me, my love.')

Five Go to Smuggler's Top ('Oh, Kenneth, darling.')

Five Go Off in a Caravan ('Can you imagine? Just the two of us!')

Five on Kirrin Island Again. ('It's my wildest dream, Kenneth.')

Five Go Off To Camp ('Bring your torch, dearest.')

As it happened, none of these books had been stolen. However, other equally precious volumes had disappeared. Who had been stealing such treasures from the library at

Green Hedges? Fatty now needed to work a little more pur-
posefully at coming up with an answer to that question.

As Fatty headed out of the lounge, he caught sight of himself in a mirror. A middle-aged woman with bright eyes and
a big nose rubbing her hands in scarlet-taloned glee. Crikey,
sometimes he even scared himself.

'I'm just going into the library,' he said to the rest of the
Find-Outers. But he couldn't resist adding, 'I may be gone
for some time.'

CHAPTER FIVE

IN AND AROUND SWANAGE

1

The train doesn't go all the way to Swanage. A ten-mile stretch of railway line – from the coast as far inland as Wareham – was removed a few years after Enid's death, perhaps to stop people doing exactly what Kate and I are doing today: following in the author's tracks.

When I planned the trip, I thought we could start exploring at this post-train stage. But I now realise that we need to get rid of our bags before we do anything else. The arrangement I've made to book in at the B&B around four o'clock now looks daft.

From the bus stop I phone Sunny Bay House. The landlady answers and I explain that we will be in Swanage earlier than planned, and would like to drop off the bags if possible. She offers to pick us up at the bus station so that we don't need to carry our bags up the hill. But I tell her that won't be necessary, and end the call.

'You turned down a lift?' asks Kate. 'We don't know how far it is from the bus station. And we could do with saving our energy for a proper explore this afternoon.'

True enough. So I phone again and accept the kind offer.

'Happy now?'

Well, Kate is happy, because our bus has arrived, bang on time. We get on board and dump our bags in the luggage rack and then

Kate disappears upstairs. I follow. But I'm not too relaxed about leaving our bags unaccompanied.

'Don't worry,' says Kate. 'We can watch as people get out.'

Sure enough we can do that. But then again, no one is going to interfere with our luggage. This is Enid Blyton's Dorset, for goodness' sake, where the people are as honest as the day is long.

'Look, that woman's got your bag on her back!' says Kate, from the window seat. 'You can wave goodbye to *Five Have a Mystery to Solve.*'

I peer over her shoulder. 'No, that's *your* bag she's scurrying off with. So there is absolutely no loss to literature to report and our holiday reading will proceed unaffected.'

As we approach Corfe, we get a view of the crumbling castle on top of its little green mound of a hill. It's an incredible landmark that appears and disappears as the bus winds up and down, left and right. But we get a better view of the castle once we're past it and hit a straight stretch of road. Unfortunately, this means us turning around and staring in the direction of a few youths sitting at the back of the bus. But, again, this is Dorset, so they're not intimidated, and there are no hostile remarks aimed at us. I settle down to gaze at the castle unselfconsciously. From this angle, the single remaining castle tower is on the right. Whereas when we were approaching Corfe from the north, the lofty bit was on the left. How is Kirrin Castle drawn by Eileen Soper? I try and conjure up a mental image. I think she has the stone tower on the left. What many people think is that Enid saw Corfe Castle and the hillock it sits upon, and she chose to move it wholesale, so that it sat – still sits, hopefully – in the middle of Swanage Bay.

Jill isn't there to pick us up. Yes, she is! She appears from a shop and points to her Peugeot, and up the steep hill we go, painlessly. At Sunny Bay House, Jill leaves us to settle in. The room is great. From the window there is a fine southerly view of the bay. So the ridge jutting out into the sea is the northern headland. Over that chalk ridge, out of sight, is Studland Bay and Poole Harbour, where *Five Have a Mystery to Solve* is largely set. As for the key location cluster for so many of the Five books: well, there's no sign of Kirrin Island with its castle, as yet. But give it time. Please, God, give it one full day.

Actually, Enid took years to put 'Kirrin' together. She admitted to a long-term correspondent that Kirrin Island in the Famous Five books was based on an island with a castle she'd seen on her honeymoon in the Channel Islands with Hugh in 1926. In 1931 she wrote about Corfe Castle in an issue of *Teacher's World*, following an excursion from Old Thatch to Bournemouth over Easter. However, the island and castle combination had only really come together in Enid's under-mind by 1942. So perhaps I'm being a bit optimistic expecting the finished article to emerge for me overnight.

I call Kate over and point out what is directly underneath the window. There are a dozen large carp slowly moving around a pool. A white one is enormous. And there is another with what looks like a helmet on its head, equally large. One of the smaller fish has lumps on its head and body. Some kind of illness perhaps. But that won't stop Kate and me loving it as much as we love its fellows.

Enid had a pond at Green Hedges. She mentions it in *The Story of My Life*. She named all the species of birds that refreshed themselves in its water and talked about one particular goldfish that didn't like them doing this. This special pet would butt the bigger birds on the leg, and knock against the beaks of sparrows and finches, telling them to get the hell out of its personal space.

Soon we're outside, strolling downhill towards the town centre. I check the charity shops for Blyton, but very quickly. The fact is, I've been there and done that. We buy some fish and chips to share and eat the steaming food – the batter on the fish is so piping hot that it might burn our fingers – on a wooden bench facing the sea.

Kate throws a chip to a herring gull, and we're immediately surrounded by open gullets. Any number of throats, screaming their hunger.

'What did you do that for?' I ask.

'I didn't mean to,' laughs Kate, 'because I knew this would happen.'

We walk along the shore then up the headland that we can see from our Swanage window. We're walking through yellow gorse much of the time. Kate is so tired that she lies down a couple of metres from the path. I am so tired that I lie down beside her. We were up too early this morning and haven't had enough sleep. We'd like to power-nap, but we know that's just not going to work in so public a spot. And it's just a degree or so too cool on this otherwise fine day.

Soon we're walking back towards town without having been to the top of the headland. What hopeless explorers! But while we're still on the north side of the bay we call in on the Grand Hotel. This is the place that wouldn't put Kate and me up at a cut-price rate, despite my Blyton credentials. But they're happy enough to serve afternoon tea to us as non-residents. A reviving pot of Earl Grey is brought to us as we sit in the reverentially quiet terrace overlooking the bay.

This seems like the right time to tell Kate about the Swanage of Enid Blyton. So that's what I begin to do: 'Enid first came to the town in the spring of 1940. She was accompanied by her daughters and they stayed at the Ship Inn.'

'What prompted the visit?'

'Previous annual holidays with Hugh had been spent in Scotland, or on the Isle of Wight. But the latter wasn't possible during wartime. Anyway, this wasn't a holiday with Hugh. He'd made the decision to leave his job with George Newnes and join the territorials, if you remember.'

'Silly man!'

'That's certainly what Enid thought. The whole thing about whether or not Goon is a real policeman may be a derogatory reference to Hugh in uniform, Hugh involved with the Home Guard – a real soldier?'

'So why did *she* go to Swanage with the girls?'

I don't know why she did, so we don't get bogged down in that. Instead I reveal that in the booklet *The Dorset Days of Enid Blyton*, Enid's daughter Gillian recalls visiting Corfe Castle. They travelled on the miniature railway but it doesn't run every day now, even in summer. We may have missed out on clambering over the castle. Luckily, Kate doesn't mind, she feels we've already got a handle on Corfe Castle via our double-decker bus ride. We both feel the process of moving a fortified island to Swanage Bay is well underway.

Enid went back to Swanage in the spring of 1941, where she had to stay in a boarding house because a bomb had fallen on the Ship Inn. Perhaps there was more enemy action during their holiday because Gillian says the family watched the Inn burn down. It was in this spring too that Enid was first introduced to Kenneth Darrell Waters, a virile 49-year-old and surgeon, while on a separate trip to Devon. According to Barbara Stoney, they were instantly attracted to each other. They were soon booking a hotel for overnight stays together in London, though he wasn't part of the Swanage trip that year. In the summer of 1942 the family came back to Swanage for the third year running and this time Kenneth *was* among the party.'

'Were they married by that time?' asks Kate.

'Enid got her divorce from Hugh in December 1942. It was made absolute in June the next year, by which time Kenneth was also free to remarry. The wedding actually took place in October 1943.'

'The change-over period took a while, then?'

'Depends how you look at it, and from whose point of view. Enid effectively transferred her loyalties from Hugh to Kenneth in the spring of 1941, though according to Enid's daughters it wasn't until a while later that Kenneth started to become a regular visitor to Green Hedges. However, Imogen and Gillian only knew about the marriage a few days before it happened, and both girls were upset to learn they'd never see their real father again. They hadn't seen him for over a year by then, so they must have been primed for such news.'

'It's hard to say whether Enid had their best interests in mind or not.'

'I think she did. But that's not the most important issue as far as I'm concerned.'

'What is?'

'The books.'

I explain to Kate that – for Enid – Swanage, Kenneth and the Famous Five were tied up as closely as Hugh and *The Zoo Book*: 'The first visit to Swanage was in spring 1940. The first meeting with Kenneth and the second visit to Swanage were in spring 1941. The first Famous Five book must have been written in the months after that, because it was published in September of 1942. So I'm intrigued by the thought that when Enid, Kenneth, Gillian, Imogen and chaperone Dorothy visited Swanage again in the summer of 1942, they may have had a proof copy of *Five on a Treasure Island* to hand.'

'Five in the party. I wonder who represented Timmy.'

'Newly beloved Kenneth, I reckon. Anyway, in July of 1943 the second Five book was published, just a few months before the October marriage.'

'Enid's wedding present to Kenneth?'

'Yeah, why not. From then on, year after year, the Darrell Waters came back to Swanage and stayed at the Grosvenor Hotel. And every year a Famous Five book was published in the summer or autumn.'

'Where's the Grosvenor Hotel?'

'Not far from our Sunny Bay House; that side of the bay anyway, though directly overlooking the beach. It was an ugly modernist high-rise according to Imogen, and has since been demolished.'

Jumping ahead about ten years and the same number of FFs, I tell Kate that in 1952 the family switched from the Grosvenor to the very Grand Hotel in which we sit. Imogen discusses the move in *A Childhood at Green Hedges*. One night during the annual holiday, the 16-year-old and Gillian joined a party – mostly comprised of students working in the hotel for the summer – for a late night swim and picnic on the rocks. When Enid found out about this, she was outraged that her daughters had been consorting with such low-life. And that was the end of the Grosvenor as far as the Darrell Waters family was concerned.

'What was her problem with the midnight swim?' asks Kate. 'That sort of thing happened all the time in the Malory Towers books.'

'A class hang-up, it looks like. Yet that same year she published *Five Have a Wonderful Time* where her fictional teenagers get pally with circus folk who are camping in the same field as they are. Though it's true to say that the circus folk give the Five a rough time, until ragamuffin Jo – a mutual friend – shows up and acts as bridge-maker.'

'Perhaps Enid was worried about the boy-girl thing too,' says Kate.

'Well, I think that's spot on. Imogen tells another story of how – when she was just about to follow her sister to St Andrew's University, so she'd have been seventeen – she was going out with a boy who also lived in Beaconsfield. Enid was not at all happy about the relationship, even though he was a respectable young man, very much of their own class. Imogen reports that she was meant to overhear her menopausal mother when she remarked to her stepfather: "Imogen thinks of nothing but boys now. Don't you think it is disgusting, Kenneth?"'

Kate's smile is a warm sight on the otherwise austere terrace.

'I don't think it is disgusting, Enid,' she calmly says to me. 'Sexual intercourse is the very thing that a girl needs before going up to university.'

It's my turn to smile in the glamorous spaciousness of the Grand. I'm glad Kate hasn't used her Scottish accent, though. But then why should she use that? Hugh is no longer in the picture.

Hugh was Enid's first love, and that relationship was naïve and romantic. Kenneth was a different kettle of fish. He was a sportsman and a surgeon, I keep reminding myself. Not the same doctor that dealt with Enid's underdeveloped uterus, but the link between the smooth working of her reproductive organs and the medical profession may have been in her mind. Certainly, it's there in mine and I try to sow the seed of such a notion in Kate's.

Together we build up a picture of Enid and consultant Kenneth in Swanage. The annual holiday being the one time that Enid took a break from her writing. According to Imogen, Kenneth was adamant that she went on holiday without her typewriter and had a rest from the usual routine. What did she fill her hours with instead? Well, they were both good swimmers and tennis players. After accompanying Kenneth around the golf course, Enid enthusiastically took up the game herself. And in the evening there were dances twice a week, a bridge drive, billiards and ping-pong. But after all that healthy exercise? In the privacy of their bedroom suite? Ah, that's the real question!

In passing I tell Kate about some of the Freudian slips that began to creep into Enid's work in the forties. At the end of *The Island of Adventure*, published in 1944, Philip's mother is given an enormous flask by the story's father figure, Bill Smugs. She takes it with a squeal, declaring that she's never seen such a giant. And in the following year, a *Sunny Story* called 'The Wonderful Torch' begins with the assertion that George was given a torch for his birthday. A lovely one, about eight inches long, which went on and off when he pushed the knob up and down.

Soon we are sharing a vision of a very different bed from the one shared by Binkle-Enid and Flip-Hugh. Indeed, according to our shared picture, Kenneth and Enid are going at it like porn stars in a room at the Grosvenor:

Me: 'How does that feel?'

Kate: 'Oh, Kenneth, It feels as if you're up to my throat.'

Me: 'Thorax, Enid, thorax.'

Kate: 'Oh, Kenneth, it feels as if you're up to my *thorax*.'

I wish that Kate hadn't said the word 'thorax' with quite so much relish. The word is bouncing off the windows. Our period reconstruction of goings-on at the Grosvenor is echoing around the Grand, here and now.

In due course, we walk back into town. We have a leisurely drink, but after that, it's supper we want, so we order soup and a pie. When we emerge it's dark outside, and just past nine o'clock. Back to our digs for an early night? Well, yes, but we'd better take some more alcohol with us. I ask a group of boys if they know of an off-licence, and they look blank. Stupid of me, they're obviously straight out of an Enid Blyton series. But one of them does offer directions, and sure enough there is a place that's open and it sells me a bottle of white wine. Next we have to negotiate the hill.

'Can't you phone for a *Peugeot*, Dunc?'

I tell her I can't.

'Why not?'

'Well, one reason is that my mobile was swallowed earlier on by a giant carp.'

Kate is not impressed by this answer. At least she replies: 'Duncan thinks of nothing but unfeasibly large fish now. Don't you think it is disgusting, Kenneth?'

But I am Kenneth, for present purposes, and I don't think it is disgusting. I think this stuff, discomfiting as it can be, is important to face head on. Almost everyone of Enid Blyton's generation was a victim of sexual repression. But I don't think Enid was a victim because she turned it, like so many other things in her life, to huge advantage in her writing. It's this I hope to demonstrate to Kate tomorrow.

We get right to the top of the hill before we realise we've lost our way. The shock clears my head sufficiently for me to find the street we're after. And there it stands as it did earlier in the day: Sunny Bay House.

Soon we're in bed. I could only manage a single glass of wine, sipped slowly as Kate undressed. Theoretically, I am ready for a decent night's kip. But I'm much too excited to settle for that.

'What about a story first?' asks my bed-mate. After all, wouldn't Kenneth and Enid have read stories to each other in their Swanage bedroom before getting down to it? Stories by you-know-who.

I establish that Kate wants a chapter from *A Story-Party at Green Hedges*, which I have in my suitcase library and which we dipped into on the train. It's a beautiful 1949 first edition of the book that I bought through the internet for £20, which tells of the story-party given by Enid in the rooms of her Beaconsfield mansion. It's got a transparent plastic cover protecting the dust-jacket that reminds Kate of a condom. With great pleasure and no little anticipation, I carefully open up the delicate object, and between us we choose 'The Teddy Bear's Tail'. We go for that one because it is sub-titled, *A Tale for Kenneth*. I try and follow Enid's bedtime story as I'm telling it...

The teddy bear was always grumbling about something. He wished he were a rubber ball that could bounce. But he wasn't, so he grumbled about this shortcoming. Then he wished he had a key and could be wound up. But he didn't have a key, and so he grumbled about not being able to be wound up like the clockwork mouse. Then he realised that he hadn't got a tail. He was amazed! Where on earth had his tail gone? The other toys assured him he had never had a tail but he wasn't happy about that. No, he wasn't at all happy about this 'no tail' business. Especially when the dog, the pink cat, the clockwork mouse and the monkey – who had the longest tail of all the toy animals – came out of the toy cupboard and proudly wagged their tails in his face. Eventually he grumbled about his tail-lessness so much that the golly decided to give him one.

'This is lovely,' Kate assures me. 'But if you were to open the window then the toy carp could hear the story as well. I'm sure they'd be fascinated to hear about the teddy bear who didn't have a tail. It would have them proudly swishing their own tails as they swam around the pond, listening to Enid and you.'

'Oh, they can hear me all right. They've fixed up my mobile using carp technology so that it works as a sort of intercom from here to the pond… You don't mind that our bedroom is bugged, do you?'

'I don't mind a bit if the room's bugged. As long as it's our friends the toy carp that have done the bugging.'

'Well, it is. Now can I carry on?'

'Mmmm. Please do.'

So I read on, following the story as I speak it aloud into the four corners of the room, the four corners of the pond.

Golly asked for a volunteer to donate a tail. The dog had been wagging his tail for a long time and intended to keep doing so for years to come, so no deal. Indeed, no toy would give up his or her pride and joy. Eventually the old toy kite, who couldn't fly anymore, said he would donate his tail as it was no longer any good to him. The golly took a look and was a bit dubious about the tail's suitability as it was made of paper twists tied onto a string. But the kite insisted. He suggested they didn't ask the bear's opinion about it and that they simply tie it on to the grumbly one's bottom when he was asleep. 'He's always grumbling about not having a tail. Well, let Grumble-Bum have this one!' insisted the toy kite. The other toys giggled. And at night, when the bear was fast asleep on his front, golly tied the long stringy tail with paper bits onto the furriest backside in the toy cupboard.

'I can hear the carp giggling outside. They're loving this!' Kate assures me. So I read on in the knowledge that I have my primary audience in the palm of my hand.

Next day, the bear wondered what the rustling noise was when he walked. When he found out, he was horrified. He hated his tail! The rustling noise was bad enough, but the tail kept getting tangled up in table-legs. It even tripped him up! Being tripped up by his own tail made him very angry indeed. But for all the bear's fury, he couldn't do anything about it. And none of the other toys would help him because he'd brought his plight upon himself. However, when the little boy who owned the toys discovered the teddy had got himself tangled up with the kite's tail – or so he thought – he took it off at once, much to the bear's relief.

'Shame,' says Kate, touching me under the covers. 'I liked it best when teddy had a tail. And so did the carp.'

I finish the story quickly.

'The toys teased the bear in such a way that the bear realised he needed to learn to be happy with what he had. He decided he wouldn't grumble any more about himself. And he didn't. He was a much friendlier bear from then on, popular with most of the other toys. But there was one type of toy he would not speak to, and that was THE TOY CARP IN THE POND.'

Kate scolds me for messing up the ending, and for spoiling the whole story for the fish. I put my arms round my partner and tell her I know a similar Blyton story about a teddy bear that wanted two tails, one front and one back, and who was always grumbling that he didn't even have a front tail.

Kate wants to hear the story. But not right now, because it is too late, too late for another story. Which is a pity because Kate admits the new story would no doubt have a few great lines in it. Like the bit where Enid – lying in a double-bed in her bugged suite at the Grosvenor in period Swanage – says by way of 'goodnight' to her second husband: 'Imogen's teddy thinks of nothing but having front and back tails, nowadays. Don't you think it is disgusting, Kenneth?'

Silence.

'Dunc?' says my partner, breaking into my train of thought.

'Mmmm.'

'Do you never stop working?'

'It's not really work. As a child Enid used to lie in bed entertaining herself with what she called night-stories. That's sort of what I'm doing at the moment. It's ridiculously easy.'

'Well, you can stop right now.'

And I stop telling myself a night-story. So that I might carry on with my analysis with renewed vigour in the morning.

2

Kate and I are sitting at the breakfast table as fresh as two daisies in spring. There is an array of individual packets of cereals spread over the far end of the table. A packet of one of them is fine to be going on with, but being in a hotel or a B&B triggers off an expectation of a full English breakfast in both of us. That's what we want!

Jill comes in. We order tea and full Dorset breakfasts. She comes in again shortly after that with the tea and some toast to be getting on with. She wonders if we had a good time yesterday and we assure her we did. I compliment her on her carp pond and she tells us that a fish went missing last year. When it's hot, and the carp are sexually active (for just a split second I wonder if our hostess is alluding to the noises she may have heard from our room last night), it's possible for the fish to jump right out of the pool. So perhaps – thinks Jill – it is connected with the disappearance of the biggest fish from the pond.

Well, that gives us something to mull over while we're eating the protein-rich part of our meal. After breakfast I go up to our room and lie on the bed. I intend to read from our Five book, but I can hear Jill and Kate talking down by the pool as our landlady feeds the fish and Kate smokes a roll-up, so it won't be easy. As it happens, *Five Have a Mystery to Solve* takes off in chapter six. Or is it because I'm reading it on my own today, with a well-rested mind?

Soon Kate and I are walking towards the cliff coastline. It's then that she gets a chance to fill me in properly on what Jill was telling her. Apparently, Jill was sunbathing in the garden last summer when suddenly there was a terrific splash. A large carp had jumped out of the pool and was writhing about in the middle of the lawn. Jill, covered in sun-tan lotion, had to try and deal with the two-foot fish which wriggled and slipped about in a most unmanagable way. But eventually she got the monster back into the pool. What a vivid picture I am getting! I stay with the two-footer for a moment before asking:

'So she thinks this is what may have happened when a fish disappeared?'

'Yes.'

'But the back garden has fencing all around it.'

'She thinks a fox could have dragged it away.'

'But no fox could have got it out of the garden. Foxes can't climb fences.'

'Perhaps there is a hole in the fence and the fox pulled the fish through the gap.'

'There are no gaps in the fence as far as I'm aware. And we do have a bird's eye view of the whole back garden from our window.'

We walk along the cliff path, a warm sea breeze in our faces. Then I speak again:

'Of course, another possible scenario is that one of the guests – someone like us – came back and stole one of the big, valuable fish, after checking out. What I mean is, having sussed the set-up from the view that is available from our room's window, he would know exactly where to park his vehicle and how to gain entry to the garden. Then all he'd have to do is catch the fish.'

'That wouldn't be easy to do in the dark,' says Kate.

'You saw them first thing this morning. Absolutely dead in the water! It takes the cold-blooded creatures much longer than us to wake up. From midnight they would be sitting ducks for anyone with a landing net.'

As we walk on, there is a bird singing its heart out. I look around until I spot the spirited songster, a blackbird. We're walking south today (although I think of it as west – towards Devon), our aim being to explore Tilly Whim caves. The Famous Five get involved with caves and tunnels in just about every book in the series, so to do some caving of our own in the area is a top priority this trip. Oh, we don't mean to do anything too adventurous. But we do at least intend to get underground.

We stop for a rest at a bench overlooking the cliff. Someone has placed a bunch of flowers there for some reason. The next bench on the coastal path also supports a floral tribute. This may or may not relate to the dedication on the bench which reads: 'GONE BUT NOT FORGOTTEN: John, a devoted father, Kori, beloved wife and friend, Suzie and Benji, canine companions, and Spike, finest of ferrets.' This reads like the cast of a series of Enid Blyton books I have not yet come across. A small bunch of tulips has been tied with raffia to each end of the bench but the tulips are drooping now – they've been there for a while. Kate and I sit down and it dawns on me what these tributes are all about. From here there is, in theory, a fine view of Kirrin Island to our left. The flowers are a tribute to Enid Blyton's imagination, to her Famous Five, and, in particular, to George's rock-solid island. Yes, I can see it all!

We keep walking and come across a funny little hut called 'Dolphin Shelter'. There's one high window and one low window. There is nothing to see through either window, except for blue sea in the distance – the sun glints off it – and sea birds flying through it. Gulls, fulmars, and suddenly what I take to be an Arctic skua. It dives so fast, like a bow in shape and like an arrow in speed.

At the back of the shelter is an information panel. A group of bottle-nosed dolphins called the Durlston Five are regularly seen in this stretch of coast. Their names are Nick, Bob, Lumpy, Spot and Echo. Kate chooses to tell me now that according to Jill, the carp in the pond is covered in cancerous lumps but that the cancer is not infectious and so Lumpy is left to swim around with the other fish. I'm processing this Sunny Bay info, as I stare at the poster of the Durlston Five, when a couple wander by and tell us to come out of the shelter and see some dolphins in real life.

Yes, there they are! Apparently a shoal of about a dozen bottle-nosed have been swimming about in the vicinity since early morning. Just shuffling backwards and forwards, as they play among themselves. As we walk on we feel we have dolphins for company, not to mention Kirrin Island. It is just a matter of looking for first one, then the other, because they're there all right!

Walking on, we come to Tilly Whim Caves. The entrance is fenced off and there is a warning for the public to keep out. I expected this but I have been told that if we just keep on walking we'll come to another entrance. This will also be blocked off but in fact the wall is perfectly climbable, and local youths and others certainly do enter the caves this way. We come across the wall from above, looking down on it just as we look down upon the carp pool from our room in Sunny Bay House. We're standing on top of the caves, as it were. I point out to Kate how we can scramble down to the wall, and then walk along the wall to the lower end of it, and jump off into the enclosed space in front of the cave.

Kate looks dubious. 'I'm not sure.'

I am sure. And I demonstrate just how easy it is to get from point A on the cliff top to point B in the mouth of the cave. In no time at all we are exploring the cave together. It's the result of quarrying from before Enid's time, so she would have seen this. Great hunks of rock have been pulled out, and the roof of the resulting cave consists of horizontal slabs of rock held up by enormous pillars of the self-same rock. It's dark and echoing inside. We explore all corners. There is no tunnel leading off, which is a shame. From the piles of small stones on the floor, it's obvious that there are roof falls from time to time, and of course it would only take a single stone falling from a few feet above head-height to cause devastating injury to a human skull. I put up the hood of my jacket. It serves as no real protection, but nevertheless I intend to keep it up all the time we are in the cave and encourage Kate to do the same.

We sit close to the entrance of the cave from where we can see Tilly Whim lighthouse just a hundred metres away. I think this is the precise setting for *Five Go To Demon's Rock*. I read that story quite fast, and I summarise it very quickly for Kate. Cave, tunnels, treasure. Mid-summary, we spot the dolphins again, still moving up and down in a solid group, half a dozen of them showing above water at any one time.

'It looks like they're wearing wetsuits,' says Kate.

I talk to my companion about the caving theme in the Famous Five books. (Wet caving sometimes, but never with the aid of wetsuits.) There are always tunnels. Torches are always being switched on, or being flashed around, as Julian, Dick, George and Anne pass through a series of underground passages in single file. 'Of course, it's all gynaecological,' I can't help adding. Indeed, I can't help concluding – though it may be a bit presumptuous – that the trauma of losing her father, whom she loved wholeheartedly, had an effect on Enid's sexual development.

'It doesn't usually work like that,' says Kate.

'I don't suppose it does. But Enid was an unusual child. Anyway, it is a fact that the grown-up Enid was worried about the condition of her intimate parts. Only after a thorough investigation and a series of hormone injections was the condition of her "underdeveloped uterus" successfully treated. Or perhaps the injections weren't the key thing because it wasn't until three years later that Gillian was born. Four years further down the line, Imogen popped out. Eight years after that, Enid's other children – those of her imagination – were exploring inside Mother Earth at every chance they got.'

After a pause, Kate asks thoughtfully: 'Is there really an exploring of caves and tunnels in every book?'

'Well, let's see. Book one, *Five on a Treasure Island*. Much exploration of dungeons and passageways under Kirrin Island. Next, *Five Go Adventuring Again*. A long dark tunnel is found which goes from the study in Kirrin Cottage to a room in Kirrin Farmhouse. Then, in *Five Run Away Together*, the Five are again in the tunnels and womb-like dungeons under Kirrin Island where they come across a little girl who's been kidnapped and imprisoned down below. Next, in *Five Go to Smuggler's Top*, the Five stay in a mansion on a hill which is riddled with a network of tunnels, indeed Timmy spends most of the book underground. Then, in *Five Go Off In a Caravan*, the children park their caravan right on top of the entrance to a tunnel which they later explore in great excitement. Next, in *Five on Kirrin Island Again*, well, that's the one where George's father gets imprisoned in a dungeon and Timmy manages to rescue his valuable papers and run with them through the fabulous tunnel that leads from Kirrin Island to the mainland. So, six out of six feature tunnels, big-time! I think it would also be close to twenty-one out of twenty-one if I could be bothered to go to the trouble of remembering all the books. Enid just couldn't stop exploring her own body through the creatures born of her imagination.'

'Is that how you see it?'

'Enid was absolutely fascinated by nature, whether it was the flowers in her garden that she filled her house with or the birds and plants she found in the wild and about which she wrote field-books, or her own body in all its mysterious conjunction with her furiously fertile mind.'

'Where does Kenneth fit in?'

'The Famous Five books are firmly based in Swanage. And for Enid, more than anything else, Swanage meant time spent with her second husband, a very physical man. Her holidays involved regular intimacy with him, while her children played happily in the sand or along the coastline. (In the summer of 1943, for example, Imogen was nearly 8 and Gillian 12. There's an undated picture of Imogen on the beach at Swanage perhaps a year or two later, looking just like Anne does in Eileen Soper's line drawings of the Five.) So Enid gets back to Green Hedges, pleased to be home even though she knows she's had just what she needed: a total break and relaxed sex. She gets the typewriter out of its cupboard and lets her imagination rip, completely unconscious of the link that exists between the sex she's been enjoying and those mysterious underground passages she feels compelled to write about. A couple of weeks later and – hey-presto! – another Famous Five romp ready for the printing presses.'

'Really?'

'I don't mean that quite literally, and because of the loss of her diaries and logs from the end of 1940 I don't know exactly when she wrote a given book. Perhaps she would feel like mentally revisiting Bourne End again straight after coming back from Swanage. Perhaps after two weeks in the company of Kenneth, her undermind would feel like spending a fortnight writing rude things about Hugh in the form of Goon. In which case, a Mystery would be the book she wrote immediately after Swanage. It's quite possible that the Famous Five books wouldn't be written until she was beginning to long for Swanage and seaside fornication again.'

Kate makes a circuit around the cave on her own. On her return, she makes the point that early books such as *The Book of Fairies* and *The Enchanted Wood* involve plenty of tunnels, caves and towers and that these were published when Enid was with Hugh.

'True. But the tunnels and passages in these early books are of a different kind to the later ones. Symbolic, perhaps, but in a nonsexual way. With no sensual or visceral aspect to the exploration that the very young or non-human protagonists make.'

Kate takes her glove off and rubs the roof of the cave at a place where the cave is just six feet from the floor.

I carry on: 'However, it is also true that Enid was beginning to write the kind of book that involved adolescents exploring passages and tunnels in the late thirties. In *The Treasure Hunters*, published in 1940, three children plus Rags the dog are involved in a story that involves them going down into a hole, finding treasure there and being pursued by villains. And in *The Children of Kidillin*, also published in 1940, four children and a dog called Paddy go down a pot-hole, and in the heart of a Scottish mountain find evidence of the activities of a couple of German spies. Perhaps the best example of the tunnel theme, pre-Kenneth, is *The Secret of Spiggy Holes*. In that book, the same set of children who made a life on a secret island in the first book in that series, find a secret passage that allows them to move between key locations on the Cornish coast. The secret passage allows them to escape danger on a couple of occasions, though it's their flight to the secret island of the earlier book that ultimately foils the kidnappers.'

'So how does your theory account for the existence of these books?'

I shrug. 'Enid was still developing in the late thirties, as a person as well as a writer. And as the relationship with Hugh began to break up, she may have felt on some level the urge to express something she was longing for, that is, a more rewarding physical relationship with a fellow human being.'

'Was there no one else in that period?' asks Kate, still rubbing her palm against the rock.

'Perhaps there was. The nurse Dorothy Richards entered Enid's life at the birth of Imogen, and it has been suggested that there may have been a sexual relationship between them. Imogen, in her book, refutes the idea, but she was only eight when the friendship between the women finished shortly after Enid's marriage to Kenneth (though a less intense friendship resurfaced years later). Dorothy did not attend the wedding ceremony.'

'Was this marriage the reason Enid and Dorothy's friendship fell apart?'

'Well, ostensibly not. Barbara Stoney recounts how, in 1942, some members of Dorothy's family, who'd been bombed out of their London home, were invited to stay at Green Hedges. But Enid soon changed her mind about this hospitality when the presence of so many additional people severely disrupted her writing routine. She was rude to her guests and they left Green Hedges after only a few days. Apparently, she was unrepentant when confronted by Dorothy about her behaviour.'

'Perhaps one or other of them used it as an excuse to break up their affair. Was Dorothy Richards a lesbian? Did she go on to have affairs with other women? Did she marry?'

'I don't know, I haven't followed that up. I plan to write a book called *Looking For Enid*, about the influence of the men in her life. Somebody else – perhaps someone who's particularly interested in those books set at girls' boarding schools – can write a book investigating the impact of Theresa Blyton, Mabel Attenborough and Dorothy Richards on Enid's life and work.'

'*Looking For Enid*, by Kate Clayton.'

I can't help smiling. 'I would love to read your book.'

'If only it would write itself.'

As we walk on, I tell Kate about a sad incident in Kenneth and Enid's married life. Enid miscarried their baby in 1945 or 1946. It was in 1945, according to Barbara Stoney, who states that Enid found out she was pregnant in the early spring of that year and miscarried five months later, after a fall.'

'She says "early spring" and then "five months later".'

'Yes, it's a curious way of giving a date. Imogen claims the miscarriage was in 1946, and that the fall took place at Easter of that year. Apparently, she shares the memory with Doris Cox, who only joined Green Hedges as parlour-maid in February 1946, and has gone on to be a life-long friend.'

'Which date is correct?'

'I don't know. I trust Barbara Stoney as a biographer. But her book came out in 1974. Imogen's version of events appeared in 1989. Stoney refers to its existence in a postscript chapter added to the second edition of her book, but doesn't make any changes as a result, which would suggest Stoney was sticking to her 1945 date. Then, in an article published in the *Enid Blyton Society Journal* in 1996, Doris Cox refers to coming to Green Hedges for an interview on 13 February 1946, which would seem to back up Imogen's dates.'

'Does it matter?'

'Well, first let me tell you what happened, whether it was in August 1945 or April 1946. The Darrell Waters kept apples in a loft above the garage at Green Hedges. Enid went to fetch some in a wooden basket. She took Imogen with her because Kenneth had banned her from climbing ladders while she was pregnant. But when they got to the garage, Enid did the climbing after all. Half-way up she gave a cry and fell down onto the concrete floor. Imogen fled to the garden where she cried for some time before creeping back to the house.'

'Oh, great.'

'Yeah, I know what you mean. Meanwhile someone else had found Enid and helped her into the house. And so when Imogen entered Green Hedges again her mother was lying on the sofa in the lounge with a rug on top of her. Enid was taken to hospital, and soon came back her usual cheery self. But the baby was lost.'

'Sad about Imogen's behaviour.'

'Yeah, poor kid. But sad all round. As far as the date thing is concerned – it does matter, I think. I mean, Enid's books are facets of herself, as she said. I feel the miscarriage – or the pregnancy – might have fed into the Famous Five books, consolidating the underground tunnel theme. The third adventure, which features a young child found in the womb-like dungeon in the depths of Kirrin Island, was published in October 1944.'

Kate looks thoughtful, then suggests: 'Too soon to be affected by the miscarriage or the pregnancy itself.'

'True. Though perhaps she was already thinking about having a child with Kenneth by then. After all there wasn't much time to be lost, she was 47 in 1944. But in any case the fourth book, *Five on Smuggler's Top*, which has Timmy trapped in tunnels in the body of a hill for much of the story, was published in October 1945. Let's say there was six months between the delivery of a manuscript and its publication; that implies that the pregnancy – not the miscarriage – might have fed into the writing process.'

'Assuming Barbara Stoney's dates to be the correct ones.'

'That's right. The next Five book, *Five Go Off in a Caravan*, published in November of 1946, does have its underground exploration, but it has a far lighter feel to it. Assuming Stoney's dates, Enid might have written *Caravan* a few months after the miscarriage. Assuming Imogen's dates, she would only just have miscarried, which doesn't feel right to me. In the *Caravan* book there are bags of treasure hidden deep in the hillside, including gold-plate, a diamond tiara, and a china vase that looked so fragile it might be broken by a breath of air. And as I said that book has a lighter, more celebratory feel about it.'

'A pregnancy book?'

'Yeah, why not. And if you assume for the moment that Imogen's dates are correct after all, and that there was a full year between writing and publication, which I've been told is typical, that would place the writing of *Five Go Off in a Caravan* at the early stages of the pregnancy.'

'Can't you find out which dates are correct?'

'The logs in which Enid recorded details of her day-to-day writing were destroyed by Kenneth. Her diaries went the same way. I suppose I could ask either Barbara Stoney or Imogen Smallwood what evidence they have for their respective views. But to get an answer I'd have to explain to them what I'm doing. That might be tricky. Also it would interrupt the creative process I'm engaged in. I think I'll settle for the bigger picture. And part of that bigger picture is this... Whether it's the biographer or the daughter who's got the dates right about Enid's late pregnancy, and whether the time between the writing of a Five and its publication was six months or a year, the next Famous Five book, *Five on Kirrin Island Again*, was written between four and eighteen months after the miscarriage. To me that makes sense in that the book is more serious, a working-through of deep-seated anxieties. It's not a shining treasure that's underground, instead it's something to do with the wisdom of Enid's father. It's a wider and darker consideration of the parent-child relationship, which ends triumphantly. And that book is the only Famous Five title that's dedicated to anyone.'

'Who's it dedicated to?' asks Kate, quietly.

'The daughters she didn't miscarry: Gillian and Imogen.'

We leave it there, and we walk on arm in arm. The lighthouse is much less interesting close up than it is as a symbol of the light-house in *Five Go To Demon's Rock*. Besides, it's private, and you can't get into the structure itself. So we don't linger. Further on, we're still walking along the coastal path. There is a strong scent as we pass through gorse. And a sniff of the yellow flowers confirms what young Anne says in *Five Have a Mystery To Solve*, that the yellow gorse smells of coconut. It did fifty years ago on Studland Golf Course, a few miles north of this stretch of coast, and it does right here and now.

We keep walking until we come to a secluded spot where we can eat the bananas and oranges we've brought with us from the breakfast table. Also we need to have a rest after having walked for a couple of hours. No, it's more than that, it's mid-afternoon! So we lie down on soft grass studded with dandelions. I'm trying to remember the very best example of Enid and her secret passageways. It's in *Five on a Secret Trail*, which is from 1956, when Enid was staying at the Grand. I think it through in as much detail as I can, then I put the case to my chum, but first I check that she wants to hear about it.

'Sure. I'm fascinated.'

'The Five are involved in an archaeological adventure close to Kirrin Cottage, and are on the hunt for a secret way into the earth. They think the secret way is behind a stone slab, but they just can't move the hefty stone. There is a spring just behind the slab and they get wet trying to move it. More splashing about, but the stone slab finally moves a little. They carry on tugging, pulling, panting and puffing. They need more appropriate tools. Their new friend Harry assures the Five that he has the right tools with him. He comes back with his tool-bag and Julian gets stuck in with a big jemmy-like tool.'

'Is that Enid's phrase?' asks Kate, turning her head towards me.

'Yes. Basically what I'm recalling is the bits I highlighted with a yellow marker in my copy of the book. In fact, it was after marking up the passages that I realised I would have to be careful not to quote too much from them in my own manuscript, as I'm not certain I can get permission from the copyright owner to quote at length.'

'Why not?'

'My book will be very pro-Enid. But it will also be very much out there. I would like to think that Chorion Ltd – who have bought the rights to Blyton's literary estate, the books and stories anyway – would wholeheartedly support what I believe is going to be a serious and worthwhile study of Enid Blyton, a book which champions her as a unique creative phenomenon. But I can't assume that that will be their perspective.'

'And will it work for you – only using the odd actual quotation?'

'Sure. I only really want to paraphrase the books. Enid was a brilliant writer, but not so much on a line-by-line basis. She just used sentences to efficiently record the film she was watching on her own private cinema screen, if you see what I mean.'

'Mmm, I think so. So get back to the story, please.'

I see my way back to the white pages with their yellow high-lights, or rather to the sequence of events they've left me with: 'Soon the stone is prised out of the bank, and falls into the water channel. The Five stare into the exposed opening. Julian confirms there is a big hole there. He gets his torch out and shines it into the gap. The tunnel widens out behind the entrance. Everyone is too thrilled for words. Faces are glowing, eyes are shining. George gives Dick a friendly punch. Anne pats Timmy on the head so hard that he whines. Dick reckons they'll have to make the hole a bit wider before they can get down it.'

'Dick would!'

'George's eyes are shining at the prospect of exploring the juicy hole.'

'Does Enid use the word juicy?'

'Can't remember. I'll try and stick to the facts.'

'They don't need embroidering,' says Kate, who tells me that the story is resonating in her mind. Presumably, she means it's oscillat-ing in her imagination between gynaecological operation and sex-ual adventure, just as it is in mine.

'The next chapter is called "The Secret Way". All the children are jostling for position at the entrance to the tunnel. Julian makes them stand back and he alone applies himself to making the entrance wider with a tool. Ha! Even Julian, the biggest of the boys, can get in now. He stands panting, smiling broadly, tool in hand.'

'I bet Enid doesn't say that he stands there, tool in hand!'

'Sorry, can't stop the flow of the story... Julian insists he should go in first. He wants to know if everyone has a torch in hand because a working torch will be needed – after all it is pitch-dark in that tunnel! George follows Julian, then Anne, then Dick...'

'What about Timmy?'

'Timmy is with George, of course, pushing and shoving like the rest. Everyone is excited and no one can talk in a normal voice.'

The highlighted quotations spring to mind. I really can't resist using them; after all they're just one-liners. Besides, Kate wants me to tell it how it is:

'"One good shove and you're in."

"I say – isn't it dark!"

"Timmy, don't butt me from behind like that."

"What size of rabbit do you think made this burrow?"

"What a crawl! I feel like a fox going into its den."'

Kate and I are lying together, spoon-like, a couple of metres from the edge of the lush ledge we're resting on, high above the waves that I can see out of the corner of my eye. What a curious day this has turned into, full of mystery and adventure, bird flight and dolphin dive, sensual ease and literary exploration.

I nod off, thinking about Enid and Kenneth loving each other, both before the miscarriage and afterwards. Or I nearly nod off. Kate brings me back to planet earth with a question. But she'll have to repeat it if she wants an answer.

'What did the Five find in the tunnel that they had so much trouble gaining access to?'

Oh, yes, they found something, all right. What was it again?

'They found a leather bag that they couldn't open. So they took the bag back to Kirrin and a police inspector opened it for them with his – now let me get this right – small, strong-looking tool.'

'Couldn't Julian have opened the bag with his big jemmy-like tool?'

'Perhaps he could have, if he'd persisted.'

'OK, so the inspector got in there thanks to his small, strong-looking thingy. What did he find?'

'It was empty.'

'EMPTY?' shouts Kate, loud enough to disturb any cliff creatures that happen to be still napping.

'But the policeman, give him his due, poked around and found that there *was* something hidden under the lining. So he slit it open with a knife.'

'Oh, dear! That's a bit surgical.'

'But worth it, because under the membrane-like lining were blueprints. Scientific papers that George's father was then asked to go down to the police station and look at. To his astonishment, he recognised the blueprints as the only copies of originals he had in his own safe!'

'I don't understand. Nor do the dolphins. Explain!'

'What is there to explain? It's just a huge coincidence.'

'Set it out in plain English. For the sake of the slowest of the swimmers.'

'The safe of a colleague of George's father had been burgled and the papers – copies of George's father's own ones – had been stolen. Somehow these had found their way into an underground hole just a stone's throw from Kirrin Cottage… It doesn't make much sense, does it?'

'Why not just make it Quentin's papers themselves that had been stolen?'

'I think Enid would have been conscious that George's father's papers had been stolen a few times already over the years, which is significant in itself.'

Kate is silent.

I tell her about the earlier book, *Five on Kirrin Island Again*. That's the key Five text in some ways. George's father has been working on his scientific research at the end of the tunnel that no one knows exists and which links George's island with the mainland. I explain to Kate that while taking the air at Loch Clunie, I made a leap from George's father's island dungeon to Enid's father's island library. And I explain how I got from there to Enid writing book after book to make sure her father had the best underground library in the world.

So Enid wrote. She even had enough about her to marry and raise children of her own while she got on with her mission in life. Then Hugh did the same thing to Enid's children as her father did to her.

Kate interrupts: 'But didn't she want Hugh to leave, and want to *stop* him from seeing the girls?'

'Yes, perhaps; that's a complicated one. For years Enid did not want Hugh to get ill, or opt out, or leave, and tried hard to make the family work. I think she only wanted Hugh to stay away once she had established "Uncle Kenneth" as a surrogate father, someone who could and did take over the father's role for her daughters from the day of their marriage in 1943.'

'OK,' says Kate, still thinking about it.

I realise there's more to say about these Famous Five books, something that's just crystallising for me right now. I try and keep Kate abreast of where I'm heading:

'Quentin is George's father. He is also the uncle of Julian, Dick and Anne. The words "Uncle Quentin" keep coming up at the start of the first book and in several books after that. Now as it happens, when Enid started inviting Kenneth Darrell Waters to Green Hedges, the girls called him Uncle Quentin.'

'Uncle Quentin?'

'Sorry, I mean Uncle Kenneth. The connection isn't that close! Now the first Five book was published in September 1942. Enid would have probably been writing it somewhere around September of 1941...'

'Was Kenneth referred to as "Uncle" by that stage?'

'As with the miscarriage, there's a discrepancy in the records. It depends which of the daughters has got it right. According to Gillian, who, as the 10- or 11-year-old, should have the more reliable memory, Kenneth didn't come to dinner until the late spring of 1942, when he would have been introduced to the girls as "Uncle Kenneth". But according to Imogen, the visits started before the autumn of 1941. Also, she has what she describes as a persistent and strange recollection of "Uncle Kenneth" wanting to join the Home Guard and wishing to get Hugh's advice on the matter. But as Hugh didn't leave the country until June 1942, that doesn't help me to date events.'

Kate considers this: 'Even if Gillian was right and Kenneth didn't really start coming to Green Hedges until late spring of that year, he may well have just turned up on the odd special occasion. At Christmas or New Year or on Enid's birthday. So with these dates I can quite believe in "Uncle Kenneth" coinciding with the Uncle Quentin business... But did Imogen and Gillian not have other uncles? Would the term "Uncle" have been bandied about quite a lot at Green Hedges?'

'I don't think it would have been. Enid wasn't in touch with either of her brothers then. Visits to Hugh's family would have been annual affairs at most, though Hugh did have a brother who subsequently told Gillian that Enid did have a lot of trouble with Hugh's heavy drinking around 1940... Anyway, it's clear that Uncle Quentin and his relation to Anne, Julian and Dick echoes the relationship between Kenneth and Enid's daughters. This was an important structure in the author's life and an important structure in her new book. Quentin is described as tall, with an aversion to noise – that is, the complete opposite of Kenneth who was on the short side and very hard of hearing. That's Enid covering her tracks, whether subconsciously or not. More significant perhaps is that both Quentin and Kenneth have rather a strained relationship with the youngsters. In Kenneth's case it is because of his partial deafness (he could hear Enid's pellucid voice all right). In Quentin's case it is because of the noise-irritation thing.'

'If I remember rightly, Uncle Quentin's main contribution is to scowl and urge the children to keep quiet or, better still, to get out of the house.'

'Yes, that's pretty much it. But Quentin, like Fatty in the Mysteries, is playing a double role. Quentin sometimes personifies Enid's father, sometimes Kenneth.'

'Enid's father? When?'

'Quentin is Enid's father when he relates to George. That George is based on Enid is certain. She admitted it to her foreign agent. Also, in *The Story of My Life*, there is a line illustration of George and Timmy placed side by side with a near-identical photograph of Enid and her dog, Laddie. The juxtaposition is clearly deliberate and this is in a book the very personal nature of which means that the illustrations would certainly have been decided by Enid herself. The images strongly suggest – though stopping short of crassly saying: "I am George and George is me".'

'She doesn't actually say it, then?'

'No. But the text at that point is admitting that George is based on a character in real life, a girl who is grown up now. A girl who was stubborn, bold, hot-tempered and loyal.'

'That's our Enid! And subtle too.'

'All the stuff about Quentin being a scientist, with important secrets that need to be saved is Enid writing about Quentin as a symbol of wise Thomas Blyton, whereas Quentin stands for Kenneth when he relates to Anne, Julian and Dick, who in turn are a version of Gillian and Imogen. When the children are playing in the tunnels, what is Uncle Quentin doing? Well, Quentin is married to Fanny. And when the children are out playing, they have Kirrin Cottage to their adult selves.'

'Not quite to themselves. Don't forget the cook who has sent the Five out with a packed lunch,' says Kate.

'Yes, Fanny – that's grown-up Enid – might have to keep the noise down in order not to upset the cook. One way of looking at all the running up and down of tunnels that the Five do is to take it as a metaphor for what Quentin and Fanny are getting up to in Kirrin Cottage.'

'Or what Enid and Kenneth are getting up to in the hotel while Imogen and Gillian are playing on the beach.'

'Exactly.'

'Kirrin Cottage is quite a complex set-up, then,' says Kate, tentatively. 'There are really two families living there at the same time. There's the old Beckenham family: Enid and her parents. And as well as that there's the new Beaconsfield family: Kenneth, Enid and the girls.'

'That's right. Uncle Quentin, Fanny and Julian-Dick-Anne are Kenneth, Enid and Gillian-Imogen. That's one household. Simultaneously, Uncle Quentin, Fanny and George are Enid's father, her mother and Enid herself. That's the second household. And with Kenneth free of his Uncle Quentin duties, as it were, I feel Timmy, George's sensual companion, the main digger out of tunnels, the main explorer underground, is good old Kenneth.'

'Phew. Can Kenneth be in two places at once?'

'Of course he can, in Enid's infinitely flexible imagination! Kenneth can play the role of two characters; moreover Enid's main character can slip between her childhood self, with her main relationship with her father, and her adult self, where the main relationship is with her lover.'

'Phew, again.'

'Hugh again? Well, not quite, there's no anagram this time. But there are many lines like this one in *Five Go Adventuring Again* where George thinks: "Nobody could possibly know how much she loved Timothy."'

Kate looks thoughtful.

'Of course in the first book George makes the relationship clear

THIS IS HER
KENNETH

He suddenly bent down.

when she tells her cousins that Timothy is her greatest friend and that she couldn't do without him. The cousins haven't met Timothy at that stage. "Who in the world can Timothy be?" wonders Julian, some kind of fisher-boy?'

'Some kind of surgeon?' says Kate, catching on fast.

'That's why Enid loved writing about Kirrin. She was writing about *the* essential elements of her own life. And as for where Julian, Dick and Anne normally lived when they were not on holiday with George, that's supposed to be London in the first book. But I don't think Enid was comfortable with that. So in the first chapter of *Five Go Off in a Caravan*, which has the Five starting off from the family home of Julian, Dick and Anne, it is quite obviously in the countryside. I would say Beaconsfield, although Enid was at pains not to say that.'

So where are *we*? Lying on this grassy ledge near the top of a cliff, in a cocoon of concentration. In order to press on, let me recap where we've got to.'

'Enid's definitely still brooding about the Hugh business when Kenneth comes along. Enid is as bowled over by him as she was by her father, though in a different way. And that's when the whole library project starts in earnest. That's when she's writing a Five book *for* Kenneth, about adolescents and a dog, a Mystery book *against* Hugh, about adolescents and Goon, and twenty-odd other books a year. All for her father's library. That's when her passionate attachment to three separate men drives her on.'

'The dolphins are listening.'

'From the spring of 1941 onwards: Kenneth lights up Enid with his wonderful torch. Autumn 1942: the publication of *Five on a Treasure Island* which climaxes with the rescuing of gold, that most precious of natural elements, from the dungeons underground on Kirrin Island. Summer of 1943: Kenneth pours tea for Enid from his formidable flask as they both enjoy reading the newly published *Five Go Adventuring Again*. In that book, the Five discover a tunnel from Kirrin Cottage to Kirrin Farmhouse. They explore the tunnel – Timmy leading the way – grab George's father's precious papers, and run back to base where they reinstate them in George's father's study. From the mid-forties, Kenneth and Enid come to Swanage with the girls every year, and they also come on their own in the summer and autumn. Why? So that they, the adults, can have an even fuller and franker sexual relationship.'

'YOU say.'

'Certainly, I do! More fresh Five books are most definitely the result, but it wasn't until 1947 and the publication of *Five on Kirrin Island Again* that the union between Kenneth and Enid bears its ripest fruit. Only then does Enid manage to write about the tunnel that goes between the mainland and Kirrin Island. Turns out that an undeveloped uterus was only part of her problem. The vagina was in altogether the wrong place!'

'Eh?' says Kate, determined not to let me get away with anything obscure.

'Look, I know that on one level this is speculation. I can't prove these things, exactly. But just bear with me and see how convinced you are by where we end up.'

'Go on, then, Professor.'

'I think that Kenneth straightened things out for Enid, sexually. He got Enid's psychic tubes all linked up the way they should be. Everything was in excellent working order, and Enid is over the moon about that on a nightly basis. Any pain from the desertion she felt at adolescence, and again when Hugh and she messed things up, has been transformed into pleasure with another man. "Woof!" Actually, the pain had long been turned into literary productivity. But now it's turned into personal ecstasy as well. "Woof! Woof!"'

'What about the miscarriage?'

'I'm assuming that was just a blip in their happiness. From the development of the books, I've no reason to suppose that the misfortune had a permanent impact on the relationship between Kenneth and Enid.'

Kate nods.

'In effect, what was on a number of occasions deposited in Enid's fictional tunnel was male secrets, the spark of life, written by her altar ego's father, rescued by her altar ego's animal companion.'

'The dolphins need to hear that bit again.'

'In several of the books – notably *Five Go Adventuring Again, Five on Kirrin Island Again, Five on a Secret Trail* – the scientific secrets of George's father are taken up a tunnel. In these books, the father's wisdom – his personality, his passion – is taken up a tunnel and deposited in a womb-like place. And it takes Enid – or the teenage characters she's created, or the dog that symbolises her beloved – to search out the wisdom and expose it to the outside world.'

'Giving birth to it as books?'

'Yes, on one level. But where does the wisdom come from originally? It comes from the mind of Enid's father or from the tower that George's father erects on Kirrin Island in book six, or from the lighthouse in *Demon's Rock* which was situated directly above a tunnel into the earth.'

'Tower and tunnel?'

'Phallic and vulvic symbols. But listen: what are these important secrets all about? What is the wisdom in question? Well, in one of the early books, George tells the rest of the Five that her father is working on an invention that will give free energy to the world! Now what is it that could give the world free energy?'

'Nuclear power?'

'I don't think so! Try again. Keep it simple to start with but allow it to become an Oedipus complex! Enid and her father, a love gone wrong. Then Enid and Kenneth in a Swanage bedroom. Or, if you prefer, Quentin and Fanny in Kirrin Cottage. Or, if you must, George and Timmy running together in a tunnel. Visualise!'

Kate is visualising. I help her by stroking her arm.

'PEOPLE POWER!' she shouts.

After her shout, Kate lapses into silence.

'The key to the future is us. Thanks to our parents' forethought. Thanks to our sexual partners. Thanks to our children, real and imagined.'

'Sexual healing!' says Kate, smiling.

'The saviour of the planet is going to be the human race. All we need to do is to remember to love one another. Enid's father knew this. And he made sure the knowledge was passed on to Enid. Enid in turn has passed it on to us in the most scintillating way.'

'The dolphins are loving this. But they've had enough for now. They've swum out from the coast to deeper, cooler water to mull things over.'

That's fine by me, because right now I've got nothing more to give.

3

By the time we get back into Swanage, we are starving, but we've got our evening meal all worked out: we'll go to the Indian restaurant on the High Street and have a coconut-orientated feast. That is, we'll have lamb or chicken korma with coconut rice and a couple of vegetable dishes.

And that is exactly what we do. Happily, we don't order too much. Just the right amount, fringed with the yellow flowers that we've pinched from the prickly branches of gorse. What pretty platefuls of food we're eating! What a lovely smell of coconut and Tiger beer throughout! So that when we step out of the restaurant, we feel mellow fellows, the both of us.

It's dark. There are lights on in the town, but the headland at the northern flank of Swanage beach is invisible now. What was a prominent landmark during the day has now merged with the night. Sky and land as one dark mass. Despite the dark, there is activity on the beach. A squad of young men are training. Sprints then push-ups, then more sprints, then more exercises on the spot. Also, there are a couple of school parties on the beach. And plenty of people strolling arm-in-arm, as we're doing. At nine o'clock on a weekday evening at the beginning of August? What's going on? My theory is that it's the effect of the island. People are attracted to the sea-front at Swanage as it's as close as they can get to Kirrin Island, which is right now being continuously circled by dolphins. Kate and I decide to walk all the way along the beach, at one with the school of bottle-nosed islanders.

The last Five book comes to mind. Perhaps because it features one last trip to Kirrin Island which takes place at night. Most of the book takes place in a house in Big Hollow – not Kirrin, which is just a bus ride away. The Five are concerned about valuable scientific papers, which are at risk of being stolen – by circus folk – from their friend Tinker's father, who has stored them in his vulnerable tower laboratory. Why not Uncle Quentin's tower? Well, Kenneth is in his early seventies by this time, so perhaps Enid needs to look elsewhere for her phallic symbols.

The Five decide to hide these papers on Kirrin Island. But George feels really rather territorial about the island, so she gets up in the middle of the night – before she and the others are scheduled to – and makes the night journey alone to Kirrin. Well, when I say alone, she is of course accompanied by the ever-young, ever-lithe Timmy. George is scared by the lights of oncoming cars and urges Timmy to stay on her left. He obeys, and without too much trouble she gets to Kirrin in two pieces: herself and her animal mate.

Kate and I stop and look out into the bay. Only when I spot the island (first you bring it to mind by an effort of imagination, then you just relax, and after a few seconds you check that it's still there...) do I continue my description of the book:

'The sea is dark, as now. And the island is an even darker patch.

Then George spots a light on her island. She's furious that someone has had the audacity to trespass there of all places. She stuffs the papers under the tarpaulin cover of a fishing boat where they'll be safe enough, then gets her own boat into the water and rows off to Kirrin Island with Timmy for the last time.'

Kate and I are still standing there, arm-in-arm, imagining the boat making steady progress across the placid sea.

'Does she not come back?'

'Oh, yes, she comes back. But first she rows out to the island. She and Timmy deal with the corrupt circus folk who have overheard the Five's plan to hide the papers on the island for safe-keeping. Then she rows back to the mainland where Julian and the others are there to tell her off for going all alone, and to congratulate her on making such a great fist of doing it.'

'And that's it?'

'Yes, that's it. Though I think that at the time of finishing *Five are Together Again*, Enid intended that there should be more books. Her plan was to first write six novels and then, due to popular demand, six more. Then, due to persistent public clamour, she decided the Five could go on adventuring underground forever. That was never going to happen, of course, those sensual, energising holidays in the Swanage area had to come to an end. But I suppose Enid knew that.'

When we get to the end of the beach, we keep going. Leaving for dead our tired selves from yesterday afternoon, we walk uphill until we are on top of the ridge separating Studland Bay from Swanage Bay. What an overview! From here it is so easy to imagine the dolphins going round and round Kirrin Island. Then, once in a blue moon, they go up the coast and slip through the narrow harbour entrance and into Poole Harbour, second largest natural harbour in the world after Sydney. And there they swim around Brownsea Island a few times, until it transforms into the Whispering Island of *Five Have a Mystery to Solve*. We will get an even better view of Whispering Island from the golf course that we're going to walk over tomorrow morning: the golf course that Enid bought for Kenneth when they were in their Swanage prime. In *Mystery to Solve*, the Five take a boat over towards Whispering Island, where they are then pushed right onto it by the strong outgoing tide. And judging by the chapter headings, they end up exploring caves and coming across hidden treasure. Of course they do! When she was writing that book in 1961, Enid would have been 64 and Kenneth would have been 73. Still virile? Perhaps, perhaps not. But, let's face it, some of the most poignant sex comes courtesy of memory, when the original feelings have been honed to a perfect pitch.

But that closer view of Brownsea Island is for tomorrow, our going-away day. Tonight, this is just such a great place to get an overall topographic perspective on Enid's last three Famous Five books, published in July of 1961, 1962 and 1963. Place *does* matter. In *Demon's Rock*, she starts the children off at Kirrin Cottage, but the Five and Tinker spend most of the book at the lighthouse a few miles south and west of here, effectively where we were this afternoon. I'm sure Enid didn't feel inclined to set the book at Kirrin Cottage itself because she was no longer staying at a hotel in Swanage. Location, location, location!

In *Mystery to Solve*, Enid doesn't start off in Kirrin Cottage but in Julian, Anne and Dick's house which is obviously located in Studland Bay, and which is where she was by the time of writing. That is, she and Kenneth would stay two or three times a year at Knoll House Hotel in Studland Bay, handy for their golf course. The book shoves the Five out to another picturesque cottage up on the golf course. This was a site that Enid knew very well by then and from here there's a great view of a new island, Brownsea Island, which you really would be aware of, if you were based at Studland. The Five explore the new island and go caving for treasure.

Finally, in the last book, Enid does again make an effort to get with the old magic, and starts the book in Kirrin Cottage. But straight away the Five are spirited off to Tinker's place. Not to the lighthouse this time, but off to his father's house (complete with tower in garden) in nearby Big Hollow, which has got to be a reference to Knoll House Hotel in Studland Bay again. Things plod along in Big Hollow and it's left to George and Timmy to make the last-gasp dash back to Kirrin Island in order to save the day – and the book. The dolphins, if they ever were really circling Brownsea-cum-Whispering Island, were – and are – on their way back to their real home. Those last three Famous Five books – which aren't the best in the series – were written with a love of the Dorset landscape that's evident on almost every page.

Kate and I need to get back to our Sunny Bay House, that amalgam of the Grosvenor Hotel and Kirrin Cottage. We both know this as we sniff the coconut bushes and stare up at the stars, all the time keeping our inner eyes on the dolphins, those endlessly circling Find-Outers.

4

We're lying in bed after some late-night activity. I hope we've not been making too much noise. Our room is next to Jill and her husband's one, and I don't really see how they could not have heard what's been going on. Oh, well, no offence meant. None taken, surely.

'Dunc?'

'Mmmm.'

'Is the intercom on?'

'Of course. Our friends the carp can hear everything that passes between us.'

'Good. Because what the carp and I would like to know, is this: given that Enid was with Kenneth when she wrote the Mysteries, isn't it likely that he influenced that series of books as well? Perhaps he's even in them in some guise.'

'I've been thinking about that. The Mysteries feature a group of high-spirited independent children enjoying themselves, so Enid's father is responsible for their existence on one level. That's point one. They're about the persecution of Goon around the environs of Bourne End, so Hugh has played a part in their conception. That's point two. And then there's the dog, Buster. Buster does not have as prominent a role in the Mysteries as Timmy does in the Fives. Fatty's protector rather than George's soul mate. But Buster is Kenneth all right, forever trying to chase off Goon who, after all, is a potential rival for his master's affections.'

'What about the jealousy between Fatty and Goon?'

'You mean with Hugh being Goon, for all intents and purposes, then Fatty rather than Buster might be Hugh's rival, Kenneth?'

'Was Kenneth clever enough to run rings around Hugh?'

I consider this. 'He might not need to be. All that might be required was for Enid to subconsciously *want* her new man to run rings around her former partner. Her fertile under-mind would then do the rest.'

'That doesn't quite work, though, does it? At least the carp don't seem keen on the idea. They're just idling in the pond. We'll be able to tell when they smell the truth: they'll start dashing around.'

'Fatty is such a vital intelligence. I don't think Kenneth was, or even convincingly could be, in Enid's mind's eye. Kenneth was a doctor, and he could play bridge and, like Enid, he had a photographic memory. That's all true. But I don't think there's any suggestion that he was an ideas man, or a joker, or a linguist. An important axis of the relationship with Enid was *his* admiration for *her* creativity. Dog-like devotion, you might say. He marvelled at what she could do by way of mimicry at the dinner table – laughing until the tears rolled down his face. Not vice versa. He marvelled at what she could come up with if left alone with a typewriter for a day. Again, not vice versa.'

'The carp can confirm that Frederick Algernon Trotteville is *not* an anagram of Kenneth Darrell Waters.'

'Thank goodness for that, though I admit that the triple name thing had me going for a moment. As I've said, I think that the Bets-Fatty relationship is essentially Enid and her father. As you know, I've also tried thinking about Fatty as Enid, and that works quite well. After all Enid *was* a practical joker as a child, with a huge appetite for fun. She could also come up with playful poetry at the drop of a hat. So yes, I think there is a lot of Enid in Fatty. It's just that I think there is a lot of Enid's hero-worship for her father in there too.'

Kate reminds me of the image that stuck in her mind from the Bourne End visit. Fatty and Goon sitting beside each other on the bench, both disguised as tramps. She goes on: 'Now you're suggesting that the Goon tramp was really Hugh, and the Fatty tramp was mostly Enid's father. I do see that. But for some reason I still want to think of the two tramps as Hugh and Kenneth. Does that make *any* sense? Can you see it that way?'

Can I?

'I see the two tramps sitting on the bench, no problem there. It's Fatty and Goon in disguise all right. Yet if I carefully unpick the disguises in the way you're suggesting, I discover that it's really Hugh and *Kenneth* sitting alongside each other. Well, well! Kenneth is aware that the fallen human being sitting beside him is Hugh. Whereas Hugh is unaware of the real identity of the man sitting next to him. Perhaps that could work?

'Hugh and Kenneth? Kenneth and Hugh? Actually, I can clearly see that pairing now. The Find-Outers recognise Hugh (not Kenneth) and stare at him from across the street. Larry approaches the bench and asks Hugh for the time. Hugh tells him how late it is, how late. Pip approaches the bench and asks Hugh if he's got change for sixpence. Hugh smiles wistfully and shows that his pockets are empty. He tells the boy that he's too late to get any money from him, about a decade too late. Daisy approaches the bench and asks Hugh if the bus to Sheepridge leaves from there. Hugh's eye takes on a nostalgic glint. He used to get on that bus with Enid, and they would ride together to the Saturday market at Sheepridge. That was before the orgy of writing an avalanche of books made living a normal life together impossible. Finally Bets approaches the bench and interrupts Hugh's melancholic reverie. "Have you seen our little dog, Buster?" she asks, dripping with charm. She asks the loaded doggy question of the man who hasn't seen either of his daughters for years. The delightful girl asks the cute-clever question of the man who hasn't seen his Imogen since she was Bets age and looked just like her. And, beside him, Kenneth the dog – I mean the tramp – bursts out laughing. Or, rather, he just manages to turn his guffawing into what appears to be a coughing fit with the use of his pocket-handkerchief. A classic tramp trick, that – to be sitting on a bench and to turn triumphal laughter into a coughing fit by the clever use of a filthy old square of grey linen.'

I'm not entirely happy with that image. I feel I'm in danger of sentimentalising Hugh's position. And I can hardly do that and at the same time constantly marvel at the comic creation that is Goon, can I? After considering the image of tramp Kenneth and tramp Hugh with a little more circumspection, I turn to my partner: 'We've got one more day in Swanage, remember.'

'What difference will that make to a pair of tramps sitting on a bench in Peterswood?' asks Kate, reasonably enough.

'Ah, you might be surprised!'

And the carp start to swish around in the confines of their pond, anticipating what the morning will bring.

5

The five Find-Outers bought their lunch from the chippie they'd discovered on the first day of their holiday, and wandered outside to a bench on the quayside. The sun splashed down on them. On Buster too.

'Funny how a cooked breakfast first thing in the morning leads you to feeling absolutely ravenous by noon,' said Fatty philosophically, slipping a big, hot, salty chip into his mouth.

'Yes, it is funny, that,' replied Bets, her eyes glazing over as she concentrated on her first mouthful of battered, vinegary cod.

There was only room for a sprawling Fatty and Bets on the bench. But Larry, Pip and Daisy were comfortable enough down on the stone quay with Buster. Perhaps another of the children could have squeezed onto the bench. But for this to happen, Fatty would have had remove his copy of *Sunny Stories*. And no one was asking him to do that.

The little magazine full of Enid Blyton gems came out every Friday, but you could usually get hold of it on a Wednesday in Peterswood, and, happily enough, this was also the case in Swanage. Neither of the Daykin children, or the Hiltons, had invested in the magazine, because both families had the publication on order at their local newsagent where it would be waiting for them on their return. Fatty could read his own ordered copy in due course. But he had made it clear to his friends that he WAS NOT going to wait a few days for the latest instalment of *In the Fifth at Malory Towers*.

Fatty marvelled at the way this story was developing. It was set at a girls' school, and for this reason he wouldn't have been comfortable to be seen with the book itself, when it eventually came out; he hadn't read the first four books in the series either, because of this. But the fifth novel's unobtrusive presence in the magazine had allowed him to become familiar with the previously unknown world that was a boarding school for girls. By reading the fortnightly instalments, Fatty felt he knew no fewer than a dozen teenage girls now, each of whom had a unique personality and who contributed to the group dynamic in a different way. For Fatty, used to the hopeless selfishness of boys of his own age, it had come as a revelation to see the girls, with the support of their friends, mature through adversity: a regular revelation, Fatty realised he had eaten enough of his meal to start thinking of someone else's appetite, and Buster got his first chip of the day.

'Have you read it all, Fatty?' asked Pip.

'Naturally.'

'What does Enid say in her letter from Green Hedges?' asked Pip, thinking it would be nice to be reminded of home in this way.

Fatty didn't need to consult the magazine to answer: 'Apparently, when the names and addresses of the overseas winners of the painting competitions are printed at the back of the magazine, loads of children from this country write to them. So she's asking us not to bother, because the little for-eigners are getting overwhelmed by it all. Besides, I dare say postmen the length and breadth of Africa and Australia just can't cope.'

'Perhaps I should get a little Bengali pen-pal,' said Pip, missing the point.

'Why don't you write to Enid instead? She finishes off her *Sunny Stories* letter by stating she already gets so many letters that sometimes after the post's been delivered you can only see the topmost hair of her head. So a letter from you, Pip, would bury her completely!'

The other Find-Outers laughed.

'Who's the letter from at the back?' asked Daisy. All the Find-Outers were familiar with the format of the publication from long acquaintance. But Fatty had seen his older cousin's collection of *Sunny Stories* magazine, and only he knew that the stapled booklet had been appearing in much the same form for decades. Fatty had gazed for a long time at a particular issue of his cousin's, from the summer of 1940. Back then, the same-sized magazine had the same orange-red printing on the cover and the same cover price – 2d. It was astonishing to think that in the ten years between that issue being published and the one lying on the bench right now – the Second World War, the atomic bomb and everything else – all that had really happened was that *Enid Blyton's Sunny Stories* had become *Sunny Stories, by Enid Blyton*.

'Oh, Fatty, you've put your great chippy thumb on it,' complained Bets. 'Look at the grease mark!'

'Can't make an omelette without breaking eggs,' said Fatty brightly. Buster barked his ongoing hunger and Fatty stuffed a piece of battered fish into his gob while answering the question he had been asked:

'The letter at the back is from the seagull that appears in one of the stories.'

'What story?' asked Daisy

'It's called "The Fish that Got Away".'

'Tell us what happens,' asked two voices at once. It wasn't as if Fatty had barred the others from reading his copy of the magazine. But they preferred to have Fatty mediate between them and their favourite author while on holiday. It seemed to be an unsaid rule that they would leave it until they got back home before enjoying pure and unabridged Enid Blyton.

Fatty gave them a quick rundown of the story: 'A boy on

holiday with friends stops another boy from throwing stones at seagulls. One gull has already been hurt, though, so the nice children take it home and look after it for a day or two until it can fly off into the wild again.' Bets had started to throw chips in all directions and Fatty was only too well aware of the gulls that were circling around them. Buster was barking at the birds, concerned perhaps that the gulls were getting nosh that should have been going his way. But Fatty didn't say anything. Or, rather, he carried on with his résumé: 'Then, during a fishing contest that the children have entered, a gull appears to help out the boy who came to its rescue, by dropping a mackerel close to where he is fishing on the pier.'

Bets threw another chip in the air, which got snaffled by an agile herring gull long before reaching Buster on the ground. She commented: 'I bet Enid thought of that story when she was sitting right here eating fish and chips.'

'Perhaps she did, Bets,' said Fatty.

'So what does the letter from the seagull say?' asked Daisy.

'Well, in the story it's not clear whether the fish falling out of the sky at the boy's feet is just luck, or whether it is a deliberate act by the gull.'

'And the letter makes it clear that the gull *did* mean to pay back the boy for his kindness?'

'You've got it, Bets! And the seagull ends his letter by wishing you – ee-ew! ee-ew! – a happy holiday.'

'Ee-ew! Ee-eew! Ee-ew!' went the gulls and the children, as one.

'A happy holiday to us!' cheered Bets, throwing a chip high into the sky. The others watched it until it was inside a clever white bird. Then suddenly all the gulls were gone and Buster was growling.

'Crikey, here comes Goon!' said Larry.

The Find-Outers had been intrigued when they found out that the Peterswood policeman was going on holiday to Kirrin at the same time as Enid Blyton. Especially since they were booked to go there as well! It was almost as if there was some mysterious link between the two places.

'Has he seen us?' asked Fatty, making Buster come to heel and telling him to shut up.

'No. He's got a big floppy hat on. I don't think he can see anything except the sand he's tramping through.'

'Good,' said Fatty, slipping off the bench and picking up Buster. 'You stay here and talk to him. Let's go for Plan A. Buster and I will catch up with you later.' Fatty slipped away, pleased that he hadn't given away how excited he was about what he had lined up for the rest of the day. Today was going to be so special!

As Larry, Pip and Daisy squeezed excitedly onto the bench beside Bets, they tried to remember what Plan A was. Soon Bets concluded: 'So there is no Plan A that any of us can recall, and we'll just have to play things by ear.' She bided her time, swinging her legs to and fro on the seat, then shouted: 'Hello, Mr Goon. Fancy seeing you here!'

The off-duty policeman stopped, lifted his sagging sombrero, and stared. He was not in the least pleased to see the troublesome kids from home. But once he'd established that Fatty wasn't among their number, or his pesky dog, he relaxed slightly. Truth is, Mr Goon was lonely. On his own in Kirrin, with no police work to keep him occupied, he found that his summer holiday was hanging heavy on his hands.

'We're staying at the Grosvenor, Mr Goon,' said Bets. 'Our rooms have lovely sea views. Same floor as Enid Blyton from back home, as it happens. What about you?'

'Up the hill there,' mumbled Goon. 'Always stay at my aunt's place because it's a lot cheaper than a fancy hotel.'

'Bed and breakfast! How exciting!' said Bets. 'Will you show us?'

Mr Goon didn't think it was so very exciting to be sent out in the morning with only tea and toast under his belt. But he was going that way now for a lie-down after his heavy lunch, and if the kids wanted to accompany him then he had no objection. Might even help him get up the hill. Lordy, why did his aunt have to stay at the top of such a mountain! If he could have afforded a room at the Grosvenor that's where he'd be all right. Nice big lounge and people on hand to get drinks and snacks for you all day long. That's what Goon would have called a holiday. And if he'd bumped into Mrs Darrell Waters of an evening then it would have been the most natural thing in the world to have fallen into conversation with her. But who was Goon kidding? That brilliant lady would not give him the time of day. In a different league she was. Trouble being, Goon just couldn't get the great author and her fine womanly figure out of his mind!

Half-way up the hill road there was a woman sitting on a stool with a table in front of her. A big woman, fearfully wrinkled, dressed in colourful but heavy clothes. A sign in front of the gypsy told the policeman that she was a fortune-teller. Goon was about to ask to see her street-trading licence when he remembered he was on holiday, and outside his jurisdiction. What's more he was completely out of breath, and to sit down on the free stool on the other side of the table was exactly his intention. If that meant he had to pay tuppence to have his hand read by the shabby old crone, then that was more than worthwhile. Besides, Goon believed in fortune-tellers.

'You would like to take the weight off your *beeg* feet now, yes?' said the woman, apparently reading the policeman's mind. 'You would like me to read your *beeg, beeg* hand – and you will cross my old hand with silver?'

Goon looked at her outstretched paw, fat and wrinkled...

'Silver! I don't know if I can run to silver!'

'Go on, Mr Goon. Find a sixpenny-bit in your shorts,' said Bets at her most persuasive. 'What is your holiday money for, if not for spending on treats like this?'

Goon looked over his shoulder. He'd forgotten about them children. Still, what did it matter if they heard what the old woman had to say? Perhaps they'd even keep her honest. She was a sharp one was Bets.

The gypsy woman took Goon's hand and traced the main lines of it. She shut her eyes and seemed to lose herself in concentration. Then she suddenly announced that his name was Theophilus Goon and that he was a Chief Inspector of police. Goon was impressed that she'd got his name spot on. And if she'd made an error in respect of his rank, well, that just showed the children that there was more to Police Constable Goon than they sometimes gave him credit for.

'Hmm. What else do you see there?'

The old woman – who everybody except Goon realised was Fatty in disguise – told him a couple of tit-bits that had the others putting their hands to their mouths to stop any sound of laughter from being made. Fatty was just warming up, though. They all knew that, and it was this that account-ed for the delicious tension in the air. Such holiday frolic!

'Aha! Zees is a vairy pee-culiar thing I see!' said Fatty, moving more boldly into the French pronunciation that Goon had lapped up more than once before. The police-man really did seem to have extraordinary powers of sus-pension of disbelief.

'I see a fat boy – a beeg fat boy.'

Larry and Pip just managed to smother their laughter.

'Oh, Fatty,' Bets wanted to announce, 'you're pretending you see yourself in Mr Goon's hand!'

Goon was not slow to react either: 'What! That toad! Tell me more!'

'Oh, tell us more, Fatty,' urged Bets, silently.

'BEWAAAAARE of zis fat boy. There is something feeshy about heem. Ze fat boy and ze feeshyness are togezzer!' Fatty paused and twinkled round at the others while the policeman kept staring intently at his own fat hand.

'What? Something fishy going on? A mystery! Go on – tell me about it. What mystery is it?'

'All I can see iz a book, a priceless book and the feesh, a beeg sleepery feesh. Zey are togezer. But BEWAAAARE of ze beeg, fat boy with the bee-ee-eeg slee-ee-eepery fee-ee-eesh.'

That was the end of the hand reading, because Buster could contain himself no longer in the presence of the policeman he loved to hate. The Scottie was out from under the table, barking and snarling for all he was worth. To his great joy he successfully pursued Goon up the road. 'Keep that blasted hound away from me,' shouted Goon, aware that his holiday shorts left him more exposed than the serge of the uniform he normally wore.

Goon panted while kicking out at a barking, sniffing Buster. He was sweating like a pig, he admitted that, but why should he have to put up with this humiliation at the snout of a dog that by rights should be a hundred miles away from here? 'CLEAR-ORF!' said Goon in near desperation, feeling Buster behind him. Things couldn't get much worse for an off-duty policeman down on his personal hygiene. No, things couldn't get much worse.

As they all got to the top of the hill, Larry managed to get Buster under control. As Goon unlocked his aunt's house, Buster was tied up to a fence post. Goon noticed this with approval, and turned to walk up the narrow stairs to his room. He had reverted to thinking about what the fortune-teller had told him about the fat boy from back home, and wasn't really aware that the other kids were still following him. He only realised it when he sank down onto his bed and, looking round, realised that his room seemed even smaller than usual because it was child-infested. Larry was sitting in his armchair, Daisy was in the washroom, Pip was at the window, and Bets was admiring the room's only decoration – a large model donkey made of unpainted plaster of Paris.

'What a lovely big seaside donkey,' said Bets, who wanted Goon to relax. 'And what a cosy room,' she added, just as Goon was about to tell the lot of them to scarper.

'Bit small,' Goon conceded, politely.

'Of course, you've got a whole house to yourself back in Peterswood. So the single room must take a bit of getting used to.'

'This bleeding bed,' said Goon, moving his back to the accompaniment of a great groan from the mattress. 'That's what takes a bit of getting used to.'

Larry sat on the end of the bed and bounced up and down. It creaked chronically.

'Hoy, don't do that! Idiot! There's enough of that sort of thing gone on over the years. You'd think my aunt would change the mattress once in a blue moon. But, no, there's no point according, to her.'

'No point, Mr Goon? What can she mean?' asked Larry. 'Gah, forget it. And please excuse me.'

Goon lumbered to his feet and disappeared into the only feature of the room that he was truly happy with, his en suite. He didn't suppose they even had these at the Grand, swish though that place was. For some reason his aunt had got ahead of the local competition in terms of luxury appointments, if only in this one respect. He locked the door behind him with a proud and emphatic clunk of the bolt.

Daisy had already had a look round the washroom. 'It's tiny,' she whispered.

The Find-Outers all sat or stood motionless as they heard Goon undo his belt and let his shorts fall to the ground with a swish. More little sounds – including sighs, intakes of breath, peeling noises – meant that they were aware of the stage-by-stage process by which Goon's underpants were gradually being detached from about his person. Pip tried to stop certain images coming into his mind. But he couldn't.

Next came the sound of Goon sitting down on a wobbly toilet seat. None of the Find-Outers budged in case by their moving they should topple Mr Goon from his precarious position. Their wide-eyed gazes went from one to another's faces, and soon each Find-Outer could do nothing but assume that he or she too was sporting the same look of horror as was each of their companions. They all had ghastly thoughts about what was coming next. 'Let's get out of here,' thought Daisy, Bets, Larry and Pip, individually and collectively. And yet none of them could move an inch.

Fortunately for the Find-Outers, Mr Goon was only resting, and the four find-Outers were relieved when they heard a stream hitting the bowl of water that Goon was surely now standing above. They were relieved because this new noise brought a different image to mind. Or at least it dispelled the previous imagery, which had taken their innocent minds just about as far as they could go in a certain direction. Pip put his hands to his mouth to stop himself giggling aloud. Larry put his hand to his brow and felt his forehead to be steaming hot. The trouble was, thought Daisy, the stream was going on and on. Bets was beginning to wonder if Mr Goon had a horse in there with him. She'd seen a racehorse peeing once and that had been pretty sensational. But just as suddenly as it had started, the stream came to an end, only for a resounding release of trapped wind to break the subsequent silence. This was too much for Bets who fell onto the bed as if shot. As she lay there in silent hysterics, Larry tried the door handle.

'Occupied!' shouted the voice of authority.

'Oh, sorry Mr Goon. I didn't realise there was anyone in there.'

The kids were killing themselves laughing. Or rather, everyone was killing themselves trying not to make the slightest noise. There was more and more silent laughter. Larry's face was red with the suppressed excitement of it all. Daisy felt they needed to get out of Mr Goon's bed and breakfast accommodation before something truly disturbing happened – and indeed all the kids felt this. And as they listened to Goon in the toilet – it sounded as if he was bouncing off the walls at this stage of whatever operation he was now involved in – Bets wondered again why they didn't just scarper.

But, no, horrified curiosity kept them rooted to the spot as before, their ears working overtime... When Goon eventually emerged from the loo wearing a new pair of white flannels, he smiled in a surprisingly sane manner. 'Would you like a cup of tea?' he asked of his young guests. This downright hospitable enquiry was very nearly the last straw, but in fact some threshold had been crossed and it calmed everyone right down. Bets noted the kettle on the floor in a corner of the room, beside the bed which Mr Goon would have to sit on in order to access the tea paraphernalia. In a little jar on the bedside table there was a packet of tea and a few sugar cubes and a tiny jug of milk;

barely enough for Mr Goon, never mind his unexpected guests. And there was only one cup and saucer. It came to Bets just how lonely Goon must be. She didn't know how old he was, but shouldn't a grown man be on holiday with somebody else? Shouldn't he have a lady friend of his own age? Bets wished with all her heart that he did and suddenly it wasn't funny any more. Well, it had stopped being funny the instant Mr Goon had emerged from his en suite. Now it was ever so sad. Bets was going to burst into tears the moment poor Mr Goon sat on the bed and bent down and stretched over to switch on the kettle. She knew she would.

Pip saved Bets. He saved them all by looking out of the window and noticing what was happening at the pool. 'Stone the crows!' said Pip, followed by: 'I don't believe it!'

'What's s'matter?' asked Goon, moving towards the window. Seconds later everyone in the room was struggling to get some sort of view of what was going on outside.

'That toad! The fish! The old woman was right!' cried Goon.

The policeman struggled with the window, failed to get it open, then ran out of his room. He was thinking fast. If he could foil Fatty's attempt to steal his aunt's fish, then surely he'd be made a bit more welcome in the house. He imagined evenings in the lounge downstairs, cooked breakfasts, those kind of treats. But first things first. That toad of a boy was not to get away with stealing a giant carp from under his very nose. It was a matter of professional pride. There was probably a priceless book hidden in that carp! So if he retrieved it for Mrs Darrell Waters then he'd be in her good books too. Also, if Fatty did get away with the theft of the fish, then his aunt might never allow Goon back into the house again! Goon clomped down the stairs as fast as he could, images of fish and book swirling around in his head, as if they were chasing one another.

Bets and Larry took over the large space vacated by the policeman, fast enough to see Fatty standing on the patio with the largest carp in his arms. Its tail was flapping from side to side, and the carp still in the pond were swimming around frantically. 'How did Fatty manage to catch it?' asked Bets. 'A neat bit of work with the landing net,' said Pip. 'The carp didn't know Fatty or the net was there, then Fatty made a sharp noise and the big carp swam straight into the net. What a whopper!'

'What on earth will he do with it now?' asked Larry.

'Dunno. But we'd better go down and help him deal with old Goon who seems a bit put-out,' said Pip. And the four Find-Outers fled the room.

No one was by the pool by the time Pip, Larry, Bets and Daisy got there. Where had Fatty and Goon got to so quickly?

'Get Buster, he'll know where they've gone,' said Bets.

But it took time before Buster could be untied and brought to the pool. And it took a minute before the barking dog finally realised what he was being asked to do. Chase Goon! No, he wasn't being asked to do that. He was being asked to follow his beloved master. Well, Buster would do that all right. He would follow marvellous Fatty to the ends of the earth if required.

Buster ran round the garden and made for the moor behind. The Scottie ran on swiftly, occasionally turning his head to make sure everyone was following. He led the way to a hollow they'd explored the previous day.

'The quarry! Did Fatty come here then?' said Pip. 'But why?'

The Scottie disappeared down the middle of the quarry,

slipping and sliding on the steep slopes as he went. The others followed as best they could, trying to imagine that Fatty had been down here just a minute or two before, with a large carp in a bucket of water, followed by an outraged Goon wearing clean flannels.

Buster went straight to a shelf of rock and disappeared underneath it. They heard him give a short bark as if to say gruffly: 'Look sharp! This is the way.'

'There's a tunnel under there,' said Pip. 'The one we thought we might explore yesterday, but didn't.'

'I'll go first,' said Larry, and wriggled through the hole, which was slimy. It smelt of seaweed. It was an exhilarating smell and he shared the enjoyment of it with the others. They all tried hard to believe that either Fatty or Goon could have squeezed through the gap. However, Larry was soon through to a wider bit, and then came out into a part where he could stand. He walked a little way in the pitch dark, hearing Buster bark impatiently. Luckily, Larry had been given a torch for his birthday, and since then it had gone everywhere with him in a pocket of his anorak. He pushed up the knob and the light came on. Obviously Fatty must have had a torch as well, for it seemed that he had thoroughly planned his escape with the fish. But Goon must have had a torch as well, otherwise surely he couldn't have followed Fatty into the bowels of the earth.

To begin with the children had to walk along in a stooping position, which was tiring. But the roof gradually became higher, and Larry, constantly flashing his torch around, saw that the walls and floor, instead of being made of soil were now made of rock which gleamed with moisture. He tried to think where they were.

It was not until Daisy pointed out the curious booming noise that Bets realised they must be under the rocky bed of the sea. They were walking to the island! How wonderful!

'Woof!'

'All right Buster – we're coming!' said Daisy.

Soon they came to where the tunnel split into two and Buster took the right-hand fork without hesitation. And when that split into three again, the Scottie dog again chose an option without hesitating.

'Marvellous, isn't he?' said Larry. 'His master went this way, so Buster's following him by scent as easily as if Fatty had used a knife and forceps to leave a trail of his own body organs to follow.'

Daisy wondered aloud why her brother was choosing such imagery. 'And stop sticking your torch into me! Keep it pointing forward – that's where we want to go.'

'We just need to hope that Fatty's going the right way,' said Pip. 'Seems to me we could all end up lost.'

'Well, if we did,' said Larry, 'we'd just make sure Goon didn't give Fatty too hard a time of it, and then let Buster lead us back the way we've come.'

'I wonder if Goon really is succeeding in trailing Fatty. After all he's not got a dog's nose to show him the way,' said Bets.

The Find-Outers all stopped for a minute to discuss this.

'Perhaps he's close enough to hear Fatty,' said Pip.

'Or to smell the fish,' said Larry.

'I cannot believe Fatty did that with the carp. The poor thing will be drying out even if half of it is in a bucket of water,' said Daisy.

'I think perhaps if it curves around on itself it could just about all be under water,' said Bets. 'It's an especially wide bucket.'

'Remember this issue's *Sunny Story* about the fish that got away?' said Pip. 'I bet that's where Fatty got the idea for all this.'

Larry agreed. 'Yes, obviously he had seen the fish pond before taking up his position as a fortune-teller. Which would explain why he went on about the "beeg feesh" when he read Goon's hand.'

Bets giggled in the darkness.

'Crikey, Fatty's a sharp one,' said Pip.

'I've always thought so. But this is absolutely barking,' said Larry. He switched his torch off to save the battery and they listened to the booming of the sea high above them. Bets could have sworn she was listening to her own heartbeat. After a minute, Larry asked: 'So here's a question for us down here in the dark. Who do you think is the nuttiest on today's evidence? Fatty or Goon?'

'Fatty at the pool or Goon in the toilet! Which is the stark, raving maddest?' asked Pip.

'Fatty!' said Daisy.

'Goon every time,' said Pip.

'It's just *got* to be Fatty,' said Larry.

They discussed this matter for a while longer. Then Buster's impatient barking prompted Larry to push up the knob of his torch again. They plodded on.

Suddenly they heard an excited yapping. 'CLEAR-ORF,' said a disgruntled voice. And as the Find-Outers rounded a corner they saw Buster barking at Mr Goon, rivals to the very end of time.

'Heel, Buster,' shouted Larry. But Buster didn't want to come to heel. He still had a deep-seated loyalty to obey. The Scottie shot past Mr Goon and made for the patch of light that everyone could see just ahead.

Soon the Find-Outers were going up a steep flight of stairs cut out of the rock itself. And from those stairs Larry, followed by the others, stepped into a sea breeze. 'Kirrin Island!' he said, looking around.

'And there's the castle,' pointed out Pip. There were jackdaws, disturbed by the unexpected activity. And Buster running through the ruins to the far side of the island. What would they find there? They half dreaded finding out.

They came to the far shore. They couldn't see Buster though they could hear his excited yapping again. 'Isn't that a cave just beyond that big rock there?' said Pip, pointing. 'It looks like one to me. And I think that's where the barking's coming from.'

So they cut across the mass of rock and made their way towards the jutting out part of the cliff, where the cave seemed to be.

'It is a cave!' said Pip, in delight. Its floor was spread with white sand, as soft as powder and perfectly dry. Suddenly a figure emerged from the shadows of the cave entrance, a tall man with an air of authority. The Find-Outers were surprised to see their old friend Chief Inspector Jenks. But they weren't the only ones taken aback:

'Cor! – it's the Chief!' muttered Mr Goon, stumbling up behind the children.

'Hello, Find-Outers, pleased to see you again. Good day to you, Goon. My word, look at your trousers! What on earth have you been doing?'

Goon looked down at his flannels. True enough, they were in a right old state. He hadn't realised the tunnel had been so muddy. Somehow the kids seemed to have emerged from the tunnel just as clean as they'd left his room. Goon decided he'd better repair the first impression he had given to the Chief:

'We're after a pretty desperate fish thief, Chief. Have you seen a fat boy with a large ornamental carp in a bucket?'

'Carp in a bucket!' scoffed the senior officer. 'Never mind that nonsense, Goon. Instead say hello to the boy who has solved The Mystery of the Stolen Books. Step forward, Frederick!' And Fatty walked out of the cave and stood demurely by the Inspector.

Goon was nonplussed. Had the Chief gone mad? 'There was a carp!… In a bucket!… On this island!… Brought here by this… this so-called Frederick!'

Fatty spoke in the quiet way he had when he wanted to make Goon feel particularly foolish. 'As for carp in buckets. All I would say, is that if anyone thought they saw me with such a thing, then I can only assume they were seeing what they wanted to see rather than what was actually there.'

This baffled Goon. 'Woof,' went Buster, pleased to hear his master speaking with all the apparent wisdom of Solomon. The chief took a step towards Fatty and patted him on the back. 'Congratulations again, Frederick,' said the Chief. 'You really are cut out for a top job on the force as soon as you've finished your education.' The Inspector turned to the rest of the Find-Outers. He had a special smile for young Bets. And then he started to explain:

'I was just about to tell Frederick about the interview I have recently conducted with Mr and Mrs Darrell Waters at the Grosvenor Hotel. As you're all here now, you might as well hear what I've got to report. Indeed Frederick asked if he might bring you along for just such a briefing. I should add that we're only having this conversation in this out-of-the-way spot because it was my own wish that I should get to plant my feet on Kirrin Island while my work took me to this neck of the woods!'

'We're listening, sir,' said Larry. They all were.

'As advised by Frederick, I put to Kenneth Darrell Waters that he had been placing large bets on horses. The horses are legitimately owned by his and his wife's business associate, Eric Rogers, all of whose horses have a certain thing in

common as you'll soon hear. The first book to be sold for
such a purpose was *The Enchanted Wood*. Frederick, you might
as well fill in some of the details?'

'Certainly, sir. On the 1st of June this year, a horse belong-
ing to Eric Rogers called The Enchanted Wood was in the
starting line-up for the two o'clock Handicap Chase at
Haydock Park. Earlier that day, Mr Kenneth had sold a special signed copy of *The Enchanted Wood* for £40 to the owner
of a second-hand bookshop on the Charing Cross Road in
London. He had then returned to Peterswood by train and
placed a £40 bet on the horse at the betting shop on the
High Street.'

Everyone was listening. Goon was listening so hard he
couldn't blink.

'Did The Enchanted Wood win?' asked Bets, hoping it
had for some reason.

'Fourth, Bets, fourth,' said Fatty, happily. 'Mr Kenneth lost
all the money.'

'Oh,' said Bets, realising that Green Hedges had lost the
wonderful book as well.

The Chief took up the tale: 'Though uncomfortable
about his wife hearing about this sequence of events, Mr
Darrell Waters did not try and deny it. Nor did he deny what
I put to him about *Adventures of the Wishing-Chair*...
Frederick?'

'Yes, sir,' said Fatty, enjoying himself immensely. 'On the
14th of June, another horse from the Eric Rogers stable,
Wishing-Chair, was under starter's orders for the three
o'clock at Cheltenham. Earlier in the day Kenneth had sold
an inscribed copy of *Adventures of the Wishing-Chair* to the
same dealer on Charing Cross Road as before. He had
returned to Peterswood where he had placed a bet – £50 on
the nose – on Wishing-Chair.'

'Did the horse win?' asked Bets. Not knowing if she wanted it to or not.

'Trailed in last, Bets,' said Fatty, with a distinct grin on his face.

Goon seemed to recall that he'd had a little money of his own on that damned Wishing-Chair. He'd liked something about the name. Come to think of it, Kenneth Darrell Waters had been in the betting shop that day. He'd tipped the horse to romp home, and had impressed the regulars with the way he'd put his money where his mouth was. Goon shouldn't have listened to the fool, though. Should he tell the Inspector about the coincidence now? No, perhaps not.

Together the Chief and Fatty went through the misfortunes of several racehorses running under the colours of Eric Rogers. The animals boasted such fine names as The Boy Next Door, Teacher's World, Those Dreadful Children, The Naughtiest Girl in the School, The Naughtiest Girl Again and Hello, Mr Twiddle.

'Did none of those horses with such lovely names win?' asked Bets.

''Fraid not,' said Fatty, grinning again. 'It seems that Mr Eric Rogers had not selected a very good trainer. Funny, that. He made most of his money through backing a brilliant author, but lost a packet by not repeating the magic when it came to choosing a trainer of racehorses.'

'Oh, dear. And is Mr Kenneth going to prison?'

'Not at all!' said the Inspector, brightly. 'All he's done is waste police time. He's also offended his wife. Mrs Darrell Waters was furious that her husband had sold her books. His defence was that some of the books were gifts to him, and that she would not have let him make the bets if he'd consulted her. She rounded on him then. "Of course, she wouldn't have encouraged him to make the bets. Betting on

horses was not a fit pursuit for adults. It was contemptible".
Actually, she went on like that for about five minutes. Almost
made me feel sorry for the little man. Made me see why she's
a writer, though: an endless stream of words, and all of it
very much to the point. When she'd had her say, she stormed
out of the room.'

'Golly,' said Pip.

'However, she caught up with me in the lobby of the hotel
on my way out. She had calmed down and got the situation
in perspective. She was very pleased that the mystery of the
disappearing books was solved. She congratulated me on my
work, and I explained that the Find-Outers, and in particular Frederick, had helped solve the case. And I told her
exactly how.'

'How?' asked Bets, clapping her hands.

'Yes, how did you do it, Fatty?' clamoured Daisy, Pip and
Larry.

Fatty tried to look modest. In fact, he did feel rather
sheepish. He began: 'Remember, the night we visited Green
Hedges and I left you to work on the manuscript of *The Ship
of Adventure*…'

'Yes!' shouted four Find-Outers as one.

'Well, I slipped into the library to see what was what. It was
obviously someone with everyday access to the house that had
to be taking the books. They were all more or less equally valuable volumes, so why had some been taken and not others?
Money didn't seem to be the main motive, though the value of
the books was clearly a consideration. I didn't rate these find-
ings at the time, but I think I did tell you what I'd seen.'

'You did,' said Bets.

Fatty continued: 'The next day I was in the police station
talking to Mr Goon about a few… er… damp spots on some
books of my own. He had the racing paper on his table, as

usual, and a horse's name had been circled with a red pen. It was upside down, but of course I just had to try and decipher it. And I found I could: The Naughtiest Girl Again. I enquired if that was the name of one of the Enid Blyton books that had gone missing from Green Hedges, assuming that was what had attracted Mr Goon's attention to the name…'

Fatty paused. He wondered if he should be acknowledging Mr Goon's presence more directly at this juncture. But he decided it was for the best if he didn't. Meanwhile Goon could not believe what he was hearing. If it wasn't for the presence of the Chief he'd be sure that the fat boy was making it up for the sole purpose of humiliating him. The hated voice drawled on: 'But Mr Goon just looked at me blankly, and said he'd had a hot tip from him at Green Hedges.'

That bit rang a bell, realised Goon. Oh, Lordy – perhaps it was all true!

'Everything just fell into place at that instant,' said Fatty. 'And it was just a matter of going through old copies of *The Racing Post* and betting shop records to put the whole story together.'

Goon groaned. He wasn't sure just how stupid he'd been for weeks on end, because there was no way he was thinking clearly right now, standing in this sandy cave on this stupid island in the middle of these kids. It was pretty obvious that the fat boy had made deductions that by rights he should have made himself.

'Anything to say, Goon?'

'No, sir. Nothing constructive.'

'Well, as *I* was saying, Mrs Darrell Waters, actually Enid – I think I can call her that when I recollect how much friendlier she had become by this stage – was most impressed with what she'd heard, and asked me to wait in the lobby while she got something from her rooms. She returned with advance copies of her new book, which she tells me is to be published in a fortnight. She only had four to sign for you, but she had a copy of an earlier book as well, and she hopes that you, Bets, will accept it until she returns to Green Hedges and signs another.'

The Find-Outers were each presented with their books. Fatty, Larry, Daisy and Pip were given brand new copies of *Five Fall Into Adventure*. Daisy inspected the cover: George was pulling Timmy up a cliff by hauling on a rope. Pip inspected the cover: George was on the end of a rope, letting Timmy down towards the beach. Larry inspected the cover: he assumed he was looking at a cliff and beach that could be found on this very island. Fatty opened his book and stared at the title page:

FIVE FALL INTO ADVENTURE

By
ENID BLYTON

Illustrated by Eileen Soper

To Frederick Algernon Trotteville.
Congratulations on solving a
real life Mystery!
Love from Enid Blyton xxxxx

Fatty felt… How did he feel? He didn't know. So he pulled himself together and told the chief: 'Oh, this is a fantastic gift, sir. Thank you so much. What can I say to her? I must write to the lady this very afternoon.'

Inspector Jenks nodded. 'She has gone back to Green Hedges. Write to her there.'

Bets was regarding her own book with deep affection: *The Further Adventures of Josie, Click and Bun*. 'I love Josie, Click and Bun, Inspector Jenks,' said Bets quietly. 'They were my absolute favourites when I was little.'

The Inspector smiled at Bets, who still wasn't that big as far as he was concerned, and asked her what it was about.

Bets brought her own much-loved, sadly soiled copy to mind. There were two beautiful drawings printed on each page. And under each picture, two or three lines of words. It was amazing what Enid Blyton – helped by her illustrator – had been able to put across in such a simple way. The book featured three unforgettable characters. Josie, the cute doll with heart-shaped face and enormous eyes; Bun, the adorable bunny; and Click, the tiny little clockwork mouse.

Fatty looked up from his own gift book. Someone had told him that Enid's nickname for Hugh had been Bun. When were the Josie, Click and Bun books written again? Fatty knew that the strip cartoon had first appeared in *Sunny Stories* in 1939, just after the family's move to Green Hedges. That is, just a short time before Hugh and Enid's final split.

Bets continued to recall the story as she flicked through her precious new book. The bit that really got to her was near the end. She wanted to tell the others about this, so she said: 'Bun – that's the rabbit – is alone in the Tree-House and has found a box of pencils with which he is drawing on the wall. He is having a great time scribbling away. But when Josie and Click get back from the shop they are angry at the mess he's made on the walls. Bun shows them a drawing he's done of Click the mouse's face. But instead of getting them to laugh along with him, Josie the doll gives him a sharp ticking off. "We're going to have to pay someone to clean the walls," she shouts and she makes Bun go upstairs to bed.'

Fatty looked thoughtful. In fact, everyone seemed to be

paying attention, even Goon. So Bets carried on telling the story that was etched in her mind by words and pictures viewed time and again: 'Bun goes upstairs to the bedroom as he's told to. But he's very angry and doesn't go to bed. Instead he paces back and forth about the room with a stroppy look on his face. In the end he sits down and writes a furious letter to Josie and Click claiming that they don't love him any more, and that as a result he's running away. He packs his suitcase, takes a rolled-up umbrella with him in case of rain, and goes off to live with a relative.'

'He leaves Old Thatch,' said Fatty thoughtfully.

'He left the Tree-House,' corrected Bets.

'Poor Josie and Click,' said Daisy.

'Poor Bun,' said Fatty.

'He goes to stay with his Aunt Floppy,' said Bets. 'When Josie finds the note, she's in tears. She says to Click: "Fancy Bun thinking we don't love him any more just because he was naughty." But then she goes on to make the same mistake, because she claims that Bun must have stopped loving Click and her because they were cross with him! Whereas, of course, Bun still loved Josie and Click!'

Pip shook his head at the impasse.

Bets continues: 'Bun doesn't find it easy at his aunt's. She doesn't especially like him and she makes him work hard for his keep. Poor Bun soon forgets his crossness with Josie and Click, and misses them terribly. But when he gets out his writing things, he finds he can't put pen to paper. He is too ashamed of himself for scribbling nonsense on the wall of the little Tree-House and for running away.'

Fatty was trying to keep up with the story behind the story. It seemed to him that round about 1940, Enid was thinking about the possibility of her first husband leaving the family home. She would be sad to see him go. She was hoping that he might be sad about such a prospect as well. And then it actually happened! But Fatty realised he should keep listening to Bets:

'Josie and Click are so upset at seeing Bun's empty bed each night that they think they will have to sell the Tree-House where the three of them were so happy for so long. But before they do, they try and get a message to Bun. Bun eventually gets the message, and in a desperate hurry he tries to travel back to the Tree-House before it is sold. He misses the bus, so has to run all the way through the wood. Bun knows his heart would break if he arrived too late and the Tree-House was empty or had been sold.'

That's right, thought Fatty. Enid was sad to see Hugh go. And hoped that Hugh would be sad enough too to want to return to Old Thatch or Green Hedges, whichever one it was.

'Tears were running down Bun's cheeks as he ran through the wood with his suitcase with "BUN" writ large over it, and his furled umbrella, which he was still carrying in case it should rain, though that was the last thing on his mind.'

Everyone was now standing in a big circle, picturing Bun with his rolled-up umbrella like a city gent's, hurrying through the wood as fast as his little legs would take him. Bets went on:

'At last Bun came to the Tree-House. Josie and Click were still inside, packing up the last of the things for their removal van. Click saw Bun running towards the house and gave a squeak. He said: "Oh, look Josie, there's our dear, darling, old Bun!"'

As far as Fatty was concerned it was Imogen or Gillian speaking, and she was saying: 'Oh, look, Mummy, there's our dear, darling, old Dad!'

Bets knew she was quoting the very words on the page now. She couldn't help it, they were etched into her mind, as was the drawing of the coming together of the three creatures: '"Well, dear me, the hugs and kisses and squeezes and squeals and tears and laughs that went on!"'

Pip, Larry, Daisy, Fatty, the Inspector and even Goon stared towards Bets, all lost in admiration for the story and the storyteller. Though only Fatty was lost in admiration for Enid as well as Bets. As for Buster, he was not at all pleased that Bets was holding Goon by the hand.

'"Friends always forgive one another," said Josie, hugging Bun. "Nothing else matters if we all love one another, you know."'

'Nothing else matters if we all love one another,' said Fatty, testing the line for sincerity. In reality, while Enid was waiting for Hugh to come back to Green Hedges she met Kenneth and quickly became involved with him. Kenneth took Hugh's place in Enid's affections. Isn't that what had really happened? Fatty had a question for the Inspector. 'I wonder if you can remember what her last words to you were, sir?'

The Inspector looked sharply at Fatty. Yes, Mrs Darrell Waters had said something else to him in the lobby after handing him the books. What was it now?

But Fatty couldn't wait all afternoon for the Chief to come up with the goods. 'Was it something like this?' he asked. And putting on his crystal-clear Enid Blyton voice, Fatty gave it his best shot: 'Forgive me, Inspector. But I must now return to that husband of mine and make him realise that just because I think him an imbecile does not mean that I don't love him any more.'

Buster barked joyfully. The Inspector stared at Fatty. Had the boy been hiding in the lobby of the Grosvenor Hotel when the meeting actually took place? As far as the senior policeman could recall, those had been Enid Blyton's exact words of parting.

CHAPTER SIX

IN GEORGE MACDONALD

1

I'm sitting at the computer in my study. I'll be here for the duration. By which I mean I won't be leaving home until my *Enid* is completed. No need for anyone to worry, though. This will be one smooth roller-coaster slide from start to finish, especially if the October robin outside the window keeps up his pep-song.

Also keeping me company is the Enid Blyton Society. One of the topics I posted on its Forum pages some months ago was: '*The Complete Letters of Enid Blyton*. Wouldn't it be great if there were such a book?' Then it went on to encourage anyone who has a letter from Enid to provide details on the site. I got a couple of supportive responses to this, but no actual letters, until the other day when a new member posted a scan of a letter from Enid to a young correspondent in 1960. The EB Society member declared the letter that she had got hold of was not that important, but, as far as I was concerned, it was. For a start, the letter was on headed notepaper. It was a thrill to read the address of Green Hedges, alongside Enid's telephone number, printed at the top of the page in raised red letters: 'Beaconsfield 1091'. In the body of the message itself, Enid apologised for not being able to answer questions about her life in a letter. She got so many such enquiries from schools that if she tried to answer them all she would have no time left for her imaginative writing for children. So she hoped her young correspondent would understand, and that he would find some of the answers to his questions in the booklet she was enclosing. Enid was being a bit more generous with her time than she was implying, the explanatory note itself taking up a whole side of Green Hedges paper.

There is another letter from Enid posted on the Forum, but not in response to my appeal. This second letter appears in the 'items for sale' section. There's no scan of the letter itself, but the message is transcribed. Apparently, it was written from the Grosvenor Hotel, Swanage, in the summer of 1952. Enid is writing to a boy reader, glad to hear that he likes the Famous Five books so much, and telling him that he should look out for the eleventh title, *Five Have a Wonderful Time*. She adds that if the boy and his brother are so keen on the Five then they'll probably like the Adventure series as well, so they should give that a go. The price of that neat example of self-promotion is £250. I'm tempted to make an offer for it. But, no, I've had my fill of Swanage and I must move swiftly on. If, however, Enid had added a paragraph about how naughty her own teenage daughters had been the previous night, and that as far as she was concerned the Grosvenor Hotel had had its day, then I might have been tempted to break into my piggy bank.

As I said, I'm here for the duration. I suppose I'm making this 'staying put' point because this year I have played fast and loose with my *Enid*. This is partly because there's no guarantee the work will get published. Far from it. The present author's name does not have a fraction of the clout with publishers that Enid Blyton's once did. So Macmillan, Hodder, Collins, Methuen and the rest are not eagerly awaiting this particular manuscript. As things stand, it's possible that not a single editor will have his or her antennae out for my *Enid*, which is fair enough. I just have to hope that my London agent, through his enthusiasm and his contacts in the literary world, will be able to pull off something on our mutual behalf.

But I have to live in the real world, which for me, for now, is the art world. So when opportunities have presented themselves to write texts for individual artists and articles for a contemporary art magazine, I've had no hesitation in stopping my work on the book and taking them. My Blyton trips – principally, to Swanage in March, and Bourne End in July – have had to work around other things. Luckily these trips took off in all the ways I needed them to take off and I feel I've retained their essence sufficiently to both write them up as individual episodes and fit them into an evolving narrative in the space that I've had between art projects.

Perhaps I've gone about the writing of this book in such a risky way because I've been inspired by the unstoppable creativity of the work's subject. In any case, one of the recent trips away from *Enid* has been instrumental in handing to me on a plate what is going to be – what has got to be – a mind-blowing last chapter.

What do I mean? I was invited by an artist friend to stay at the Scottish Sculpture Workshop in Aberdeenshire, and while I was there I met Claudia Zeiske who runs an art organisation in the town of Huntly. Next year, she is hoping to invite a writer to the town to undertake a residency with a focus on George MacDonald, the Victorian fantasist who was born in Huntly. The writer-in-residence could conceivably be me, though I've not yet decided whether I'd want to invest a chunk of time in the study of another writer. Having said that, the initial week would be in the actual farmhouse in which the author was brought up. I got tantalisingly close to Enid's homes in Beckenham, Bourne End and Beaconsfield: actually living for a while in an author's house seems like the next logical step. Anyway, when I got back here from my trip north, I sought out the following quotation in *The Story of My Life:*

'The book I loved best as a young child, and read at least twelve times, was *The Princess and the Goblin*, by George MacDonald. It wasn't so much the story as the strange "feel" of the tale, the "atmosphere" as we call it. It hung over me for a very long time, and gave me pleasant shivers.'

Enid would have first read this book while living at 35 Clock

House Road. I guess she would have read it also while living at 31 Clock House Road, given her age – 11 – when she moved there. Of course, I've read this book now, and 'pleasant shivers' doesn't begin to describe the effect it had on me. The story is absorbing in its own right, but astonishing in the context of Enid's *oeuvre*. Would I have read this book if it hadn't been for the coincidence of the Huntly connection? Perhaps not. There are still so many books by Enid that I haven't read, and I'd started to wind down my research. But what I should have noticed when I read the autobiography in the first place was that she'd read the book *twelve times!* That explains why everything about the story has evidently sunk so deep into her mind. It explains why the structures and themes and characters of this single George MacDonald book (he wrote plenty more) can be traced to any of Enid's hundreds of books. What's the word I'm looking for? A template. Or am I exaggerating its importance? Well, let's see.

The Princess and the Goblin begins: 'There was once a little princess whose father was king over a great country full of mountains and valleys.' Beckenham, circa 1905, shall we say? The father does not stay in the same castle that his daughter does, and the Princess Irene only gets to see him now and again throughout the book. He is distant, imperious, loving – in a hands-off sort of way – and has great status among everyone else. He is the king, after all.

'The princess was a sweet little creature, and at the time my story begins was about eight years old, I think, but she got older very fast.' She was about Bets' age, then, and if there is a Bets, it's only right that there should be a Fatty. There is a Fatty. His name is Curdie. He is the 12-year-old son of a miner, and he is the second main character in a book that should certainly be called *The Princess and Curdie*. More about him later. Actually, that's one of MacDonald's writing tricks. To drop in snappy little sentences like that. A bit more about him too later.

What about the mountains mentioned at the start of the book?

The third paragraph begins: 'These mountains were full of hollow places underneath; huge caverns, and winding ways, some with water running through them, and some shining with all colours of the rainbow when a light was taken in. There would not have been much known about them, had there not been mines there, great deep pits, with long galleries and passages running off from them, which had been dug to get at the ore of which the mountains were full.' It didn't take me long to realise that these caves and tunnels ran throughout the book and that much of the action would take place there with Irene and Curdie taking on a role that seemed familiar to me. Yes, the whole tunnel theme common to the set of Famous Five books may owe something to the state of Enid's relationship with her own body, as she explored it with Kenneth in a Swanage bedroom. But for sure it owes a great deal to the network of underground tunnels that she read about as a child in this most vivid of books.

One of the main pieces of action in the book is when the princess, guided by an enchanted thread, has to go underground. 'A shudder ran through her from head to foot when she found that the thread was actually taking her into the hole out of which the stream ran. It ran out babbling joyously, but she had to go in. She did not hesitate. Right into the hole she went, which was high enough to let her walk without stooping. For a little way there was a brown glimmer, but at the first turn it all but ceased, and before she had gone many paces she was in total darkness.'

Very *Five on a Secret Trail*. The princess is able to make her way through the underground network of passages, thanks to her enchanted thread, though not without difficulty. She doesn't know it, but Curdie has been imprisoned deep within the mountain in a room the door of which is blocked by a pile of stones. The thread leads her unerringly to the place, and Curdie is both astonished and delighted when he realises that Princess Irene has come to rescue him. But he's not saved yet:

"'There's such a lot of stones!' she said. 'It will take me a long time to get them all away.'"

"How far on have you got?" asked Curdie.

"I've got about the half away, but the other half is ever so much bigger."

"I don't think you will have to move the lower half. Do you see a slab laid up against the wall?"

Irene looked, and felt about with her hands, and soon perceived the outlines of the slab.

"Yes," she answered, "I do."

"Then, I think,' rejoined Curdie, 'when you have cleared the slab about half-way down, or a bit more, I shall be able to push it over.'"

Which is what happens. But how do the princess and Curdie get out from deep in the middle of the mountain? The princess puts the same faith in the thread as George and the rest of the Five put in Timmy as he unerringly finds his way from dark tunnel to sunshine and fresh air. 'Woof!'

Who had locked Curdie up in the first place? Back to the first chapter in the MacDonald book: 'Now in these subterranean caverns lived a strange race of beings, called by some gnomes, by some kobolds, by some goblins. There was a legend current in the country that at one time they lived above ground, and were very like other people.' Years after reading this, Enid wrote *The Green Goblin Book*. And she had red goblins undermining the Magic Faraway Tree in a way that reminds me of how MacDonald's goblins go about trying to undermine and invade the castle in which Princess Irene lives. In the index to *Sunny Stories* covering the years from 1942 to 1953, the word 'goblin' comes up in the following titles: 'A Bit of Luck for the Goblin', 'The Goblin Hat', 'Goblin Magic' and 'The Goblin's Toyshop'. The goblin was a concept that had well and truly entered Enid's consciousness, then, and I suppose this was partly due to *The Princess and the Goblin*.

Goblins occupy some of the underworld in MacDonald's book,

and miners occupy the rest. Miners and goblins are in constant con-
flict, and Curdie is loyal to the miners' cause. Good-natured Curdie
has learned that the best defence against goblins is to sing at them.
They can't stand that! This is the song that Curdie is singing when
Princess Irene first meets him:

> 'One, two, three –
> Bright as gold can be!
> Four, five, six –
> Shovels, mattocks, picks!
> Seven, eight, nine –
> Light your lamp at mine.
> Ten, eleven, twelve –
> Loosely hold the helve.
> We're the merry miner-boys,
> Make the goblins hold their noise.'

Curdie can come up with these songs spontaneously, we're told.
Now there are two Blyton characters conspicuous for their ability
to do exactly that: Noddy for one and Fatty for the other. Surely
they've inherited this ability from the young miner boy:

> 'Curdie: "Light your lamp at mine…"
> Noddy: "That will be just fine."'

Noddy and Fatty can produce verse at the drop of a miner's
helmet:

> 'Noddy: "We're the merry Blyton-boys."
> Fatty: "Make the robins hold their noise."'

For much of the book there is a mystery: the mystery of what the
goblins are up to. Curdie spends much of the story trying to find out

the answer to this (that's the reason he gets captured and locked up underground). It's not like a Peterswood Mystery, with Fatty leading a team of Find-Outers. No, Curdie goes it alone, in a way that Fatty doesn't usually do. It's more like a blend of a Mystery (with a Fatty and a Bets), an Adventure (because the environment is exotic and antagonistic) and a Famous Five book (because of the underground element), though without the teamwork that is common to all these series. Enid may have learned a lot from George MacDonald's fantasy, but she didn't learn teamwork from it. Apparently, as a child Enid also read *Little Women* several times, the only other novel she mentions having read repeatedly. Perhaps the 'pulling together' theme comes from that book.

But the really special thing about *The Princess and the Goblin* lies in yet another sphere. I'm sure it's this that Enid refers to when she talks about the 'feel' of the book and its 'atmosphere'. The very first thing that happens in the story is that the princess explores a part of the house she's not been in before. She goes up three flights of stairs to a floor full of corridors and doors. She gets lost, and tries to make it back to her room and her nurse, but can't find the stairs again. Eventually she does find a staircase, but this only leads up. Being a brave and inquisitive girl, Irene goes up the narrow steep stairway on all fours, and comes out into a floor that contains two doors facing each other, with a third door facing the top of the stairs.

Irene hears a low sweet humming noise coming from behind one of the doors to the side, so she enters it and finds an old lady sitting, spinning thread. But wait; I must convey the authentic George MacDonald voice in this, of all passages:

'Perhaps you will wonder how the princess could tell that the old lady was an old lady, when I inform you that not only was she beautiful, but her skin was smooth and white. I will tell you more. Her hair was combed back from her forehead and face, and hung loose far down and all over her back. That is not much like an old lady –

is it? Ah! but it was white almost as snow. And although her face was so smooth, her eyes looked so wise that you could not have helped seeing she must be old. The princess, though she could not have told you why, did think her very old indeed – quite fifty, she said to herself. But she was rather older than that, as you shall hear.'

Isn't that a tantalising stream of words? And out of copyright too. So I've been able to lift it, and the other quotations, straight from the text that the Gutenberg Project has made available on the internet, in a way that I just couldn't do for Blyton material. Besides, it's different. If I paraphrased the MacDonald prose, I'd risk losing the ingredient that gave Enid those pleasant shivers.

Before I get back to Irene, I have something to say here about the lovely Kate who has helped me so much in this book's execution. Kate is just 7 years old. Sorry, I mean Kate is just seven years older than I am. But that makes her 55. Is that old? *Kate is not old*. The 7-year-old she once was still lives within her. And some mornings she wakes up with just her jim-jam bottoms on, wanting to be a dog. That is, she moves about the double-bed on her hands and knees, shaking her platinum-blonde head, growling and wagging her tail. Like Timmy or Buster. 'Woof! Woof!' Translation: 'I can't find my pyjama top anywhere, where have you hidden it?' This is one sexy and wise 55-year-old, and I can hardly wait to be as mature myself!

Over the phone recently, Kate mentioned that she'd picked up a Blyton nature book from a charity shop. I asked for its exact title, so she told me: *Enid Blyton's Nature Book, Number 3, Discovering Nature Month by Month*. Now I'd not come across this book before, even though it was obviously a *Round the Year with Enid Blyton* sort, so I asked her to send it to me. It arrived with a pencil note on the first page: 'This book belongs to Kate Clayton and she is lending it to her friend Duncan McLaren, a fat boy who lives in Scotland.' The book arrived the same day I wrote the scene in which Goon receives a book with a coded message from Fatty.

That's an example of what I mean by Kate having helped me with the writing of my *Enid*. Another is her recent response to the Swanage chapter, which included the question, 'Is all that stuff about Kenneth selling books and betting on horses owned by Eric Rogers actually TRUE? Because if it's not then you've got to tell the reader that, when you get back to your own voice, the voice we have learned to TRUST.'

Well, it's not true, reader. Eric Rogers was a philistine and Kenneth connived with him to waste much of Enid's wealth and some of her time, and they both liked a flutter on the gee-gees, but that's as far as it went. Not true either are the inscriptions on the Famous Five books which Fatty finds in the library in Green Hedges. But surely I'm allowed some fiction in my fiction scenes? It's true to say, though, that these scenes are as close to real life as my imagination can make them.

When will I be seeing my Kate again? As soon as I've finished this final chapter. Good. Which really is going to be the roller-coaster glide I promised. Can you sense that?

So back to ageless Enid, by way of the book that made most impression on her as a child: 'While the princess stared bewildered, with her head just inside the door, the old lady lifted hers, and said, in a sweet, but old and rather shaky voice, which mingled very pleasantly with the continued hum of her wheel:

"Come in, my dear; come in. I am glad to see you."'

I suppose I should mention in passing that George MacDonald was a contemporary and an intimate friend of both John Ruskin and Lewis Carroll. Both these great bachelor writers were as much into little girls as MacDonald was. But MacDonald was married and raised eleven children, so there was a big difference. So carry on, George MacDonald, you most respectable and brilliant of Victorian writers, now sadly neglected except by the director of a contemporary arts organisation in your home-town of Huntly. Yes, carry on...

'When the old lady had got her thread fairly going again, she said to the princess, but without looking at her:

"Do you know my name, child?"

"No, I don't know it," answered the princess.

"My name is Irene."

"That's my name!" cried the princess.

"I know that. I let you have mine. I haven't got your name. You've got mine."

"How can that be?" asked the princess, bewildered. "I've always had my name."

"Your papa, the king, asked me if I had any objection to your having it; and, of course, I hadn't. I let you have it with pleasure."

"It was very kind of you to give me your name – and such a pretty one," said the princess.

"Oh, not so very kind!" said the old lady. "A name is one of those things one can give away and keep all the same. I have a good many such things. Wouldn't you like to know who I am, child?"

"Yes, that I should – very much."

"I'm your great-great-grandmother," said the lady.

"What's that?" asked the princess.

"I'm your father's mother's father's mother."

"Oh, dear! I can't understand that," said the princess.

"I dare say not. I didn't expect you would. But that's no reason why I shouldn't say it."

"Oh, no!" answered the princess.

"I will explain it all to you when you are older," the lady went on. "But you will be able to understand this much now: I came here to take care of you."

"Is it long since you came? Was it yesterday? Or was it today, because it was so wet that I couldn't get out?"

"I've been here ever since you came yourself."

"'What a long time!' said the princess. 'I don't remember it at all.'"

"No. I suppose not."

"But I never saw you before."

"No. But you shall see me again."'

Now imagine the young Enid reading that in her home in Beckenham. Imagine her reading it the only way it can be read, with the spine tingling. She would be about the same age as the princess Irene, with a similarly noble father in her background and a woman who isn't up to much when it comes to spiritual guidance in the foreground. Irene has little respect for her nurse and likewise Enid for her mother. How wonderful, then, for Enid to hear about this special female, Irene's *father's* mother's father's *mother*! Just imagine the compulsion to read on.

The princess's visit to the old lady culminates in the room opposite the top of the stairs. This room is inhabited by pigeons, mostly white ones, and Irene works out that the old lady lives on their eggs. The advantage over hens' eggs is that you don't have to feed the birds. They fly off and feed themselves! I haven't quoted the relevant passage because it's not essential. And I suppose I'm only referring to it now because there are wood pigeons in the beech tree close to the room in which I'm working, making cooing and wing-clap noises. I prefer the robin as a soloist. On second thoughts, that is not so. Nature in all its variety is what pleases me. I like to think I take after Round-the-Year Enid in that respect.

The second time the princess visits the old lady, months have passed and Irene is not sure that she didn't dream the first visit. (I wonder how much time passed between Enid reading *The Princess and the Goblin* for a first and a second time.) But the old lady is no dream, and is both delighted and not at all surprised to see Irene again. However, the princess's title for her of 'great-great-great-great-grandmother' is pushing it a bit, so they settle on the more simple title of 'grandmother'.

Actually, Kate is a grandmother. I haven't met her daughter, so haven't heard Kate being addressed as Mum. And I haven't met the two young sons of Kate's daughter. I'm not sure how I would react to having Kate addressed as Grandmother, or Granny, or whatever it is the little boys call her. Perhaps they call her Princess Kate. That would be most fitting.

Back to George MacDonald's princess: the old lady shows Irene (who has pricked her finger) her large and lofty bedroom which features a lamp as round as a ball hanging from the ceiling, and an oval bed with blue velvet curtains around it. Irene loves the room and the old lady loves having her there. Let me describe this in the original writer's way:

'"I don't think I can let you go away tonight," she said. 'Would you like to sleep with me?"

"Oh, yes, yes, dear grandmother," said Irene, and would have clapped her hands, forgetting that she could not.

"You won't be afraid, then, to go to bed with such an old woman?"

"No. You are so beautiful, grandmother."

"But I am very old."

"And I suppose I am very young. You won't mind sleeping with such a very young woman, grandmother?"

"You sweet little pertness!" said the old lady, and drew her towards her, and kissed her on the forehead and the cheek and the mouth. The little princess nestled close up to the old lady, who took her in both her arms and held her close to her bosom.

"Oh, dear! this is so nice!" said the princess. "I didn't know anything in the world could be so comfortable. I should like to lie here for ever."

"Then good night,' said the old lady. In a moment more the little princess was dreaming in the midst of loveliest dreams – of summer seas and moonlight and mossy springs and great murmuring trees, and beds of wild flowers with such odours as she had never smelled before. But, after all, no dream could be more lovely than what she had left behind when she fell asleep..."'

Let's leave Irene sleeping in the arms of her grandmother and catch up with Enid. All through the 1940s and 1950s – her own forties and fifties as well – she's been living at Green Hedges. In addition, she's been holidaying in Swanage, keeping an eye on the development of Imogen and Gillian, writing a Mystery and a Famous Five book every year, writing books, books, books – and that's not hyperbole. The Noddy titles in particular are a worldwide success and she writes a successful play based on the illustrated stories.

As well as the books, there's the magazines. She stops writing her column in *Teacher's World* in the autumn of 1945, after twenty-three years, but only because its long-term editor retires. Her loyal and full contribution to *Sunny Stories* goes on until 1952, and she only stops that in order to set up another magazine, published by Evans instead of Newnes. *The Enid Blyton Magazine* contains a letter from Enid, a serial, short stories and competitions, much as *Sunny Stories* did. A prominent part of its *raison d'être* is the support of one club and the establishment and promotion of three others. Such is the loyalty and enthusiasm of her child readers for all her ideas that these clubs go on to be a great success for the causes they are linked with. The Busy Bees is the junior section of the People's Dispensary for Sick Animals, and Enid promotes it in her magazines and contributes features to its own magazine, *The Busy Bee News*. As for the clubs actually set up by Enid: The Famous Five Club raises funds for a babies' home in Beaconsfield; The Sunbeam Society raises funds for blind children; and The Enid Blyton Magazine Club helps spastic children who daily attend a special centre in Chelsea. Glory days, then. Dream on, Queen Bee Enid.... But the dream has to come to an end and it does; slowly at first and then gradually faster.

In 1957, when Enid is 60, she is taken seriously ill. She collapses with chest pains on the golf course and the fear is that she's had a heart attack. According to the specialist it isn't her heart but a digestive problem caused by hunching for too long over the type-writer. But Kenneth encourages his wife to believe the problem is indeed with the heart, perhaps in an effort to get her to slow down.

Her final letter to children in *The Enid Blyton Magazine* in September 1959 mentions two reasons for the magazine's closure. The first is pressure of work by which she means the time she has to devote to handling the successful Noddy plays and pantomime, making radio broadcasts, putting in personal appearances at book-shops and continuing to write her many books. But it's also in this letter that she mentions Kenneth's retirement and her wish to spend more time at his side. The magazine closes, but Enid ensures that the four clubs go on and that the good work that they do con-tinues, partly through the publication of an annual *Enid Blyton Diary* which keeps readers up to date with the activities of the clubs and the charities they support.

That sounds all right, but with more time on her hands, she con-fides to Imogen that she feels her thoughts are closing in on her. Perhaps – despite or even because of all the charity work in recent years – she feels guilty about how she's treated two individuals in particular: her first husband and her mother.

Hugh had been promised access to Imogen and Gillian as they grew up, but that simply didn't happen. Apparently, Enid told over-dramatised accounts of his supposed misdeeds during their mar-riage in order to justify her own cruel actions, and having told such stories it was difficult for her to retract them. Not that I know what these stories were; Barbara Stoney's book simply refers to them having been told to Enid's friends and daughters. I imagine that all this is part of the 'tactful gaps' that Imogen says Stoney left out of the official biography, in the introduction to her own *Green Hedges* book. I would love to know what these 'over-dramatised accounts' were, to see if they could somehow be connected to episodes involving Goon. Anyway, Hugh bears it all with fortitude, it seems. He doesn't hold a grudge against Enid, as far as Barbara Stoney or

George Greenfield can make out and, for me, Hugh can never be reduced to Goon. Well, he can and he can't be – but I've explored that fully already.

In her later years, Theresa pleaded to see the daughter she'd not seen since the early twenties, but Enid declared herself too busy to make the trip to Kent. Theresa died in 1950 and Enid was not at the funeral. She'd made up her mind about her mother decades before, and if there was no going back on it when she lived, there was no reversal of attitude when Theresa was dead. If anyone had asked Enid to back up such an apparently heartless no-show, she could no doubt rattle off the names of the thirty-one books she had published that year. In fact, I'd like to make that very statement on Enid's behalf right now. She didn't go to her mother's funeral in 1950 because of being too busy publishing the following (the titles that I've actually read are in capitals):

The Astonishing Ladder... A Book of Magic... Enid Blyton's Little Book No. 1... The Enid Blyton Pennant Series (30 parts)... Enid Blyton Readers (Books 10-12)... FIVE FALL INTO ADVENTURE... HURRAH FOR LITTLE NODDY... IN THE FIFTH AT MALORY TOW-ERS... The Magic Knitting Needles and other stories... MISTER MED-DLE'S MUDDLES... MR PINKWHISTLE INTERFERES... THE MYS-TERY OF THE INVISIBLE THIEF... The Pole Star Family... The Poppy Story Book... RILLOBY FAIR MYSTERY... ROUND THE YEAR WITH ENID BLYTON... Round the Year Stories... RUBBALONG TALES... The Seaside Family... SECRET SEVEN ADVENTURE... THE SHIP OF ADVENTURE... Six Cousins Again... Tales about Toys... The Three Naughty Children and other stories... Tricky the Goblin and other sto-ries... WE DO LOVE MARY MOUSE... Welcome Mary Mouse... What an Adventure... THE WISHING-CHAIR AGAIN... The Yellow Story Book.

But time passes and the brain cells of a genius die just as surely as all mothers do. Enid's productivity falls off at an alarming rate.

1961: the fifteenth and last Fatty and Bets book: *The Mystery of*

Banshee Towers. This is a book I was advised not to read, such is the fall-off in quality. I did read it. And it's not too bad. To get into Banshee Towers the Find-Outers have to go through an underground tunnel in Banshee Hill. The whole story has a Famous Five feel to it. That might be all right, it might be fitting even, for the two series to come together. After all, haven't I had the Find-Outers doing their thing in Famous Five territory in the previous chapter? What is not so easy to stomach is that in *Banshee Towers* Fatty is just a shadow of his former self. And I don't think Goon even puts in an appearance. Or if he does, it's not significant. Ghost Fatty and Ghost Goon: how sad is that?

1962: only eight books were published this year, including a Famous Five, a Secret Seven and a Noddy – the penultimate one of each series.

1963: only five books were published in all, including the twenty-first and last Famous Five title and the fifteenth and last Secret Seven.

1964: the twenty-fourth and last Noddy book comes out. *Noddy and the Aeroplane* is delightful, I have to say. But a year or two later, Enid tells Imogen that she's written another Noddy book. Alas, when her daughter looks at the notebook, there is nothing there but a few disjointed sentences.

So what happens? Perhaps she gets distracted by the rise of the Beatles and the success of the Apollo Moon missions. It would seem fitting if the great enchanter gets some enchantment from the rest of the world in her declining years. But it doesn't happen like that. It is to some kind of pre-senile dementia that Enid succumbs. The wheels come off in Enid's once all-powerful, kaleidoscopic mind from about 1960. Soon she has difficulty accessing her child-infested inner life. Without fantasy to fall back on all her waking hours – as has been her lifelong habit – Enid feels bereft.

She potters about in the real world as best she can and, according to Barbara Stoney's biography, Enid regrets not having made her peace with her mother and now talks positively about both her parents. She bucks up when she is visited by Gillian's children – Enid is a grandmother! And she bucks up again when she gets letters of any kind from children who have read and been transported by her books.

Kenneth tries to protect Enid in her decline, in all sorts of ways. Burning her diaries is one of his more dubious contributions. But he is failing too, undermined by arthritis, and in 1967 he dies aged 75 of kidney failure brought on by prescribing himself too many painkillers. According to Stoney, the only concise and clear entry in Enid's diary for that year reads: 'My darling Kenneth died. I loved him so much. I feel lost and unhappy.'

In her final year, when her mind continues to collapse under the weight of its past achievements – if I can put it like that – it is to Beckenham that she longs to return. She wants to be with her mother and father, to explore the woods and fields of her youth.

Enid's brother Hanly hasn't seen Enid for seventeen years when he gets a phone call from her in 1967 asking him to come and visit her because she is 'desperately lonely'. I dare say she's been desperately lonely ever since she fell out of her Magic Faraway Tree. No Kirrin Island... No House-For-One... No Peterswood. The everyday world must seem so flat. No Fatty... No Timmy... No Kiki... The everyday world must seem so *quiet*.

Hanly dutifully travels from his home in Kent to Green Hedges only for Enid not to recognise him when he knocks at the door. Mr Twiddle is it? Mr Meddle? NOT PINK-WHISTLE, SURELY? Eventually his identity is established and she begs him to take her back to Beckenham. He doesn't that day, but he does another day, just to show her that the old Beckenham doesn't exist and that her true life is the one she has made at Green Hedges. But hang on! Does Hanly not take her up the stream where the kingfisher sits stock still and totally turquoise to this day? Does he not take her to the house on Chaffinch Road opposite whose front windows the trees go *wisha-wisha-wisha*? To numbers 31 and 35 Clock House Road where gardens can be compared and contrasted? To the three-storey house round the corner where the postman no doubt still delivers coded messages, if required? To Elfin Cottage where Binkle and Flip were – and always will be – good bunnies? Of course, the old Beckenham is still there! It's still there to *this* day. Which might explain why, as soon as they are back at Beaconsfield, Enid talks once more of 'returning home'. If Hanly had his wits about him, he'd buy his sister a copy of *The Princess and the Goblin* and save himself a fortune on petrol money. But I'm getting carried away, because he only drives her to Beckenham once.

Irene pays her grandmother a third visit in the middle of *The Princess and the Goblin*. It's got all the atmosphere of the first two visits. It's the author at his most atmospheric:

'"Mightn't I stay and sleep with you tonight, grandmother?"

"No, not tonight. If I had meant you to stay tonight, I should have given you a bath; but you know everybody in the house is miserable about you, and it would be cruel to keep them so all night. You must go downstairs."

"I'm so glad, grandmother, you didn't say 'Go home,' for this is my home. Mayn't I call this my home?"

"You may, my child. And I trust you will always think it your home. Now come. I must take you back without anyone seeing you."

"Please, I want to ask you one question more," said Irene. "Is it because you have your crown on that you look so young?"

"No, child," answered her grandmother; "it is because I felt so young this evening that I put my crown on. And I thought you would like to see your old grandmother in her best."

"Why do you call yourself old? You're not old, grandmother."

"I am very old indeed. It is so silly of people – I don't mean you, for you are such a tiny, and couldn't know better – but it is so silly of people to fancy that old age means crookedness and witheredness and feebleness and sticks and spectacles and rheumatism and forget-

THIS IS HER
GEORGE

George kicked and fought and struggled.

fulness! It is so silly! Old age has nothing whatever to do with all that. The right old age means strength and beauty and mirth and courage and clear eyes and strong painless limbs. I am older than you are able to think, and –"

"And look at you, grandmother!" cried Irene, jumping up and flinging her arms about her neck. "I won't be so silly again, I promise you. At least – I'm rather afraid to promise – but if I am, I promise to be sorry for it – I do. I wish I were as old as you, grandmother. I don't think you are ever afraid of anything."

"Not for long, at least, my child. Perhaps by the time I am two thousand years of age, I shall, indeed, never be afraid of anything. But I confess I have sometimes been afraid about my children – sometimes about you, Irene."

"Oh, I'm so sorry, grandmother! Tonight, I suppose, you mean."

"Yes – a little tonight; but a good deal when you had all but made up your mind that I was a dream, and no real great-great-grandmother. You must not suppose I am blaming you for that. I dare say you could not help it."

"I can't always do myself as I should like,' said Irene, beginning to cry. 'And I don't always try. I'm very sorry anyhow."

The lady stooped, lifted her in her arms, and sat down with her in her chair, holding her close to her bosom. In a few minutes the princess had sobbed herself to sleep. How long she slept I do not know. When she came to herself she was sitting in her own high chair at the nursery table, with her doll's house before her.'

When Enid comes to herself she is sitting in her own high chair with her doll's house before her. What I mean is, Enid spends her last three months in a Hampstead nursing home. By this stage she has entirely lost her short- and medium-term memory. The physical and psychological effects of this are profound and she needs to be cared for around the clock. According to Imogen, every night Enid tries to run away to the parents that had let her down sixty years before.

Enid dies on the 28th of November 1968. A psychiatrist reports to Imogen that her mother's last words were recorded as: 'I am going to my father! At least I think I am.'

2

Bets woke up feeling strange. Where exactly was this bed she'd been sleeping in? She had a feeling she wasn't in Peterswood. But if she wasn't in Peterswood, then where in the wide world apart from Peterswood was she?

The name of her home village seemed to have got stuck in Bets' mind, so she turned onto her back and tried to think through her position in another way. She had a feeling she wasn't going to see Fatty that day. Certainly nothing had been arranged. But was that because Fatty was away at school? Or was it because Bets was away at her own school? Perhaps both Bets and Fatty were away at their separate boarders. Unfortunately, whichever was the case, it looked like Bets wouldn't see Fatty until the end of term even though it seemed like *ages* since Bets had last talked to Fatty.

Wide awake now, Bets had got out of bed and dressed and was determined to explore this strange dorm she was all alone in. She looked out of the window and saw that it was autumn. She wouldn't mind exploring the fallen leaves, just to see exactly what tints and toadstools had been laid out for her delectation. But first she wanted to have a good nose through the big school or house or whatever it was – this ancient place she'd woken up in.

Up the curious old stair of worm-eaten oak she went. Up and up she skipped – such a long way it seemed to her – until she came to the top of a third flight. Here she paused because there was a poem she intended to read out to Fatty when they next met, and if she was going to get it exactly right she knew she had better practise it. Fatty was the one who could come up with a poem off the top of his head. But Bets was good at looking through old books and finding a ready-made one that suited her purpose down to the ground. Like this:

> 'When a night in November
> Blew forth its bleared airs
> An infant descended her birth chamber stairs
> For the very first time,
> At the still midnight chime;
> All unapprehended
> Her mission, her aim.
> Thus, first, one November,
> An infant descended
> The stairs.'

Bets was delighted. Word perfect!

> 'On a night in November
> Of weariful cares,
> A frail aged figure
> Ascended those stairs
> For the very last time:
> All gone her life's prime,
> All vanished her vigour,
> And fine forceful frame:
> Thus, last, one November
> Ascended that figure
> Upstairs.'

Not a single mistake or hesitancy so far! Fatty would have been impressed with her. Bets glided across the floor, but she didn't go through any of the doors on this intermediate floor, because she knew it was exactly that – an intermediate floor. She wanted to go straight to the top of the house. Accordingly, she found her way to a tower staircase. When she got there, the stairway was so narrow and steep that she proceeded like an animal on her hands and feet. The unusual thing about this four-legged creature, she told herself, was that it had an old poem by Whatsisname going round its head:

> 'On those nights in November -
> Apart seventy years -
> The babe and the bent one
> Who traversed those stairs
> From the early first time
> To the last feeble climb -
> That fresh and that spent one -
> Were even the same:
> Yea, who passed in November
> As infant, as bent one,
> Those stairs.'

Bets was nearly at the very top of the house. Who knew – she might even find Fatty there! It would be just like Fatty to be lording it over everyone in the highest room of the house, a room that Mr Goon couldn't have reached in a million years. Oh, but Bets mustn't put it like that! She had made it up with Mr Goon. They were all the best of friends these days though Bets was beginning to suspect she would never see Mr Goon again.

'Wise child of November!
From birth to blanched hairs
Descending, ascending,
Wealth-wantless, those stairs;
Who saw quick in time
As a vain pantomime
Life's tending, its ending,
The worth of its fame.
Wise child of November,
Descending, ascending
Those stairs!'

Happy that she would be able to recite the poem to Fatty even if she came across him unexpectedly, Bets let it slip to the back of her mind, and put her ear to one of the doors at the top of the tower. No sound of spinning. For some reason she'd been expecting to hear the sound of spinning. Somehow she knew that, usually, all through the day, the sweet gentle bee-humming of someone – probably Fatty – could be heard spinning. She opened the door and went inside. There was the spinning wheel, but with no one at work. There wasn't any unspun thread about the room, either. Usually – funny word, 'usually', and one in which Bets was beginning to lose confidence – there was some unspun material and in the daylight it shone like silver, but it tended towards grey rather than white and only glittered a little. Fatty had told her that it was a spiderweb of a particular kind. Fatty's pigeons brought the material here from over the great sea. According to Fatty, there was only one enchanted wood where the spiders lived who made this particular kind – the finest and strongest of any.

On a shelf close to the spinning wheel were some finished jobs. A row of shimmering balls each about the size of a pigeon's egg. Bets took one in her hand, and looked at it all over. It sparkled and shone here and there. It was of a sort of grey-whiteness, like spun glass. How many such shimmering balls were there? When Bets came to count them, she realised that there were hundreds! Hadn't Fatty – or whoever it was – been busy? Bets certainly didn't have time to stand there and count them all, never mind unwind them as they were supposed to be unwound. She supposed she could have an adventure underground if she unwound the thread and followed where it led her. Or she could have an adventure up a faraway tree in an enchanted wood. Or an adventure in dear old Peterswood. But not today. She stood in the middle of the room for a while, gazing out of the window, listening to a robin. It was the only songbird that sang from September to December. What a big chunk of the year that was! Luckily, the bird seemed to shoulder its singing responsibilities lightly. The robin with its puffed-out winter plumage reminded Bets of Fatty. Bets listened, and as she listened she imagined walking with her friend through the lanes of Peterswood. When her robin went quiet, Bets kept listening out for a while… Then she turned on her heel, left the room, and looked into the one opposite.

'Come in, my dear. I am glad to see you.'

Bets did as she was told, stepped inside the door at once, and shut it gently behind her.

'Come to me, my dear.'

Bets approached the old lady, stood by her side, and looked up into her face with her blue eyes with their deep dark centres.

'Why, what have you been doing to your eyes, child?' asked the old lady.

'Crying,' answered Bets.

'Why, child?'

'Because I couldn't find Fatty.'

'But you could find me.'

'Not at first – not for a long time.'

'Your face is streaked like a zebra's. Hadn't you my hand-kerchief to wipe your eyes with?'

'No.'

'Then why didn't you come to me to wipe them for you?'

'I should have remembered to do that. I will next time.'

'There's a good child!' said the old lady.'

'Isn't Fat... Aren't you working today?'

'No. I knew my granddaughter was due to pay me a visit, so I thought I would take the morning off and make myself look nice for her.'

Bets saw that the old lady's hair was silver. Not grey-silver, like unspun spider thread. Rather, sun-silver, like water sparkling in the light of a summer's day.

'You look lovely, grandmother.'

'You look very well yourself, princess. But let's go over our names again. It's very important that we get that right before we go on with our chat. Do you know my name, child?'

Bets hesitated. 'No, I've forgotten it,' she finally admitted.

'My name is Enid.'

'That's my real name!' cried the princess.

'I know that. I let you have mine. I haven't got your name. You've got mine.'

'How can that be?' asked young Enid, bewildered. 'I've always had my name.'

'Your papa asked me if I had any objection to your having it; and, of course, I hadn't. I let you have it with pleasure.'

'It was very kind of you to give me your name – and such a pretty one,' said Bets, who had decided to go on calling herself by the name Fatty knew her by.

'Oh, not so very kind!' said Enid. 'A name is one of those things one can give to any number of worthy children and keep all the same. I have a good many such things. Wouldn't you like me to remind you who I am, child?'

'Yes, please.'

'I'm your father's mother's father's mother.'

'Fatty's mother's Fatty's mother? Oh, dear! I can't understand that,' said Bets.

'But that's no reason why I shouldn't say it.'

'Oh, no!' answered Bets, beginning to like the idea of it anyway. *Fatty's* mother's, Fatty's *mother*. She liked it so much she began to giggle.

'I will explain it properly to you when you are older,' Enid went on. 'But you will be able to understand this much now: I came here to take care of you.'

'Is it long since you came? Was it yesterday? Or was it today, because I couldn't find Fatty?'

'I've been here ever since you came yourself.'

'What a long time!' said the princess. Then she bowed her head: 'I don't remember it at all.'

'No. It seems not.'

'But I never saw you before.'

''Nonsense, child. But you are seeing me now, and that is what matters.'

Bets shivered. She didn't know why she shivered, because she knew it wasn't a cold day. It was a fine autumn day, with a wind from the south and a cover of clouds to keep the warmth of the land from rising off into… into… Bets shivered again.

'I've lighted a fire; you're getting cold,' said Enid.

Bets looked, and saw that what she had taken for a huge bouquet of red roses on a low stand against the wall was in fact a fire which burned in the shapes of the loveliest and reddest roses, glowing gorgeously between two bookcases. And when she came nearer, she found that the smell of roses with which the room was filled came from the fire-roses on the hearth. Enid was dressed in the loveliest deep-red velvet, over which her hair, no longer white, but of a rich raven colour, streamed like a cataract. Her face was that of a woman of twenty-nine.

'Bun!' sighed Bets.

'Pardon,' said the lady.

'You're supposed to say: "Little Bunny",' said Bets, sadly.

'Try it again, then.'

'Bun!'

'Yes, Little Bunny?'

Bets was suddenly so bewildered that she couldn't speak, and timidly withdrew into herself, somehow feeling dirty and uncomfortable. Enid was seated on a low chair by the side of the fire, with hands outstretched to take her, but the princess hung back with a troubled smile.

'Why, what's the matter?' asked Enid. 'You haven't been doing anything wrong – I know that by your face, though it is rather miserable. What's the matter, my dear?' And still she held out her arms.

'Dear grandmother,' said Bets, 'I'm not so sure that I haven't done something wrong. I ought to have… Or rather I ought not to have…' But shame prevented Bets from turning her thoughts about Bun into sentences.

'You were taken by surprise, my child, and you were not so likely to do it again. And indeed you didn't do it again. It is when people do wrong things wilfully that they are more likely to do them again. Come.'

And still Enid held out her arms.

'But, grandmother, you're so beautiful and grand with your crown on, and I am so grubby with dust and dirt from the corridors and the stairs. I should quite spoil your beautiful red dress.'

With a merry little laugh Enid sprang from her chair, far more lightly than Bets herself could, caught the child to her bosom, and, kissing the tear-stained face over and over again, sat down with her in her lap.

'Oh, grandmother! You'll make such a mess of yourself!' cried Bets, clinging onto her.

'You darling! Do you think I care more for my dress than for my very own girl? Besides – look here.'

As she spoke she set her down, and Bets saw to her dismay that the lovely dress was covered with dust and stains. But Enid took a book from the fireside bookcase, and, stooping to the fire, held it to the flames. When its pages were alight, she passed the book once and again and a third time over the front of her dress; and when Bets looked, not a single stain remained.

'There!' said Enid, 'You won't mind coming to me now?'

But Bets again hung back, eyeing the flaming book, which Enid still held in her hand.

'You're not afraid of the book – are you?' she said, about to replace it on the shelf it came from.

'Oh! don't, please!' cried Bets. 'Won't you hold it to my frock and my hands and my face? And I'm afraid my feet and my knees need it too.'

'No,' answered Enid, smiling a little sadly, as she slipped the smouldering book back into its place. 'This book is too hot for you yet. It would set your frock on fire. Do you see that bath behind you?'

The princess looked, and saw a large oval tub of silver, shining brilliantly in the morning light.

'Oh, what a big one! I've never seen such a bath.'

'Go and look into it,' said Enid.

Bets went, and came back very silently but with her eyes shining.

'What did you see?' asked Enid.

'The sky, and the moon and the stars,' she answered. 'It looks as if there's no bottom to it. It feels as if there is no end to everything.'

Enid smiled a satisfied smile, and was also silent for a few moments. Then she said: 'You are very tired, my child. Your hands hurt from the climb, and I have counted nine bruises on you. Just look at you!'

And she held up to her a mirror which she had picked up from the floor. Bets burst into a merry laugh at the sight. She was so bedraggled from creeping through narrow places that if she had seen the reflection without knowing it was a reflection, she would have taken herself for some gypsy child whose face was washed and hair combed only once in a month. Enid laughed too, and lifting her up onto her knee again, took off her cloak and night-gown. Then she carried her to the side of the room. Bets wondered what Enid was going to do with her, but she asked no questions. She only started a little when she found that she was going to be laid down in the large silver bath; for as she looked into it, she saw no bottom, but the stars shining miles away in a great blue gulf. Her hands closed involuntarily on the strong arms that held her.

Enid pressed her once more to her bosom, saying:

'Do not be afraid, my child.'

'No, grandmother,' answered the princess, with a little gasp; and the next instant she sank in the clear, cool water.

When Bets opened her eyes, she saw nothing but a lovely blue over and beneath and all about her. Enid and the beautiful room had vanished, and she seemed utterly alone. But instead of being afraid, she felt more than happy – perfectly blissful. And from somewhere else came Enid's voice, singing a strange, sweet song about an island – her own island – a beautiful living island. Bets could distinguish every word but could not make out the sense of the song; she had only a feeling – no real understanding. Nor could she remember a single line after the singing ceased. It had vanished, like the poetry in a dream, as fast as it had come.

How long Bets lay in the water she did not know. It seemed a long time – not from weariness but from pleasure. But at last she felt the gentle hands lay hold of her, and through the gurgling water she was lifted out into the lovely room. Enid carried her to the fire, sat down with her in her lap and dried her tenderly with the softest towel. It was no different from her father's drying.

'I don't think I can let you go away tonight,' she said. 'Would you like to stay with me?'

'Oh, yes, yes, dear grandmother,' said Bets, clapping her hands.

Enid drew Bets towards her, and kissed her on the forehead and the cheek and the mouth. This done, Bets was ready for bed. Goodness, what a short day! But, oh, what a delicious bed it was into which Enid laid her! She hardly could have told she was lying upon anything: she felt nothing but the softness.

Enid having undressed herself lay down beside her.

'Why don't you put out your moon?' asked Bets.

'That will go out soon enough,' Enid answered.

'I hope it will never go out,' said Bets.

'Shall I take you in my arms again?'

The little princess nestled close up to Enid, who took her in both her arms and held her close to her bosom.

'Oh, dear! This is so nice!' said Bets. 'I should like to lie here for ever.'

But after a minute Bets began to feel that her grandmother was holding her too tightly. When Bets looked, she saw that her own shoulder was little more than skin and bone. It was her grandmother's shoulder that looked plump and tender. Bets realised with a lump in her throat what had happened. She had aged. Or, rather, she had got mixed up. It must be her own granddaughter she was holding. Bets had got hold of the wrong end of the stick entirely. It was Bets herself who lived up at the top of the house next to the old spinning-wheel. It must have been her own granddaughter who had come all the way up the stairs to see her today! Why had she got so badly mixed up? Perhaps because she had aged so much, so fast? Perhaps because she was still telling herself stories after all these years?

The precious infant in her arms was sleeping.

Bets realised something peculiar. In the mirror she had seen her own young face. And that had only been minutes ago! Ah, but that hadn't been a mirror. That had been a trick she'd played on herself. Bets had been looking at her granddaughter's face through a glassless oval.

The child slept soundly in Bets withered arms.

It hadn't seemed like a second ago that she had been a child herself, living in Peterswood. And now she was an old lady who would never walk Peterswood's lanes again. What a funny pain that was! A pain that came and went as her thoughts went in and out of focus.

Was it all right what had happened? Was it all right that it seemed like *only yesterday* that Bets had been eating her porridge in a state of high excitement? Or had that just been in a story? Well, in her memory it seemed real enough. 'There's no need to gobble your porridge, Bets,' her mother had said. But Bets had pointed out that there was *every reason* to gobble her porridge, because Fatty was coming home from school that morning and Bets was due to meet him at the station.

Dear Fatty.

What else could Bets remember?…

Nothing.

Try again… .

No, nothing.

Oh, dear. Was that really all that was left of a full life just lived? Was that the fundamental thing that had happened to her? She'd sat at her parents' table, rushing her breakfast, with a sense of anticipation about meeting up with Fatty. And now she was never going to see Fatty again in this world, whatever world this was. And if she was never going to see Fatty again then she might as well revert to her Enid name.

'Oh, my dear child,' said Enid, though not loud enough to wake the sleeping babe. 'I must say a final farewell to someone special.'

But suddenly it wasn't clear just who Enid was saying goodbye to, let alone who exactly saying goodbye. Was it Bets or Enid saying goodbye? And was it a real goodbye? Perhaps it was just a goodbye in one of the stories that she felt part of her mind was still coming up with? Anyway, how could 'goodbye' be the right word when she had recently had so many millions of words at her disposal?

What better word could she remember?

Nothing.

Oh, dear. Try again…

Nothing.

Nothing was even worse than goodbye.

Goodbye! She wanted to shout something aloud. But did it really have to be that? Enid went on trying to think of another word until she realised that what little energy she had been holding on with was about to leave her. 'Goodbye,' she whispered, stroking the cheek of the child. 'I am going to meet Fatty. At least I think I am.'

ENDINGS

1

This isn't exactly my idea of an Enid Blyton Day, a meeting held inside a brick-walled hall. But, then, I've had more than my share of breezy, outdoor, Enid Blyton Days in the last year so I'm happy enough to have made the trip to the Berkshire town of Twyford to spend a few companionable hours with fellow members of the Enid Blyton Society.

Besides, Kate is here with me, looking fresh and happy. Nina and Karen from last year's coach trip are also here at my invitation, so the day is something of a second Proust reunion. They are currently working at a historical re-enactment society where they start by surreptitiously filming what's going on, then break cover and negotiate permission to film. It wasn't hard to persuade them to come along today since in a sense the adults here are re-enacting something of their childhood. That's what I said, anyway. Not that they needed much persuading; they are both switched on to the possibilities that a get-together such as this may offer. Are they filming the event? I don't know and I don't want to ask.

The hall is set out with enough seats for a couple of hundred people, and at midday, and again after lunch, speakers will entertain us. But between half past ten and noon this fine morning is a chance to mingle and to poke around the various stalls full of Enid Blyton merchandise. I dare say most people in the hall are mem-

bers of the Enid Blyton Society. Is 'Old Bourney' here? 'Nesta'?
'Anita'? 'Kirrin'? 'Kiki'? 'Viv'? 'Fatty' from Mumbai? 'Oldbookfan'
from Australia? Perhaps I'll meet 'Belly' as the day wears on. She's
the only person who responded to my posting on the Forum about
'The Men in Enid's Life'. And that was just to say that she doubted
that Enid's relationships would have had much of an impact on her
writing, because Enid was incredibly driven and self-motivated. So
that's my book rubbished, then. Somehow I feel I can still face the
world.

I point my guests towards Stella Books. I've done business with
that South Wales bookshop, because they have the habit of placing
scans of the cover and spine alongside any book they offer for sale
on Abebooks.co.uk. When I was buying Methuen Mysteries I
became quite fussy about how the cover looked, after receiving a
copy of *Spiteful Letters* where some former owner had made the
mistake of writing the number '4' on the spine of the book. He or
she had used red biro against the red linen, so it could have been
more unsightly. But I still say 'mistake'.

Kate comes up to me and asks: 'Which book has Fatty and Goon
sitting on the bench in Peterswood, both disguised as tramps?'

Nina is taken aback by Kate's relaxed use of the name 'Fatty'. But
she needn't be. Here it is normal to speak of Fatty and Goon, of
Twiddle and Pink-Whistle too. But in particular, the hall's rafters
resound with the hallowed name of 'Fatty'.

'*The Mystery of the Invisible Thief*,' is my answer to Kate's question. 'And over there is a copy with a dust-wrapper.' But Kate's
attention has been caught by the cover of *The Mystery of the
Vanished Prince*, featuring as it does Bets, dressed as Princess
Bongawee, sheltering under the magnificent State Umbrella.
Leaving Kate to choose between such riches, I take a step back from
the milling crowd. I notice that Nina and Karen have already melt-
ed away into different corners of the hall, blending in and soaking
up.

Later, I will try and talk to Tony Summerfield who is co-hosting the event. I must ask him how he's getting on with his Illustrated Bibliography. He has already published parts one to three of this, which I believe list all Blyton publications between certain years, with photographs of the covers of various editions. Tony is holding back on the 1963-1974 instalment, on the grounds that he has lost money on publishing the earlier parts. Another possible course of action would be to charge an exorbitant amount for the new book, but that would just reduce sales to a negligible figure. Well, nobody said it was easy being a writer. Actually, perhaps Enid said exactly that, in bed with Kenneth any time during that golden period from 1943 to the mid-1950s. Right then, she, if anyone, would have been entitled to claim that.

Nina catches my eye. She and Karen are dressed in old-fashioned school uniforms: white shirts, dark skirts and ties. Very Malory Towers, very Whyteleafe, very St Clare's. It brings to mind the completely different fancy dress they wore in the video they made for our entertainment on the Proust trip. I've watched it so many times on my DVD at home that it is now quite easy for me to adapt their dialogue to fit the scene in front of me now:

First, Nina dressed as Evelyn Waugh, standing in front of David Schutte's bookstall:

'Darling Nancy, I am reading Blyton for the first time – in Deans of course – and am surprised to find her a mental defective. No one warned me of that. She has absolutely no sense of time. She can't remember anyone's age. And as for the jokes – oh, the boredom of *Bimbo and Topsy*.'

Good: minimal slippage in the crossover from Proust. Now where is Karen? There she is, standing in front of two elderly women, with her nose in *The Enid Blyton Book of Fairies*. In the scene I'm both shooting and playing back, her fashionably dressed Nancy Mitford replies to Nina's Waugh on the private cinema screen in my mind:

'Darling Evelyn, I am sad to think of you reading Blyton in Deans – there is not one joke in all their 48 "classic" volumes. In the Adventure series and the Mystery books one laughs from the stomach, as when reading you. I don't remember what you say about time. I am an inattentive reader, I fear. The later books are more enjoyable, and I began on the Mysteries, but you must have read the earliest ones to get the best out of them.'

Actually, Waugh – whose novels I read when I was 17 and who I may make the subject of my next book – was dead by the time Dean and Son got round to publishing their new editions of Enid's books in the mid-sixties. So that dialogue needs to be re-cast.

The two elderly ladies behind Karen are Gillian and Imogen. If I was to cast them as famous writers, Gillian would be Enid herself – she has inherited many of her mother's facial features – and Imogen would be Samuel Beckett. She's a tall, elegant, gaunt woman. I read somewhere that the sisters don't get on particularly well, or at least don't see each other socially. Right now they seem fine with each other. They're both widows, so they've got that in common. Perhaps Imogen's book about her childhood at Green Hedges caused distance between the sisters for a while. Or perhaps it acted as a catharsis and allowed them to see what they had always had – and still have – in common: Mother Enid.

Neither Gillian nor Imogen had any idea about the existence of their grandparents – Enid's mother and father – until Enid published *The Story of My Life* in 1952. Enid had always told her children that she'd been brought up by the Attenboroughs. How had Enid felt able to mislead her daughters in this way? Surely it was because Enid's own mother had persuaded her to lie about the disappearance of her loving father to neighbours and peers and, having done that, it became easy, in due course, for Enid to blot out both her parents – the beloved and the barely loved – until the time seemed right to acknowledge them again by way of a book. When her daughters, aged 16 and 20, finally learned about her grandfather and recently buried grandmother, it must have come as a revelation.

It would seem that Gillian in particular has learned to be wary of the kind of book I'm involved with. And if retaining the copyright on Barbara Stoney's official biography of Enid is one sign of that, having an afterword added to Imogen's *A Childhood at Green Hedges* is another. In that postscript, Gillian argues that her sister puts Kenneth's visits to Green Hedges at too early a date, when Hugh was still around. Clearly Gillian believes (or is more comfortable with the idea) that Hugh was properly out of the picture before Kenneth became Enid's lover. Hopefully, if and when Gillian ever reads *Looking For Enid*, she will find it treats her father as sympathetically as it treats her mother. Decent, able Hugh and bloody incredible Enid.

In the late nineties, Imogen spoke at the Enid Blyton Society Day; her talk was entitled 'Our Books are Facets of Ourselves'. She published an article based on her speech in a subsequent issue of the *Society Journal*. It struck me as a balanced and mature judgement of her mother's writing. She pointed out that both Fatty and Bets displayed aspects of Enid's character. And she saw in George and Julian's rivalry for leadership of the Five the same sort of tussle for dominance that took place at Green Hedges between Enid and Kenneth: Enid eventually used to give way to her partner in most things, on condition that she retained control of the 'peace and quiet' factor which enabled her to work. Her own Kirrin Island, as it were. In later years, I imagine Kenneth was able to bet on horses till the cows came home. 'Our Books are Facets of Ourselves'. I wonder what Imogen would think of my Hugh = Goon thesis or of my Quentin-Kenneth-Timmy connections. But most of all I wonder what she would make of my Fatty.

Imogen's daughter Sophie is keeping an eye on the EB Society stall. She's a writer too. Or at least I recently read her review of David Rudd's book, *Enid Blyton and the Mystery of Children's*

Literature. It was good to be reminded that Rudd's book concentrates on Noddy, the Famous Five and Malory Towers. By consulting with child readers, and getting veteran Blyton readers to fill in questionnaires, his research counters previously touted opinion that Blyton was racist, sexist, class-ridden and bland. Well played, that man! He also identifies the Malory Towers books with Malory's *Le Morte d'Arthur*, claiming that Malory Towers is the equivalent of a medieval court, where the girls are tested for their worth like the Arthurian knights, but are not bogged down in male competition. As well as that, the Rudd book puts emphasis on Blyton being part of an oral tradition – her father used to tell her stories and she used to tell stories to her pupils at school. In other words he cites a Homeric tradition. All of which is fascinating, even if I can't go along with it. But especially interesting to me, now that I've got to the end of my own book, is that Rudd's stuff hardly even overlaps with my approach to the subject. No doubt more Enid Blyton books will be written, showing just how complex a character she was. How about: *Enid Blyton and the Philosopher's Stone; Enid Blyton and the Chamber of Secrets; Enid Blyton and the Prisoner of Azkaban*. Books dedicated to Thomas, Kenneth and Hugh, respectively.

I wonder if David Rudd is here. Silver-haired Barbara Stoney is, and I would dearly like to ask her a question or two. My first question would be: 'What stories did Enid tell about Hugh in private?' Yes, this might be the time to make such an enquiry. But I wouldn't like to give the impression that this is an academic meeting or an excuse to do more research. Children are playing with each other, admiring the displays, shouting and laughing. Timeless joy is what I can hear, when I really get down to listen. I hope Gillian and Imogen can hear it too. I hope Gillian at 74, and Imogen at 70, are aware of the warmth in the room and the singular source of that warmth.

Enid was a cold mother did you say, Imogen? Surely that's not how it feels right now, standing there with your sister smiling at you, surrounded by thousands of your mother's books and generations of her readers. I should think you were as warm as toast.

Suddenly, Kate is standing right in front of me, handing me a glass of ginger beer and smiling into my face. It must be noon. 'Didn't I talk to you at last year's event, young man?'

It's Kate as Gillian. I sip from my chilled glass before replying: 'Yes, we did have a short chat.'

'Did you write that book about MY MOTHER?'

'Mmm. Just finished it, as a matter of fact.'

'And what are its CONCLUSIONS?' asks Kate, intensely. 'You know – what juicy new perspective have you come up with? Was my mother a lesbian? Can we think without words? Does the brain need food? Why is a raindrop round? Will frogs and fishes some day turn into animals like horses?'

I'm laughing. Kate has read my book. She loves every word. Or so she tells when not in party mode. But right now she is in a party mood which always makes me either rise to the challenge or retreat into banality. At this moment it seems to be the latter, which is why I can manage nothing better than: 'Enid was born with a huge talent…'

Kate's Gillian doesn't seem massively impressed with this remark: 'Well, anyone in this room could have told me THAT.'

OK, try again. 'But it wasn't until your mother was in her midforties, when certain life experiences seemed to gel in her mind, that she was able to focus her talent on writing extraordinarily vivid, emotionally full books whose structures and characters reflect the relationships and places that had most affected her in real life.'

'Our books are facets of ourselves! My mother said that once. And my sister wrote it in the Enid Blyton Blooming Journal. And now you're just saying the same old thing. HONESTLY – you academics!'

I sip from my glass and give it one last shot. 'If we were playing a word association game right now and you came up with the name "Isaac Newton", my response would be "Enid Blyton". That's how highly I rank her.'

'Oh, never mind that now. I want to know about a more important matter than rank. The coach trip! Have I missed it?'

'I'm still setting that up. I've got the coach painted, though. That's always the main thing.'

'Buttercup yellow?'

'Yip.'

'With "WE ARE NOT AFRAID OF ENID BLYTON" down one side, and "MR PINK-WHISTLE'S PARTY" down the other?'

'Sorry, no. I've gone for two quotations instead.'

'TELL ME, TELL ME, TELL ME!'

'It says "LOVE ONE ANOTHER" down one side.'

'P-FF-FF-FF-FFFFF!… And down the other?'

'"THAT TOAD OF A FAT BOY."'

'Good! I am very partial to a bit of Goon. Do you like a bit of Goon yourself?'

'I love Goon. And I admire his creator. More than I can say when faced with her ravishing daughter.'

Kate takes me by the arm. 'I think my mother would have liked you as well. She had a soft spot for funny little web-footed, pigeon-toed Scottish boys, you know.'

2

The man walks into the girl's bedroom. The walls are lined with rainbow-spined books, which pulse and glow. But the 12-year-old lies on her bed, white and motionless. Her dark curls fall over her forehead. The man is moved as he looks down on the child lying there so still.

After a minute, the man looks up again and regards the books that colour the walls. What a vibrant scene! His eye picks out a title at random: *The Boy Who Looked Back*. He knows that this is the retelling of a bible story. Nearby is another similar-sized book, the spine of which reads: *The Man Who Stopped to Help*. That would be a modern version of The Good Samaritan. But these are only two titles on a single shelf, and all four walls of the room are covered in shelves from floor to ceiling. The room is lined with myriads of books written by a single, named individual. One person wrote all these?

The man looks down again on the little girl with awe intermingled with compassion. What should he do? He knows that both the books and the individual can't be teeming with life. He has to choose between them. He hesitates for a few seconds, unsure as to how to proceed. Eventually, the man does what he knows he has to do. He puts out his hand and takes the child's cold one in his. Then he speaks lovingly:

'Get up, darling.'

The little girl opens her eyes. She looks up at the man with eyes full of love and trust. She sits up and rubs her eyes. Has she been ill? She feels quite well again now! She wants to get up. She wants to walk and run! So she jumps out of bed and skips out of the room, singing.

Once she has quite gone from view, and the man can no longer hear her happy voice, he surveys the cold, white walls of the room, now empty of books. How does he feel? He feels that by a simple act of human kindness he has somehow committed a crime against humanity. He feels he has undone a miracle.

Do you belong to
THE FABULOUS ENID CLUB?

Have you got
THE FABULOUS ENID BADGE?

There are friends of FABULOUS ENID all over the world.

Wear the F.E. badge and you will know each other at once!

The badge was designed by artist Nicola Atkinson in 2006
using an original illustration from 1948 by Elsie Walker in
The Little Girl at Capernaum

Duncan McLaren
will wear one too, so that you will know him. The lovely little
badges cost one shilling. Any profit made will go to THE
CHILDREN'S CONVALESCENT HOME in Beaconsfield.

Send a postal order for one shilling and an envelope addressed
to yourself inside an envelope addressed to THE FABULOUS
ENID CLUB, Green Hedges, Penn Road, Beaconsfield,
Buckinghamshire.

You shall have your badge as soon as possible and a letter telling
you about THE FABULOUS ENID CLUB.

Good luck to you all from

Duncan McLaren

This is the image that appears on the FABULOUS ENID BADGE. That is, a view of Enid both before and after she set the Thames on fire.

"SHE IS ASLEEP."

ACKNOWLEDGEMENTS

Barbara Stoney's official biography of Enid Blyton was always to hand during the writing of this book.

The Enid Blyton Society (www.enidblytonsociety.co.uk) is an excellent source of information and opinions on Enid Blyton. Thanks to Tony Summerfield and Anita Bensoussane for reading the manuscript of *Looking For Enid* and letting me have their comments.

The Proust coach trip that is mentioned in the text is loosely based on a coach trip to Zlin in the Czech Republic, origin of Tomas Bata's shoe-making empire. This event was organised by artists Nina Pope and Karen Guthrie. Details of the resulting film, *Bata-ville: we are not afraid of the future*, can be obtained from www.bata-ville.com.

Thanks to John Wilson for telling me at an early stage in the book's conception that it was Enid's childhood he wanted to read about, not my own. Thanks to Peter Hobbs for providing a most helpful 'tough read' of the first draft of the book.

Thanks to Ed Jaspers at Conville and Walsh Ltd for persisting with the notion that my work deserves an audience.

Thanks to Philip Gwyn Jones at Portobello Books for investing in a manuscript that several people have put a lot of thought into.

Thanks to my parents for continuing to give house space to my Enid Blyton library.

Thanks to Kate Clayton for repeatedly wandering into the Enchanted Wood with me and climbing the Faraway Tree to investigate what fresh world of mystery and imagination Enid Blyton had in store for us.

The day before the first edition of this book went to press, I learned that Gillian Baverstock, Enid's elder daughter, had died. Although we meet in the pages of *Looking For Enid*, at least imaginatively, we never met in real life. However, I know she was a long-term supporter of her mother's memory and her mother's work and I can only repeat the hope expressed earlier in these pages that if she'd had a chance to read this book she would have seen it as supportive of Enid and much that Enid held dear.

For news about current and forthcoming titles
from Portobello Books and for a sense of purpose
visit the website **www.portobellobooks.com**

encouraging voices,
supporting writers,
challenging readers

Portobello
BOOKS